Distributed – Bookmasters
30 Amberwood Parkway
Ashland Ohio: 44805
(877) 312-3520 INT'l (419) - 281-5100

Also Distributed by New Leaf Distributing:
401 Thornton Rd, Lithia Springs, GA 30122
(770) 948-7845

For additional information:
www.JillsWingsOfLight.com
www.MusicForBeauty.com
www.Ancient-Music.com
www.RedBubble.com/Jill Mattson

2

Ancient Sounds
Modern Healing

Intelligence, Health, and Energy through the Magic of Music

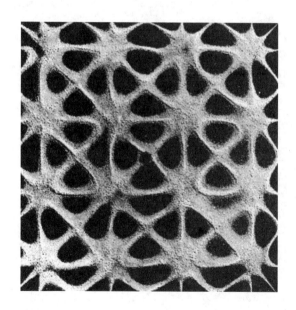

Jill Mattson

3

Also by Jill Mattson

Secret Sounds ~ Ultimate Healing
Lost Waves of Time

Musical Releases:
Paint Your Soul
Star Dust
Healing Flower Symphonies I & II
Cosmic Streams
Deep Wave Beauty
Angels, Masters and Guides
Deep Wave Body Healing

Ancient Sounds Modern Healing

Prologue

It all changed after my son, Lee, at the ripe old age of eight, won a nationwide contest on imaging computers of the future; the prize was lunch with Bill Gates!

Lee's teacher asked his class to write an essay to "Imagine the Magic" - that is, speculate what would computers of the future be able to do. Before you understand Lee's response, you need to know that Lee and his older brother, Neil, often had the job of watching their baby brother while I did household chores.

Lee penned a story about a computer projecting a hologram of Mom near a playpen… into which all good little boys could toss their baby brothers. The baby would be occupied by the hologram of Mom nearby, giving little boys freedom to play their computer games.

Little Lee visiting Bill Gates captured my imagination! Playing off Lee's idea, I started writing God's autobiography. In my story, God was the computer expert and humans were little holograms projected by the computer. The function keys were universal laws and God set in motion creation like my sons played their computer games.

I retold the *Bible*, giving the story from God's perspective. I realized God's perspective is far different than ours. For example, from a human point of view we might wonder why would God let people starve to death? In contrast, God could say, "I give them enough food to feed the entire world many times over, why won't they share?"

I squirmed as I penned stories from the *Old Testament* where I felt like I was covering for God. Why would God play games with Satan and allow Job to suffer? I believed God loves unconditionally, so why was God jealous?

In the *Old Testament* the inconsistencies of God's personality, such as swings from a merciful to a harsh God, served as a catalyst in my personal spiritual quest. I knew there were other versions of the *Bible* and I widened my search, looking for a more merciful *Old Testament* God.

I delved into a variety of Biblical translations. I discovered the *Kabala*, the *Dead Sea Scrolls*, the Essenne's doctrines, Gnostic philosophies, additional books that were written at the time of the *Bible* and stories of neighboring Middle Eastern cultures. I discovered the fascinating world of antiquity. I saw God through many people's perspectives. God's "personality" always reflected the values of the storyteller. This information led me to a shift in my thinking about God.

The God that I personally believed in was unconditionally loving, not full of human frailties. Later, when I read a passage in the *Old Testament* with an angry, moody or egotistical God, I decided that was clearly the author's input, seeing God through his small eyes.

For the first time I let go of religious dogma and I opened up to a relationship with a more loving God than the one I learned about in Sunday school. This realization was a life altering epiphany for me. My world changed. Immediately, I began to experience a steady stream of clairvoyant and clairaudient communications and my life became truly magical.

My love for antiquity and its secrets blossomed as I uncovered ideas from many cultures and ages that opened up my thinking and my heart. I read hundreds and hundreds of volumes, particularly about secret societies, such as the Tibetan monks, Christian monks, Druids, mystics from ancient Egypt, ancient Chinese, and many more.

Being a musician, my excitement grew every time I read a technique about how music was used to increase intelligence, health, energy and one's relationship with God. I filled notebooks with this information.

My life's calling finally became crystal clear: combine my love of all things musical with my personal spiritual quest. I would use my natural deep curiosity to study antiquity's secrets and mysticism - especially related to music and sound. I always had this feeling that just beyond my recollection - just beyond my fingertips resided powerful information proving that music was much more than entertainment. I just knew that people's lives could be greatly impacted, and improved, if they were opened up to the special energy that only music could offer.

I learned that in ancient societies, there were hierarchies of students: initiates, disciples, adepts and masters. Much of the information about sound and music was not written down, but preserved by verbal traditions, and passed on to only the masters. Since people could use sound to control and harm others, its powers were kept secret.

I combined and expanded upon the ancient musical techniques that I discovered. People could have more control over their own lives by carefully choosing what they listened to. This was a gift I wanted to give to people today.

I started using these ancient, musical techniques in my own composing, which was growing with leaps and bounds, especially with my clairaudient experiences hearing music that was in me, but not of me.

Inevitably, I found myself researching everything available about sound and music. I read everything available throughout the ages - from obscure ancient texts to modern state-of-the art work. I interviewed scientists and modern day masters, confirming the effectiveness of many of these techniques… and in a nutshell, that is how this book came into being.

I am deeply grateful for these magical experiences and the wonderful people who helped me along the way. For everyone seeking growth and open to new vistas, join me and "let the music play you!"

Introduction

Magic!

When the rabbit disappears inside the magician's hat, it is magic. When the magician makes a flower appear in a little girl's hair, it is magic. When something becomes invisible or visible, we can think it is magic.

What magic is to a child is well understood by adults. What was magic to ancient peoples may be understood by today's scientists.

Ancient people could perceive much scientific phenomena as magic. For example, Einstein tells us that matter and energy are equivalent. This is not what our senses perceive. We perceive an object as solid, but it is energy moving in space. It is something that we don't see. Is it magic or scientific phenomenon?

And what about sound? Today's scientific community accepts many of the benefits of sound healing.

A "sound machine" can photograph a baby forming inside a mother's womb, make a gallstone disappear or heal a fractured bone faster. That sounds like magic to me!

In addition, sound and music can lift our spirits, give us energy, calm us, heal our bodies, affect our intellect, alter our body chemistry and change our consciousness. This invisible stuff - sound and music - has got to be magic! By learning to use invisible sound waves to change our lives, we become magicians.

So, let's meet some sound magicians who will explain secrets of music that we can use to manage our health, emotions, minds and spirits. It's just magic!

Chapter One

Mysteries of the Swamiji

Crystal Hunting

"Crystals! There are special crystal rocks only about a half an hour from here," Kathy exclaimed. The words spouted from her like a fountain.

Crystals always had fascinated Kathy. One dangled from her neck as she waved a brochure in front of me featuring crystal rock formations.

Soon we were heading down the highway (back roads actually, there aren't any highways here). Kathy and I followed the treasure map to the crystals and "X" marked the spot.

Deep, deeper, and deepest into the woods we ventured, until we spotted the site... it was some sort of retreat. We could see a beautiful garden shaded in the woods, but no crystal rocks.

We parked in the large, empty parking lot and set out to explore.

We soon spied a storybook house with a stream and a waterfall nestled next to it. Flowers faithfully manned their posts in front of a white picket fence.

I watched toads by the stream while Kathy, intent on finding a clue to the crystal rocks' whereabouts, knocked on the door of the storybook house.

Out came a fairytale lady, Padma, which meant lotus flower. She pointed in the direction of the crystal rock formations, and accompanied us.

Past the waterfall and pavilions was an elegant temple built around the crystal rocks. With Padma's guidance, we finally got a long-awaited look at the crystals. I thought (but didn't say), "But they're just rocks!" Painted rocks... huge rocks, and rocks in a temple - but just rocks.

Padma invited us to just sit and enjoy the space of the "crystal" rock temple. Without noticing any change, I suddenly realized that everything became calm; my breathing was noticeably slower. Our voices were calmer - definitely softer, almost a whisper.

The temple housed many statues including Jesus, Buddha, and Shiva, and several photos. One photo was of a wide-eyed man who seemed sweet and innocent; I found my eyes riveted on the other photo of a beautiful woman with eyes like black holes. I read that black holes have been theorized to be portholes to other dimensions. Scientists have postulated that whatever goes into a black hole never comes out.

That's what those eyes were like - black holes. I wanted to go in and never return.

I don't know how long I was out of it, staring into the porthole eyes of the beautiful woman, but Kathy said about fifteen minutes had passed when she and Padma finished their chat.

I heard Padma say that Swamiji, the wide-eyed man in the other photo, healed with music.

I snapped to attention. Healed with music! (Who said nothing comes back out of a black hole? I just did.) Healing? Music? Wow!

I had spent 25 years starting and managing charities in a nonprofit agency. It was a job and life I loved until the last year or so, when I became restless and felt empty. It was time to leave. So I did. The problem was the next adventure was not in place. But I was excited about making a CD. I composed original music and I used money I earned by performing concerts to buy recording equipment. The recording studio was almost functional.

Oh, yeah, I forgot to mention that I'd been reading about antiquity for years. When reading antiquity, I feel like I am reading fairy tales - but in the history section of the library, not fiction.

When I read antiquity, my heart beats faster when I encounter insights about music. For example, I read that the Chinese, many thousands of years ago, controlled the music in their provinces as a means of controlling the sound vibrations entering the peoples' consciousness. Those in government believed this method enabled them to control the masses. While this approach may seem rather odd, we can't discount its results: Chinese dynasties did last thousands of years while we have a difficulty at times maintaining order even within our presidential terms of four years. Maybe there's something to this concept that we don't understand. Not to mention that it would be better to send our children off to band camp than to the army.

Ancient Druid traditions also utilized perpetual choirs (24/7) to preserve certain energy that they believed would help them maintain power. Ancient sages wrote that the music did indeed stop before the ancient Druids lost power during the Roman invasions.

Some ancient cultures believed that in order to stay in power, their music must not die. In contrast, Osama Bin Laden outlawed music for his people. What was the impact of these musical practices on the people? Right before war breaks out in a country, the music stops. Who wants to sing when he is afraid that war is coming? Could music stabilize, control or change the hearts of people?

I read of the gruesome slaughter of 600 people who were fighting over how to measure time and pitch! How to assign frequencies was important enough to slaughter so many. Hard to imagine what might have happened if something really big had occurred… like their football team losing the Super Bowl!

Antiquity also taught me about people who used special tones to go into deep meditative states… and yes, about music that healed people when they were ill.

"So, this Swamiji heals with music… " I pondered.

Two weeks later, Kathy and I traveled to a "healing concert," given by none other than the Swamiji in the photo who had graced the "crystal" rocks.

When Kathy and I walked into the concert hall, I couldn't help thinking it was prom night in India. The ladies' dresses were very pretty and trimmed with gold jewelry. The red dot on the forehead must be part of the dress code.

We were an hour late due to our lengthy tour of the "city", circling around to find the concert hall, but we hadn't missed a thing. In came the Swamiji.

After pomp and circumstance, Swamiji stood on the edge of the stage and just stared. He stared and stared and stared into the crowd. I thought he was looking at *me*, but everyone else thought so, too.

Now Swamiji produced a crystal stick or a crystal wand, if you will. But this was no gray rock! Swamiji stood on the edge of the stage with his arm extended, holding his crystal wand and looking like a Ghost Buster taking a reading of ectoplasm in the air. Then he used the wand to scan the audience. Slowly, the wand waved from right to left, and back again. His eyes remained closed.

Swamiji then moved to his Roland piano and stared again. Silence.

Bam! The music started. I had no idea what to expect, but I liked it. The musicians used Indian instruments, which our part of the world isn't used to hearing; there was a piano that we are familiar with. There was a violin, too. I liked that, because I'm also a violin player.

At first it was just music to me, beautiful music, but just music. Then the roller coaster rides started: I promise you, I never partook of an intoxicating substance and the only thing in my stomach was a walnut - apple salad. However, I swore there was a tornado inside and surrounding my body. I gripped my seat so I wouldn't fall off. No one else was gripping his seat; maybe it was just me.

This tornado swirled right to left - in, through, and around me. Was I in a black hole? Perhaps I was in a toilet that had just been flushed. I could feel the negative energy flushing out of me. Movement. All around. Sensations were moving from all parts of my body into my spine, down it, to my legs and into the floor. This went on for twenty-five minutes, after which, I murmured to myself, "I must be squeaky clean."

Then I entered phase II: acupuncture. I felt long, skinny needles pricking me in the oddest places, like the side of my nostrils. Each prick lasted about one minute. I imagined that the needle gathered what it wanted. The prickly sensation then went down my spine, down my legs and into the floor. I was glad I wasn't the janitor cleaning the floor after this particular concert!

The acupuncture-like sensations lasted about half an hour. I felt like Dorothy in *The Wizard of Oz*, just wanting to go home, when a new tornado arrived on the horizon.

My perception of wind gushing inside of me started again, as if I had fallen into one of those whirling teacups at the amusement park. This was different than the first tornado-like experience, because the whirlwind was in my head (…and anyone thinking of airhead jokes can just zip it.)

This experience didn't feel like it was pulling things out of me - in fact, just the reverse. I imagined something was drilling invisible energy into my head. I felt like I was at the dentist, only my whole head was full of cavities. As sensations from the swirling energy worked their way into my head, I became serene and calm.

Then it was over. The music stopped. Swamiji bowed and people were clapping.

My first impulse was to ask everyone if they had experienced the same sensations that I had, but most of the people didn't even speak English. Being shy, I looked for a reason not to speak. Oh, yes, I did not follow the dress code. I'm not wearing my Indian prom dress. I'd better not speak.

I looked at Kathy, whose eyes were bugging out. She described the tornado-like experience that seemed to take stuff out of her body and put something else back in, but she didn't experience the acupuncture treatment.

That was the first concert I ever enjoyed from the inside of my body.

Sri Ganapathy Sachchidananda Swamiji.

Magic!

Several days later, Kathy and I revisited the retreat, the home of the "crystal" rocks. Swamiji was there and so were hundreds of happy pilgrims.

The crowd was buzzing around the Swamiji. We listened in on a man wearing a white scarf. He claimed that he awakened in a morgue, after being declared legally dead for several hours, to see Swamiji's smiling face welcoming him back. I noticed the necklace of the lady in green sitting in front of me because the gold looked like bubbles of dew. I couldn't figure out how the gold balls were linked to each other. Upon inquiring, I learned she had watched Swamiji manifest this necklace, this talisman, out of thin air!

There were hundreds of people, each with their own miraculous Swamiji story. Those "crystal" rocks seemed more magical every minute.

I brought my own musical CD and gave it to Padma, who smiled as if she had been expecting it and then took me to

16

a man who organized Swamiji's appearances in the United States, Dr. Rao. He promised me an interview with Swamiji's musicians and ultimately with Swamiji. Wow! This was easy - too easy. I felt like my dog when she's expecting a juicy steak bone. I did a double-sided chop lick.

Twenty-two hours later I sat with Swamiji's organizer (Dr. Rao), Manasa (one of Swamiji's oldest friends), Jaitra (Swamiji's violinist), and Ramesh (his drum player). Between the five of us, we found words to translate our conversation, with me being the only one not contributing to the effort.

"What's the difference between Indian music and what we listen to in the Western world?" I began. "Experiencing Swamiji's concert was like hitting a baseball over the stadium's walls, never to be found. What a home run!"

For a moment, I thought I was looking at four Cheshire cats. They understood the secret powers in Swamiji's music.

Manasa opened for the Indians. "Ninety-five percent of Indian music reflects attributes of God. We sing about God within, nature that God made and other aspects of God. For example, one aspect of God may be peace and another joy. We sing, reflect on, and feel the aspects of God that we want to copy."

Dr. Rao cut in: "God is like a prism that separates white daylight into the colors of the rainbow."

It became a trio when Jaitra, the violinist, chimed in: "And the five percent of the time we are not singing about God, we are using music to prepare to sing, think and develop attributes of God."

"Music is holy. Music makes you whole," Dr. Rao mused.

I nodded, "OK. Music vibrates us. We are vibrating energy ourselves. Music can be like a prayer, changing the vibrations within us."

"All vibrations affect other vibrations. When we throw pebbles in a pond, all the vibrations of the pebbles interact. Vibrations of music interact with us literally." Manasa added.

"Music affects our moods, which can affect our thoughts," I mused. "We tap our feet to the beat of the music. Hmmm, the vibrations of music interact with us. That seems right."

Many scientists believe that our emotions and thoughts are vibrations or wave energy. Our organs vibrate and our heart beats a rhythm. (I imagined my liver doing the twist!)

What about the vibrations of brain waves? Different brain waves are associated with various states of consciousness. For example, beta waves give us the experience of our normal waking state and delta brainwaves occur when we sleep. As our consciousness changes, so does our brain waves.

I read books by Masaru Emoto, who photographed crystallized water molecules after they had been exposed to the vibrations of music. The freezing crystallized water molecules exposed to Mozart were different from those that experienced Beethoven's music. Each piece of music changed the crystalline structure of water in its own unique way.

Heavy metal music ruined the beautiful crystallized structures of the water, while words of kindness repaired broken crystallized water molecules. This experiment was even done in several languages and it still worked.

Masaro Emoto photographed polluted water molecules that were in broken crystallized shapes. Then he photographed the same water again after "holy men" had prayed several hours to bless the water. Following the prayers the polluted water returned to its pristine state, displaying a complete crystalline structure of great beauty.

The photographs showed how music, words, and even one's intent (e.g., prayers and kind words) changed the crystalline structure of water when it was freezing. Our bodies are over 90 percent water. Do the vibrations or words that come out of our mouths affect us?

Hans Jenny, a Swiss physicist, did similar experiments. He videotaped music vibrating loose sand and other materials. With only the vibrations of music to affect the matter, shapes were formed - often exquisite patterns. (Some of Jenny's experiments can be viewed on You Tube. See images of some of Jenny's work on pages 43 - 45.) At first I thought it a miracle, but there is a scientific explanation for this!

Sound Creates!

Creation stories from many ancient religions believe sound played an important role in the creation of the universe.

- "In the beginning was the Word, and the Word was with God, and **the Word was God.**" John 1:1 (A spoken word is a sound.)
- Hindu tradition states in the Vedas: "In the beginning was Brahman with whom was the Word. And **the Word is Brahman.**"
- Thot, an Egyptian God, was believed to have **created the world with his voice.**
- According to Mayan tradition, in the *Popul Vuh* (the book on creation), **humans are given life by the power of the Word.**
- In the Hopi Indian tradition, "Spider Woman" sings **songs of creation to produce animated life.**
- The *Satapatha Brahmana* of the Hindu tradition reads: "In the beginning was God with power through speech. God said, "'May I be many**... may I be propagated through subtle speech,'** he united himself with that speech and became pregnant."
- In Chinese Buddhism, **the Divine Voice calls forth the illusive form of the universe.**

Throughout the ages, the power of sound is linked with creation!

The historian in me took a back seat as the scientist in me took over, I wondered, "All those religions report that sound creates... but how?"

19

Sound, in the form of speaking (the Word), singing, or musical instruments is a form of vibrational energy. In fact, at the smallest known scales of the universe, all particles of matter and energy vibrate. Matter has *wave* properties; this is the basis for quantum theory. Einstein's $E=mC^2$ basically says that matter and energy are equivalent. I don't pretend to understand the details of how the universe was created (not even our smartest scientists are sure) - but perhaps these metaphors are simplified explanations of Creation, revealed by God again and again to various early people. A Creation story is fundamental to any faith; it is equally important as a starting point in understanding one's place in the universe. It may be that these Creation stories above are based on actual events - just simplified for our limited intellects.

In a narrower but similar sense, I remember the science lesson about entrainment that also may shed some light on the power of Sound to create. A grandfather clock with a strong sounding "tic-tock" in close proximity to a smaller clock with a weak "tic-tock" will alter the period of the smaller clock so it matches the tic-tock of the grandfather clock. In other words, a stronger vibration can "entrain" a weaker vibration.

Musical vibrations can alter the vibrations inside our mind and body. Further, sound makes patterns in physical matter. I watched it do so on Hans Jenny's videotape.

If we hear music long enough and it can influence matter like Hans Jenny showed us, what are the long-term possibilities of sound's effects on our bodies, minds and emotions?

Sound creates unique shapes in sand; Hans Jenny photographed certain shapes that correspond to specific intentions, words or music. Do shapes represent or encode information? Perhaps when we listen to music, we receive encoded information that slips past our intellectual censors. For example, could music help us experience compassion when we habitually think judgmental thoughts? When my white children sing along with black rap singers, does their musical admiration insure they will have no racial prejudice? If they love the song, will they love the singer?

If you hear something long enough, you believe it is true - that holds doubly true if you heard it while growing up. Most people prefer to listen to music they listened to as young adults. Adults enjoy the same music their entire lives. My father grooved on the big band sound until he died as an old man. Does listening to a certain musical genre give a generation a specific outlook on life? If so, what is the impact on society?

Does each generation evolve society's consciousness by selecting new musical genres? Most are not flexible enough to evolve too much in a lifetime. Likewise, most people don't enjoy a newer generation's music after they grow older. Does society need the younger generation to select new sounds to trigger changes in society? (No, my rap-loving kids did not pay me to say that!)

In his book, *Music: Its Secret Influence throughout the Ages,* Cyril Scott reported that music clears energetic pathways in our consciousness, paving a way for evolutionary progress to occur in society. Scott claims that Bach's and Haydn's mathematically perfect harmonies enabled Europeans of their time to emerge from the Dark Ages.

Scott further claimed that early classical music inspired ornate Victorian architecture and that age's highly decorative style of dress. Although this higher energy helped Europeans rise out of the Dark Ages, it also allowed them to maintain an ornate and stately appearance while their hearts remained dispassionately cold.

Later, the emotive music of Beethoven introduced compassion to the social consciousness, essential for people to grow beyond their accustomed "ornamental" good behavior. Beethoven's music rouses deep feelings of sorrow in me, helping me to understand others who have experienced great pain. Scott reports that the first charities appeared in historical records - only after many people heard Beethoven's music.

In summary, Scott claimed that music is a carrier of consciousness, enabling social evolutions.

Jaitra took me into uncharted territory as he explained, "Indian music does not have black dots on staff paper. Since Indians measure pitches the perfect way, rather than the compromised Western way, they write an equivalent of syllables of our musical notes that we call 'Do,' 'Re,' 'Me,' 'Fa,' 'So,' 'La,' and 'Ti.' For example, when the musicians see 'Re,' they play the second note of the scale."

Jaitra explained in broken English how written Indian music works, but I couldn't listen to Jaitra's words, because I was too anxious to butt them aside: "What do you mean, 'The Indians measure pitches the perfect way, and we don't?'"

But I then remembered the early classical days, the frequency for each note in the musical scale varied, depending on what key the note was played in. They used one piano for the key of "D" and another piano for the key of "G," because the "F#" in the key of "G" is not the same as the "F#" in the key of "D." For example, "F#'s" had different pitches, whereas today, "F#" has only one pitch. The pitches of the notes in the musical scale were calculated from a mathematical formula in which the frequency of the same note changed slightly in different keys. Jaitra believed that this was the "perfect" way to designate musical notes.

Having a separate piano for each musical key got expensive; one needed a big room to house a dozen or so pianos. To be practical, musicians changed the frequencies of notes in Western music so the difference between each note was the square root of 12. This was a slight compromise, but it didn't require a different piano for each key a song was played in. This was easier on the pocketbook than buying a dozen pianos that each played a different key! Western music uses this tuning convention. Today we consider this variation of the mathematical formula that produces our musical scale as the only music scale.

All the pieces of the puzzle were beginning to fit together. Remember the stories from antiquity in which 600 people were gruesomely murdered over the question of how to measure pitch and time? This is what they were fighting over: some felt that since God had created the world with sound, sound could deliver us back to God, like a lifeline. They wanted to use uncompromised mathematics when selecting pitches of the musical scale. People in antiquity believed sound was the preferred method of "travel to heaven". This concept was critical - without the "right" pitches, we would be like dogs chasing our tails, never catching the spiral wave to heaven.

Let me explain why these people believed sound could carry them to heaven. A sound wave looks like a humped-up inchworm (with wave peaks and troughs), each wavelength representing one unit of sound. There may be 100 wavelengths per second in a low note and many hundreds per second in a higher pitched note. If we sequentially numbered each hump or unit of sound 1, 2, 3, 4, 5, 6... the frequencies of sound can be used like numbers and math calculations can be applied to them.

Mathematicians enjoy discovering "magical" formulas that explain natural phenomena in quantitative and relational terms, like putting numbers in the formula $E=mC^2$. Mathematicians can also use musical frequencies as they do numbers, and have just as much fun.

The Fibonacci series of numbers produces ratios also found in solar systems, seashells, plants, the human body, and in famous architecture. The Fibonacci numbers are one of the "perfect" patterns of numbers that can be translated into pitches. Our Western music system is similar to the numerical pattern of Fibonacci numbers. However, the exact musical translation of the Fibonacci numbers can only be heard by creating tuning forks to match these numbers.

The ratios of neighboring Fibonacci numbers (or frequencies), when drawn, reveal a spiral like that found in a conch shell.[1] The compromise in Western tuning resulted in our music frequencies creating a circle when graphed. Maybe we are chasing our tails trying to find them! Maybe we are missing the spiral wave to heaven!

Fibonacci Series displayed in a Nautilus Shell[2]

Some ancient traditions believed that listening to the "spiral" pattern in sound enabled a person's soul to "quicken" and rise closer to God. According to such traditions these sound currents carve a pathway into a listener's consciousness, creating patterns to expand on.

My CD, "Paint Your Soul," that I gave to the Lotus Flower, Padma, contains the spiral Fibonacci pattern of tones in a track embedded in the music. People have written me about the stirring impact the CD had on their lives. They often experience peace flooding their being - to the point of shedding tears, realizing their worth as a person, and changing their behavior.

---

[1] We can make a picture showing the Fibonacci numbers 1, 1, 2, 3, 5, 8, 13, 21... by drawing two small squares of size 1 next to each other. On top of both of these we now draw a square of size 2 (=1+1). We can now draw a new square - touching both a single unit square and the latest square of side 2 - so having sides 3 units long; and then another touching both the 2 - square and the 3-square (which has sides of 5 units). We can continue adding squares around the picture; each new square having a side which is as long as the sum of the latest two square's sides. We can now draw a spiral in the squares. Such spirals are seen in the shape of shells of snails, seashells in the arrangement of seeds on flowering plants.

[2] Used with permission

My mind clouded over, along with my eyes. "What about the electric piano that Swamiji uses? It uses the compromised tuning of the Western world," I chuckled suspiciously. I noticed, however, that my question only produced four Cheshire cat smiles as I looked around our little circle.

Dr. Rao reveals: "The piano is really a computer, and the tuning can be changed..."

Jaitra interrupted. He had been speaking before I rudely interrupted him, and he wanted to continue explaining how to read Indian music. "Each song or 'raga' lists about six to ten notes, symbolized by the words 'Do,' 'Re,' 'Me,' 'Fa,' and so on.

"The Indians use more pitches than Western music does. We use only pitches for twelve half steps in an octave of sound, while the Indians could use hundreds of pitches in that same octave. Their pitches can be closer together than our smallest interval. So they have additional notes, such as 'Re,' 'Re +,' 'Re ++,' 'Re -,' 'Re --,' and so on.

"The Indian musician only plays the written notes, but he can play them in any order. Musicians improvise with a limited set of pitches," Jaitra explained, beaming with pride.

Poor Jaitra, I simply had to interrupt again. "How did they come up with a set of notes and rhythm patterns in the first place?" I asked. "Butting in" is one of my skills.

Dr. Rao's hand goes into the center of our circle, signaling that he is next to talk. "This is an ancient system that is thousands of years old. Your culture is only several hundred years old. This system goes way back."

Dr. Rao insisted, "The ancient people watched babies cry and mothers pat their backs, soothing babies' woes. So the musicians copied the exact rhythm of the back-pat that soothed the baby - and that rhythm could be used to calm down someone else, too. Our ancient forefathers copied the lullabies that helped the babies sleep, laugh, become cheerful and playful. They also discovered pitches that produced these desired states in people. Our ancient forefathers copied the rhythms of animals running, peaceful ocean sounds, and the spirited wind after observing how nature impacts emotions, and the psyche. By copying these rhythm patterns and inserting them in their music, they produced similar effects on listeners – as if the listeners were hearing the ocean or the spirited wind."

I recalled one Christmas when I asked my son to order me a "Kenny G" CD of velvety soft clarinet music. However, when the package arrived in the mail, the creamy Christmas music turned out to be "Kenya E" - (sounds close to "Kenny G"). "Kenya E" was African witch-doctor music! Perhaps we could play witch doctor music to dance around the Christmas tree!

The "Kenya E" CD insert included a statement of sympathy from Africa tribesmen, as they pitied the Western world that did not have access to their healing rhythms and who had to use "ridiculous" hospitals. The people who recorded "Kenya E" believed that special rhythms and pitches could heal our physical bodies, minds, and spirits. The people in Africa and the ancient Hindi shared similar ideas.

"Our Western music goes through many moods and feelings," I thought aloud now. "Indian music is not so flexible, but far more concentrated. Indian music focuses only on one specific feeling in a song."

Manasa continued for me, "Think of yourself as a bucket. As you feel an emotion, a drop of energy goes into the bucket, which becomes a part of you. For example, we focus on a feeling, like joy. We sing the raga (song) or a mantra (repeated song), while feeling joy, over and over and over. We spend years filling our buckets with joyous music, feelings and thoughts. Finally, this is who we are, a joyous person. The music made this development exponentially faster. This is why all our music is about God. We want to fill our beings with aspects of God."

Jaitra sported a huge smile. It was his finally his turn to talk. "This is how we select the limited set of pitches in our ragas. A specific set of notes produces a distinct feeling, such as joy." He smiled confidently.

"You are an instrument and the music plays you," announced Manasa.

"Something was playing me at Swamiji's concert!" I piped up.

"Just what are Swamiji's credentials?" That came right out of my mouth.

"Swamiji has no musical training, but plays 101 instruments," Manasa fired back. "He also speaks five languages without any training. What do you say to that?"

I responded with silence.

Manasa continued our conversation, "Swamiji plays for your digestion, your heart or your blood pressure."

The beneficial effects of Swamiji's music for specific body parts remind me of the work of Dr. Jeffrey Thompson, a chiropractor. Dr. Thompson popped a vertebra of a back into place with musical tones. (He plays the back like a xylophone.) Nifty discovery, but it took 30 seconds to put vertebrae back in place with a tone, and just five seconds by using his thumb. Ultimately, this was not useful for him - until he tried an experiment.

Nerves from each vertebra in our backs go to specific places in our bodies, such as organs. When a specific vertebra was out of place, Dr. Thompson took blood tests to identify problems with each corresponding organ before and after he put the vertebra into place with his thumbs. He also performed the same before-and-after tests for popping the same vertebra into place with musical tones.

The tone Dr. Thompson used to entrain the vertebra traveled via the nerve to the corresponding organ, entraining it as well. Blood tests confirmed that the organ healed when musical tones were used to put the corresponding vertebra into place. Was the body a musical instrument, with each organ struggling to maintain intonation? Was the spine like a circuit breaker, popping out whenever an organ got out of tune?

In contrast, problems in organs, noted by the blood pretest, did not correct themselves when Dr. Thompson used only his thumb to put the vertebra back into place.

Ramesh, the drum player, cocked his head. "In the ashram (Indian school – a spiritual monastery) we played harp strings fastened underneath a tabletop. Swamiji's music is played onto the backs of people needing healing."

I tried that once. What a trip, literally. I laid on the table as someone strummed strings underneath the table. In no time flat, I was "out of it" - fully immersed in my imagination. I believed I was in a jungle and later in Egypt. The experience felt real. The sun on my shoulders was warm and I smelled the freshness of the air. I could see little dust clouds float up from my feet that plodded in sand, as the softness of my leather sandals rubbed my feet.

Sound can enter our bodies several ways. It can penetrate our skin and bones just as easily as it can enter into our ears. However, when sound passes through our skin and bones, it is transmitted to the center of our brain, where our subconscious memory is stored. Things we don't want to face are pushed into our subconscious mind. Could music loosen old hidden emotions, helping us unload stored emotional baggage? Mystics say this portion of our brain also stores our past lives. I suppose they might say that my imaginings of the jungle and Egypt were of past lives as well.

Ramesh, the Indian drum player, sounded like a siren with a rising pitch. "We use earphones in the ashram, too!"

Ramesh's information brought out the scientist in me. I remembered that when different pitches enter each ear in close proximity (such as with headphones), an unusual phenomenon occurs. Let's say you hear a sound of 20 hertz in your right earphone and 40 hertz in your left earphone. (Frequencies are measured in hertz. One hertz (Hz) is one cycle per second. Hertz are used to quantify periodic things like sound waves.

Think of hertz as similar to degrees on a thermometer. As the pitch gets higher, the hertz goes up. As the pitch gets lower, the hertz gets lower. Higher Hz is the same as higher energy.)

Even though these pitches are sounded into your earphones, you don't hear the pitches of 20 or 40 hertz. Guess what you'll hear? (The suspense is killing you, isn't it!) You'll hear 20 hertz, the difference between the two frequencies.

Let's say you put a pitch of 1 hertz in your right ear and 3 hertz in your left ear; you will hear 2 hertz. Both halves of your brain work together and subtract $3 - 1$, so you hear 2 hertz. It's no big deal to hear a 2 hertz frequency. However, listening to tones created by engaging both halves of your brain with stereo headphones induces certain states of consciousness, which produce corresponding brain waves. After about five to ten minutes of listening to certain pitches with stereo earphones, you can enter a deep meditative state. It can take a monk years to learn to go into a deep meditative state that you can achieve quickly with earphones. What we hear affects our level of conscious functioning. Fascinating!

What else can sound and music do?

Dr. Tomatis, a French ear, nose and throat specialist, used sound to improve one's learning, energy and emotions. As a young doctor immediately after World War II, he observed that his Jewish patients were deaf to the pitch range of the sirens heard when Jewish people were taken to death camps. Dr. Tomatis' further investigation revealed that people, who can hear, might be deaf for specific hertz frequencies, just like the Jewish survivors of World War II. For example, a woman with an abusive father became deaf in the frequency range that included her father's voice.

We can "tune" things out! Can you hear a conversation while "tuning out" the hum of the refrigerator? Of course! We selectively hear what we want to. We can force certain unwanted sounds into the background, and eventually we don't hear them at all. So, I can tune out whoever asks me to take out the trash. No wonder so many people's hearing gets worse with age!

When we experience traumatic events, we often tune out frequencies associated with the trauma. Different cilia *(ear hairs)* in our ears perceive different hertz ranges. We can literally kill certain cilia hairs and become deaf in the hertz frequencies that we associate with the trauma. And who has not experienced upsetting emotions?

Dr. Tomatis' investigations led him to develop an "electronic ear". This machine worked by taking music of normal frequencies then electronically adjusting the treble or base of the music. In this way the cilia of the ear was "exercised". The cilia hairs in a listener's ear responded to the degree of treble or base in the sound, thereby being strengthened. It's an aerobic workout for ear hairs! Dead cilia could not be regenerated, but neighboring cilia were enhanced, allowing significant improvement in patients who used this technique.

When people recovered their full (or almost full range) of hearing through the Tomatis method, they documented associated improvements including:

- Attention Deficit Disorder (ADD)
- Attention Deficit Hyperactivity Disorder (ADHD)
- Learning problems
- Autism
- Dyslexia
- Balance and coordination
- Asperger's syndrome
- Emotional issues
- Pervasive Development Disorder (PDD)
- Down syndrome.[3]

People experienced personality changes after their hearing was repaired with the electronic ear treatments. For example, the woman who was deaf in the range of her abusive

---

[3] www.tomatis.com

father's voice never bonded with men, especially those who had voices close in pitch to that of her father's. After the electronic ear treatments cilia hairs were strengthened for deficient frequencies, these relationships returned to "normal."

Manasa reflected, "Yes, we use earphones in the ashram, too."

Jaitra changed the subject. "Get this one," he said. "At the ashram we play Swamiji's recordings to the cows to make our milk sweet and plentiful."

"I get it! Sweeter milk with sweet music?" I sighed.

This reminds me of what I have read of the French physicist, Joel Sternheimer. He discovered that "while a protein is being assembled from its 20 constituent amino acids in the 'cell factory' called the ribosome, the amino acid's (movements) are considerably slowed down…so a vibration or a frequency can be calculated…and transcribed into acoustical bandwidth as a note…."[4] Sternheimer's point is that the vibration of each amino acid corresponds to a note. If you play the notes, corresponding to the amino acids, back in the order that they are combined in a protein, a melody results. Sternheimer recognized some of the plant species' songs as familiar ones, such as "O Sole Mio" and "The Blue Danube." Better yet, when Sternheimer played the plant's amino acids' songs back to the plant, he documented up to 250 percent accelerated growth; also, resilience to drought and disease was improved.[5]

Birds sing to our plants, too! Does this help the plants to grow? Pitches affect plants and humans, so I guess cows are entitled to the benefits of music, too.

The Crystal Wand

"It was crystal rocks that got me to this deep retreat in the woods in the first place. What was Swamiji doing with that

---

[4] Jean – Pierre Lentin, Keelynet.com

[5] http://www.earthpulse.com/src/subcategory.asp?catid=2&subcatid=6 "French Physicist Creates New Melodies – Plant Songs." Sept. 3, 2005, Pg. 2.

crystal on stage? Was it his 'magic wand?'" I reflected, seeing Swamiji in my mind again, holding the crystal wand in the air in front of the audience.

"You have to tell me!" I insisted again. "What was Swamiji doing with the crystal stick?"

Dr. Rao replied, "Silicon chips in our computers are crystals. Transmitters in radios and TVs are made of crystal. Crystals receive and send information. When Swamiji waved his crystal wand and scanned the audience, the crystal was absorbing information from the audience. The vibrations of the audience's body were received into the crystal, just like we input information on a silicon chip in a computer."

I imagined all of our out-of-tune livers, wanting to hear their favorite songs.

"The crystal absorbs energy, learns what the majority of health problems of the audience are," continued Manasa. "Swamiji is a great psychic. When he closes his eyes behind the crystal that has received information from the audience, he sees colors. Swamiji uses the colors to diagnose the audience's out of tune frequencies. Swamiji analyzes the colors like we analyze information on a computer."

Here again, I remembered antiquity. Ancient Buddhists and Egyptians used color to heal people. For example, blue offered a healing experience for someone, who was stressed and angry, while red and orange energized the depressed soul. Ancient treatment rooms sported colored lighting (candles with colored fabric shades), and everything else was the same color too - clothes, furniture, even food, if possible. A pilgrim stayed in the colored rooms for up to a week, absorbing the energy needed to bring him into balance. So powerful was this treatment that it was a serious health and emotional risk to enter another color treatment until some time had elapsed.

"Does it matter what time it is in Swamiji's music?" I ventured.

I thought I had hit the big Lotto ticket! I wish you could have seen the excitement on everyone's faces when I asked such a simple question.

"Music is numbers, says the Swamiji," recalled Dr. Rao. "And numbers are time."

"And Swamiji always asks what time it is as he sits at his piano before beginning the concert," Jaitra projected.

Here, then, was the million-dollar question: "…How does Swamiji tell time?" I ventured.

I feel like I am in an animated cartoon. All four sets of eyebrows rise at the same time, maximizing the whites in the eyes below as they do.

"Not the way you do," all four voices whisper.

"You approximate the time it takes the earth to rotate around the sun to be 365 days. Your calendar is not perfect. In contrast, Swamiji uses the 'perfect' time," Manasa explained.

I guess Big Bird from Sesame Street didn't teach Swamiji how to tell time, like he taught my kids.

It takes the earth 365.2422 days to rotate around the sun. Our calendar is off by a little bit each year, with leap years correcting the differences. However, over thousands of years, our approximate calculations produce different results than the most accurate ones.

The ancient Mayans, who made many predictions about this millennium, used a more precise system of timekeeping. Various predictions, some from the Mayan culture, created the "Y2K" fear that caused many to hide in their homes as our earth passed into the year 2000. Many were not aware of the calendar difference between many ancient cultures and ours. The Mayan calendar projects that earth entered the next millennium in our calendar year 2012; thus, according to many ancient people, the predictions for our new millennium were not for the year 2000, but 2012.

"We have a far more accurate system of recording time. The Indian system of calculating time (dating back many thousands of years) is based on intense observation of solar, lunar and planetary movements. We observe the date, weekday, the ruling star, yoga, and the sum of these combined influences. This time system has astrological aspects, and we reference our activities to both," Dr. Rao added.

"The ancient Vedas (our scriptures) mention the importance of specific time periods to conduct certain activities and other times to abstain," Manasa concluded.

"A day is divided into eight time zones and there are specific ragas to play in each zone. This is to ensure balance in the listener's subtle energies. Environmental vibrations vary during the day and season, affecting plants, animals and humans. Music can balance the constantly changing web of nature's subtle energies that can affect our energy."

Manasa expanded on similarities between the energy of time and music. "There is an intimate relationship between time and music. Both are endless in nature. Both can be understood only from a reference point. Endless time is measured for our convenience in seconds and minutes. There are various methods of keeping time in music," Manasa continued.

"In the spectrum of waves, sound that we hear is only a small part. The audible and inaudible spectrum is essentially endless and infinite like time," Manasa said.

Dr. Rao sounded authoritative. "Swamiji says that music is astrology. Patterns of music are nothing but systems of numbers, like systems of numbers that are used in astrology."

I scratch my chin. Rather than getting guidance from a horoscope with our cup of coffee and morning paper, could we get the daily prescriptive song!

As silly as my wandering thoughts sounded, we are energetic beings. But what about the stars? The moon? Do they have energy, too?

Doesn't the moon cause tides in our huge oceans? In Maine the difference between high and low tide is 12 feet. The world does not have a power plant big enough to move our huge oceans 12 feet several times a day.

The moon clearly affects tides, but aren't we composed largely of water, too? Does the full moon affect us physically and emotionally? Crimes go up during full moons? Don't some people grow hair on their feet and all over their body as they howl at the full moon? …You do?

Antiquity reveals story after story of ancient musicians "playing the stars." And NO! They didn't travel around the universe and pluck the stars, creating celestial melodies. They composed their music to complement the influences of the changing energy from stars as our earth revolved on its axis circling around the sun.

According to the ancient Chinese, energy from stars affects our health, mood and energy.

Manasa confirmed this. "The energy of a star affects you based on your physical, mental and spiritual position. Music can alter the star's energetic influence, because music also changes your physical, mental, or spiritual energy, so as to facilitate or negate the star's effect on you.

"Further anecdotes would be ritual chants to bring rain or other ragas to halt rain. This is another example of ancient people using elements of music to influence nature," Manasa claimed.

I recalled that the ancient Chinese changed the music that people listened to during different times of day. As seasons changed, they also changed the keys in which music was played and they changed which musical instruments were used. Allowing only specific instruments to be used during certain times controlled the timber of the music (due to dominant harmonics for specific instruments). For example, wood instruments (such as violins) were heard in the summer and reed instruments (such as clarinets) were reserved for spring. Metal instruments were used in the fall and drums in the winter. Therefore, they tailored the dominant harmonics to control the interaction of the music with the energy of nature. In so doing this, ancient Chinese leaders altered the impact of the music on their people.

The sounds of instruments were equated with nature; musical instruments are all offshoots from nature -

(instruments are made from materials of nature, such as wood, reeds, metals, animal hides, fibers, etc.).

Many ancient people believed harmonics from the energy of nature, the seasons, and the stars (astrological influences), strongly affected their minds, bodies and emotions.

In a large church, we easily hear harmonics. Each note has a series of *"after"* vibrations that get higher and higher in pitch. This happens with all notes, but sometimes due to poor acoustics and our limited hearing ranges, we don't always hear the harmonics.

Pythagoras revealed a numerical formula of "after" or component pitches (harmonics) that accompany a base note. The pattern allows us to predict the exact frequency of the after pitches or harmonics.

- The first harmonic jumps an octave from the original pitch (an octave is twice the speed of the vibration or eight notes higher than the starting pitch); both vibrations create a ratio of 1:2. (If you plucked a string, then cut it in half, and plucked it again, the second pitch would be twice as high.)
- The second harmonic has a ratio of 1:3. (This harmonic is three times higher than the base note. The first harmonic and this harmonic create an interval of a fifth, that is, an interval five notes apart.)
- The third harmonic has a ratio of 1:4. (This harmonic is four times higher than the base note. The new harmonic is an interval of a fourth higher, that is, four notes plus an octave higher.)
- The next ratio is 1:5. (This harmonic is five times higher than the base note. The new harmonic creates an interval of a major sixth, that is, this harmonic is six notes higher than the base note).
- And so on. This pattern isn't too hard to figure out. The harmonic pitches quickly go above our hearing

ranges, but sophisticated equipment can accurately measure them.

Musical instruments differ in sound because of the intensity of their different harmonics. This is also what makes your voice sound different from someone else's, even when you sing the exact same pitch.

Playing with harmonics is like playing musical "feng shui," in that there are wood, fire, earth, water, metal and air sounds. The Chinese changed instruments seasonally, to control the harmonics people heard at various times of the year. They believed certain harmonics helped people balance the changing energy of the seasons and changing locations of the stars that rotate in the sky throughout the year.

As we were deep into the conversation on harmonics, I scratched my itchy nose, the side of my nostril to be exact, one of the many spots that Swamiji's music affected. "You're scratching a nadi point," Jaitra noted.

"A what?" I asked. "Does nadi mean nose in Indian?"

"No, a nadi point is an intersection of subtle energy channels in your underlying energy body. A nadi is a point that acupuncturists use to heal people," continued Jaitra.

In the embryo of chickens, scientists discovered an energy map or grid in place before the physical body of the chicken forms. Mystics have been referring to this energy grid for thousands of years. They believe this subtle energy body is the blueprint of the physical body and also the connection between our physical bodies and our nonphysical minds and emotions. For example, if I worry, I slow down the subtle energy in my belly. When the subtle energy grid is slow or "out of tune" long enough, my stomach becomes diseased and I get an ulcer.

Healthy energy grids are necessary for a healthy body. This is the premise that acupuncture is based on. Acupuncture "tunes" the flow of our subtle energy systems.

The major intersections of nadis that channel energy to and from the physical body are called chakras. The word chakra, means energy wheel. We are healthy when our chakras spin energy to needed areas of our body. The ancient Hindi people, the Sufi's, as well as many modern scientists, sound different vowels as one way to ensure energy is properly flowing into our chakras. The ancient Chinese people also associated the sounds of the chakras with various elements (the sound of fire, water, metal, earth and wood).

These Chinese people believed that the sound of our own voice vibrates in our body, affecting our health. The quality of our voice can be earthy (slow and deep) or metallic (high and piercing); these vibrations affect our body. They believed that exposure to too much of one type of sound causes disharmony or a weakness in a specific organ. For example, hearing too many earth elements (laughing, slow voice, drawn out, belching sounds) causes digestion problems.

I wonder if Swamiji used this information when choosing his "prescriptive" music. Manasa had said that Swamiji changes his music to improve different body systems or organs, such as digestion, the heart, the skin and so on.

Manasa had enough of my stories of Western scientists and their scientific theories and facts. With a fountain of energy spouting out of his mouth, he explained, "You can't take Swamiji's music and analyze it. Swamiji has psychic powers that we just don't understand.

"I knew Swamiji in the beginning of his career. I doubted his powers, because I wanted scientific proof. One day I learned that my sister had a brain aneurysm and must have brain surgery or die. Twenty-five years ago, the success rate for brain surgery wasn't too good in India. I was upset, but Swamiji told me, 'Don't worry. I will save your sister.'

"I was with Swamiji, several miles away from the hospital, when my sister went into surgery. Swamiji went into a deep trance during the entire time of the operation.

"The doctors reported that my sister called out Swamiji's name during the surgery. After the surgery she vowed that Swamiji was at her side the entire time of the operation. Now, I know he was not, as he was next to me in a deep trance. Later Swamiji went to the hospital with me to visit my sister. He told her, 'I gave you life.' How can we analyze what Swamiji does? He is a human being more advanced than we can comprehend."

My mind raced back to the story of the man with the white scarf who said that Swamiji enabled him to return to his body after he had legally died.

Manasa was on a roll. "When Swamiji was young, he saw people suffering with a severe fever. Out of compassion he touched them and their fever was immediately gone. In three hours, the fever showed up in his body and he would simply dismiss it. Now he doesn't even need to take the fever into himself. He just dismisses the fever in someone's body."

My mouth hung open. This sounded incredible.

Dr. Rao changed the mood by glancing at his watch.

"One more question," I insisted. "If someone just loves music, what advice would you give to him?"

A warm smile crossed Dr. Rao's face. "Enjoy it. Listening is an art. It is an active skill. Focus and pay attention. Let the music play you.

"Your feelings will be your best guide as to what music you listen to. Your feelings have a hidden intelligence. Listen to what gives you pleasure." Dr. Rao smiled again.

Jaitra added, "Swamiji won't play music for people who won't pay attention. If people don't pay attention, the music won't heal them."

Manasa noted, "Swamiji also changes the music according to how advanced a person's energy is. For example, a person who usually acts negatively or is frequently in a bad mood is affected differently by Swamiji's music than one who is kind and loving. A person that spends time in negativity slows down his energy and can't handle the intensity of some of Swamiji's music. An advanced soul can handle more intense healing and different music."

A light bulb went on inside my head. "You're saying that whoever **receives** the miracle of healing plays an active role in his own miracle? If he doesn't pay attention to the music, he turns the miracle down? The receiver is a part of the miracle!"

Four big smiles. I got this point.

I knew our time was done and I had promised only one more question, but another slipped out. This question was for me. I am a musician. "What advice would you give musicians, so they too could play music to heal people?"

The chorus started, "Same thing. Enjoy it! When you feel beautiful emotions, you vibrate in tune with them. Everyone who listens will vibrate with the beauty you create. They catch it from you. Don't play to the audience. Play to your own soul. When your music plays your soul, your music becomes a prayer of healing."

This time I smiled. "I get it. I really get it. We simply should 'be all we can be,' and that most deeply influences others. To our own selves be true!"

Four beautiful smiles beamed back at me.

www.JillsWingsOfLight.com – Art Gallery

For more information: www.dattapeetham.com

Chapter Two

Sound Made Visible

Hans Jenny created a process that allowed people to view sound shaping matter. Jenny put sand, or similar media (powders or certain fluids), on a metal plate then exposed it to sound. A crystal sound generator vibrated the bottom of the metal plate. Certain sound frequencies/collections of sounds formed shapes in the sand. Hans called this process Cymatics, after the Greek word *kymatika*, meaning, "matter pertaining to waves."

Another way to imagine this process is to imagine a boom box blasting music under a drum that has sand on its solid lid. The music will move the sand on the drum, and it may create images!

Jeff Volk, from MACROmedia, described this process, "Metal is composed of molecules, which are not uniformly distributed. Some spots of the metal plate are denser. When sound vibrates the metal plate, the vibrations go slower through places that are denser. The sound hits the edge of the plate and then reflects back in again, reflecting on other sound waves. This creates patterns of more or less concentrations of sound. The sand slows down and piles up in denser areas of sound, creating lines and shapes in the sand."

The Look of Sound
When several tones vibrate sand on a metal plate an image can be formed in the sand. People suspect sound will

produce random, haphazard and formless shapes, if any at all.
In reality, sound can create:
- Intricate geometric patterns
- Mandalas[6]
- Flower patterns
- Biological forms
- Powerful archetypes
- Images that look like stained glass
- Patterns found in crop circles.

Hans Jenny noticed that "when the vowels of the ancient languages like Hebrew and Sanskrit were pronounced (and exposed to the metal plates bearing sand), the sand took the shape of the written symbol for those vowels. Modern languages did not generate these patterns."[7]

Hans Jenny produced videos showing sound made visible through Cymatics. Now we can analyze archetypes, geometric shapes and biological forms made with sound and marvel at the relationship between sound and physical things.

Many religions tell us that our world was created by sound. As we wonder about their claims, Hans Jenny gives us a window on the interactions of sound and matter. And a picture is worth a thousand words!

Although people in different religions disagree on many points, Cymatic videos illustrate natural laws that do not rely on any belief systems. It is simple science. It is not a philosophy or religion, but an analytical observation of nature.

Take a look at the shapes that sound created from loose sand and other matter.[8]

---

[6] "Mandala has become a generic term for any plan, chart or geometric pattern that represents the cosmos metaphysically or symbolically, a microcosm of the universe from the human perspective." Wikipedia

[7] John Beaulieu. Music and Sound in the Healing Arts, Station hill Press, 1995.

[8] Images from *Cymatics: A Study of Wave Phenomena and Vibration*, copyright 2001. MACROmedia, Used by permission. www.cymaticsource.com

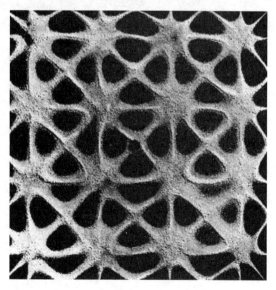

Images from *Cymatics: A Study of Wave Phenomena and Vibration*, copyright 2001. MACROmedia, Used by permission.

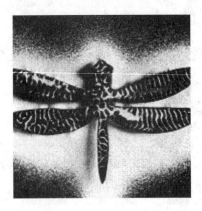

Images from *Cymatics: A Study of Wave Phenomena and Vibration*,
copyright 2001. MACROmedia, Used by permission.

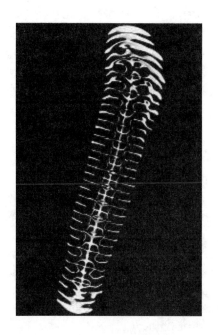

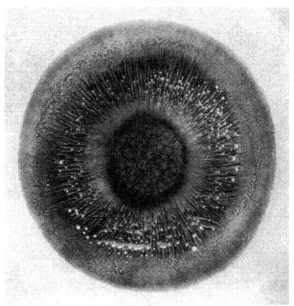

Images from *Cymatics: A Study of Wave Phenomena and Vibration*, copyright 2001. MACROmedia, Used by permission.

Creating Better "Houses of Sand!"

When a metal plate with loose sand on it is vibrated with certain pitches, the sound creates shapes in the sand that are symmetrical, intricate, balanced and beautiful.

However, tones do not maintain symmetrical designs if the pitches are raised. As the frequency of the pitch increases, new shapes organize and disorganize over and over again.

At lower frequencies, the sound patterns create simple, geometric shapes in the sand. As the frequency climbs, the lines of the simple image crack. The image falls apart at the seams! Fragmentation, disorder and shapeless sand emerge.

As the frequency continues to climb, the fragments again coalesce into a beautiful pattern. This time, the pattern is more intricate. With escalating frequencies, the sound waves again shake, rattle and roll, and the pattern disintegrates.

As the frequency continues to increase, the sand forms even more lavish and rich designs with fields-within-fields, and patterns-within-patterns.

This process reminds me of an article, written by Jeffrey Thompson, who discusses the impact in our brain when small brainwaves change into larger brain waves.[9] He writes, "These fluctuations are more than the nervous system can handle with its current structure, and the brain responds by reorganizing itself at a higher more complex level of functioning."

Why Is This Important?

Watching sound create organized shapes, which decay and then reform into more complicated shapes, mirrors life itself, helping us make sense of the difficult times in our lives. In this analogy we enjoy a simple peace, but when difficulties arise, we fall apart at the seams. After incidents shatter our thinking patterns, we pick up our pieces and learn lessons about ourselves. We remake our lives with this newfound wisdom. We achieve new stability from the more intricate and

---

[9] www.neuroacoustic.org, "The Science behind the Acoustic Brainwave Entrainment," Pg. 12.

evolved pattern in our thinking. Eventually, there is a new crisis in which we doubt our beliefs again, and the cycle continues.

Perhaps, the Cymatic videos illuminate the question, "Why do bad things happen to good people?" Crises are just part of a natural flow of energy. There is no good achieved by blaming a crisis on someone else. Instead, a crisis disintegrates our thinking patterns, which makes it easier to form new, deeper thoughts and feelings. When we surrender to the lessons which life teaches us, we can quickly change our thoughts and behaviors, recreating ourselves with more sophisticated ways of thinking and being.

Many people resist change, yet life requires change. When we resist change, we prevent new healthy energy from flowing into us. As we attempt to resist changes, circumstances may force us to alter our old ways regardless, making us create a better "house of sand."

Life in the universe flows. It is ever changing.

We Make Our Own Vibrations

In the 1960s Hans Jenny created a simple instrument that allowed us to see the human voice! The 'tonocscope' looked a bit like a small saxophone, resting on a flat base with a rubber membrane stretched over the bell, and sand spread evenly across the membrane. When you sing into the mouthpiece (no reed, just an open tube), the vibrations of your voice vibrate the membrane, animating the sand. Everything about the quality of the voice affects the subtle patterns in the sand.

You can watch your voice shape matter. Emotions hidden beneath your words are reflected in the resulting images in the sand. For example, negative emotions carried on your voice create distortion.

When we talk, sing, shout and giggle, we are creating sound, which is energy that shapes matter. We can mold matter with our spoken words! We are more powerful than we realize!

Our thoughts, feelings and words are vibrations. When we become angry, disappointed or jealous, we experience negative vibrations that we unconsciously formed. In other words, we create our world by the way we vibrate our "metal plate" with our vibrations of thoughts, feelings and words.

If we were conscious of the vibrations we form, we would choose them with more care. We can create the vibrations we want in our lives instead of unconsciously creating ones we don't enjoy.

Consciousness Increases

With the Cymatic videos, we watch cycles of creation and chaos in an evolutionary process. By improving our mental and emotional control, we attain higher consciousness. Elevating our consciousness gives us more control over things we can change, and greater understanding of things that are out of our control.

Why does consciousness increase our understanding? I sometimes imagine I am a drop of frozen water... a twinkle in a snowflake. As I become more conscious, I become aware of the whole snowflake and the beauty of all the drops of water - a greater majesty than just my one sparkle. With increased consciousness, I realize that I am part of a snow-covered mountain that is breathtakingly beautiful. Still later, I realize that my mountain is an iceberg and that "I" exist under the water as well. I marvel at what the underwater world brings to my perspective.

Still later, I realize that my existence as a sparkly snowflake is threatened as I begin to morph into liquid water. Although I am afraid of dying as a snowflake, I am reborn into a drop of water. I am morphed into the deep beautiful sea, ever changing, yet ever the same.

As my consciousness continues to expand, I see that I am also part of the planet Earth, a place with awesome wonders... and tragedies as well.

As my consciousness evolves, things appear to be different, but I am the same - the one and the all.

Can we, like the Cymatic pattern that disintegrates and reemerges into a more complicated pattern, create a more sophisticated consciousness, or increase our ability to understand our "oneness" with others and our world? Is it a matter of frequency?

Visit www.cymaticsource.com for more explorations into the visual world of sound!

www.JillsWingsOfLight.com – Art Gallery

This article was completed after an interview with Clematic expert, Jeff Volk. It includes many of his ideas and information from his web site. Jeff had Hans Jenny's videos remade and is republishing Hans Jenny's books. Jeff's 1992 video, *Of Sound and Mind and Body*, won the Hartly Film Award. For many years Jeff produced the International Sound Colloquium, a conference exploring the power of sacred sound and healing music. He completed *Sounding the Psyche: Attuning the Bodymind.*

Chapter Three

Brain Mapping

The Journey into the Wonderful World of Sound

"I give people our 'Catnap' CD to make believers out of them so they can experience the power of sound," reported Laurie Monroe, daughter of the late Robert Monroe.

"Wait!" I protested. "How did it all begin? What life paths did you follow that led to the production of a CD that makes a 'believer' out of a person?"

"I was seven years old when Daddy, a curious man, started experimenting with how people could learn while they were sleeping. After all, we spend a third of our lives asleep."

Laurie recounted the experiences of her father, Robert Monroe, who invented the Hemi-Sync® technology, and his career studying sounds. "My father produced over 40 radio shows in the New York area. At this time, my father's experimentation with the power of sound was only a curiosity, but one that would last.

"Daddy's first roadblock became a unique opportunity that gave him his purpose in life. The roadblock was teaching people how to fall asleep. As a radio producer, Daddy was familiar with frequencies and sounds, and their ability to impact people. He experimented with sounds, trying this one and picking that one, to see which specific frequencies would help people to fall into a deep sleep, a delta brain wave sleep.

"As Daddy experimented with different frequencies, certain frequencies swept him into extraordinary experiences. For example, he was conscious while flying (no airplane) and he visited people located far away, only to confirm later that the people he visited were actually doing what he saw them do. Daddy labeled these experiences as OBEs (out-of-body experiences).

"These out-of-body experiences were unexplainable to Daddy. The church and some family members saw them as macabre. Becoming frightened by his strange experiences, Daddy assumed that he was dying, going through the first step of the death process!

"After the doctor confirmed Daddy's excellent health, his thinking changed," Laurie remembered.

"'I must be losing my mind,' my father mused, as he scheduled a visit with his friend, the psychologist. If he was not dying then he must be going nuts. But after he got another clean bill of mental health, he was confused again."

Laurie recalled the day that a family friend and psychologist, Dr. Bradshaw, sat back in his chair, smoking his pipe in their living room. As Dr. Bradshaw puffed out a smoke ring he offered, "Bob, you need to go to an ashram in India and study with a guru for ten years to understand what is happening to you."

"Fat chance of that happening with a family, mortgage and responsibilities," Laurie continued, "but my father's curiosity was incurably peaked. What was this knowledge?"

Three years of intense research gave her father, Robert Monroe, peace of mind. He knew that he wasn't dying and leaving loved ones behind, because he had out-of-body experiences. He decided to enter the University of "Understand Thyself" and major in the "Power of Sound."

Sound: The Preferred Method of Travel

Laurie continued, "One day Daddy decided to share his great secret with me and tell me about his 'flying' experiences. These weren't ordinary experiences; he could fly to faraway places without an airplane and view what others were doing. Scrupulously, he confirmed that what he had observed was indeed accurate and not imaginary.

"Nervously, he told me his big secret.

"'You Fly? So? So what?' I retorted. I was ten years old and I did that, too. 'All people can fly!'" I thought.

"Now," Laurie reflected, "I think everyone had psychic or out-of-body experiences when they were younger. As we grow older, we don't believe them. These memories get cataloged as weird and tucked away in our unconscious minds, but when I was ten years old, my flying experiences were real.

"Daddy published his first of three books shortly thereafter, *Journey Out of Body*. This diary recorded his out-of-body experiences and his painstaking efforts to validate them by collaborating what he observed out-of-body with what happened in the physical world. He was amazingly accurate. For example, he would go out-of-body in Virginia and observe what a friend was doing at 2:00 p.m. in Colorado. Later, he called the friend and asked her what she was doing at 2:00, only to find he had observed her accurately.

"After several years and moves, we ended up in Charlottesville, as Daddy bought radio stations and founded cablevision companies. The Monroe Institute of Applied Sciences was opened in 1971. We just conducted research then," Laurie remembered.

"Research was conducted at the institute and at home. Guests would come over for dinner and instead of being offered a martini, they were offered a seat in the 'Box' and exposed to the Frequency du Jour. After many guests reported what they experienced from listening to the frequencies, Daddy catalogued what frequencies produced what specific experiences."

Laurie then reported how her father charted frequencies that produced different experiences. For example, with sound you can quickly experience:

- Mind awake, body asleep
- Expanded awareness beyond your senses
- The sensation of no time and no space
- The bridge to other dimensions

- What it feels like after death.

Laurie reflected, "Daddy believed the most exciting journey that anyone could ever take was within himself. There is a universe of experiences inside each one of us that we hide away in our subconscious mind, just as we put our daydream experiences away when we grow up. Sounds are the keys to different worlds that await us… deep inside of ourselves."

"In 1979 The Monroe Institute offered courses and training for people to experience the exciting worlds that people could visit in the vast universe - within themselves. Sound was the preferred transportation vehicle to all these 'marvelous vacation spots.'"

Laurie continued, "The Monroe Institute embraces a person's belief and allows him to turn that belief into something that is KNOWN. For example, I could write a book on what 'cold' is, but that will never help you understand that concept as much as experiencing what cold is.

"A person may believe that there is life after death, but when they experience a visit with a person who has passed on, and then a 'shift' occurs. Then they KNOW there is life after death - quite a different emotion than just thinking it so."

Laurie remembered, "Another big lesson Daddy learned was that people are more than their physical bodies. For example, when an athlete gets in the 'zone' for high performance, he is mastering his mind, body and spirit. People are a package deal, with different layers of experiences *(mind, spirit, and body)* comprising who we are."

The Hemi-Sync® Process and the Monroe Institute
The Hemi-Sync sound experience provides listeners with a combination of frequencies that puts one's mind, body and emotions in a desired state of consciousness. By experiencing Hemi-Sync's brain wave patterns, we expand our mind, getting us in touch with all that we are. Most people ignore the higher and better parts of themselves. The Monroe

Institute wants to reconnect a person with those greater parts found within.

I urged Laurie to tell me more about how these frequencies physically change us. "It's all about resonance," Laurie offered. "The frequency, at which the brain is vibrating at, creates brainwaves that correlate with certain states of consciousness. An EEG is one way of measuring these brain frequencies. For example, we measure the brainwave patterns of a healer and 'reverse-engineer' those brainwave patterns into frequencies. Now when one hears these frequencies on a CD, it entrains the listener's brain to vibrate at those same frequencies, which produces a specific state of consciousness. Without these auditory influences, this person may never experience such a state of consciousness."

Theta Brainwaves
Without Hemi-Sync®

Theta Brainwaves
With Hemi-Sync®

Nuero Map – viewing the Top of a Head

Laurie showed me a neuro-map, showing expanded brain usage with Hemi-sync sounds. I stared at the neuro-map. It vividly displayed that both the right and left halves of the brain were being used. In contrast, without the Hemi-Sync sounds, we normally use a small part of the right half OR the left half of our brain. When we engage BOTH halves of our brain at the same time, we increase our mental capacities - we achieve whole brain functioning.

The Monroe Institute conducted experiments for 40 years to confirm and reconfirm that their frequencies work. Actually, the scientists are not doing research, but "newsearch," as they experiment with new states of consciousness available from new combinations of frequencies. Later, they validate the frequencies by retesting over and over.

"An important consideration," Laurie emphasized, "is that the listener is in control of his experience. There is no dependence, no side effects and no subliminal messages when using Hemi-Sync to experience different states of consciousness. What you experience is up to you. It is not like hypnosis or a process that uses subliminal control. It doesn't do anything TO you.

"The Monroe Institute provides Hemi-Sync CDs to help people sleep, relax, stay focused, lessen the need for anesthesia and improve recovery time after surgery. They neither make claims that they are a medical facility nor provide medical treatment; in fact, they complement medical science.

"The Monroe Institute also offers CDs that lessen the effects of attention deficit disorders (ADD and ADHD). Surely it is worthwhile for a mother to spend $20 for a CD for ADD to see what the effects are on her child's behavior, and then decide if the medicine is necessary. If the CD works one can avoid the negative side effects of the medication.

"Monroe's Energy Dolphin Club is a program that uses auditory training so listeners can entrain their minds to other healers' energy states. We brain map healers and 'reverse engineer' their brainwave patterns into sound frequencies. This enables listeners to vibrate 'in tune' with the original healer's energy state, so they can help others to a greater degree.

"The training is miraculously fast," Laurie reports. "For example, in years past, two monks spent a week taking our residential program, entitled 'Gateway Voyage.' Later, the monks were interviewed by the *Wall Street Journal*. The monks told the world that what The Monroe Institute taught in one week, had taken them twenty years to learn.

"For thirty-two years, the 'Gateway Voyage' Program has taught people to learn that they are 'more than their physical bodies' by using sound. In 32 years, we heard person after person tell how the 'Gateway Voyage' was a life changing experience," Laurie confirmed.

After the initial training, the 'Gateway Voyage,' The Monroe Institute offers graduate programs entitled:

- Manifesting and Creating
- Lifeline (experiencing a map of the afterlife)
- Heartlines
- And many more.

"How did you get the frequencies for these programs?" I queried.

"I'll tell you how I created 'Heartlines.' In 1994, at Daddy's insistence, I spent four days with him in his cabin where he did his writing. We reminisced about everything, I mean everything. We talked about fun times and sad memories. We explored our ideas about what life was all about. There were no sacred topics and every secret we ever had was told. Our egos were gone.

"At the end of this time together, we were incredibly close. I had never experienced such intensity in my heart. We were just two essences, expressing love. I experienced what people can feel without the barriers they create in their minds - barriers from pain, lack of forgiveness and judgement. These activities separate people from the true power within. We then mapped these frequencies by measuring our own brain waves and copying them for others, so other people could access them."

"So, how does one best experience your rich frequency gifts?" I asked, summing up our conversation.

"In addition to taking our courses at The Monroe Institute, people who can't travel to Virginia, can experience CDs that we offer at www.MonroeInstitute.org. For example, we offer the 'Gateway Experience' on CDs, which is similar to the 'Gateway Voyage.'

"Our CDs give people the experience by entraining the brain to vibrate at various frequencies. Once people know what these frequencies feel like, they can recall the feeling and train their brain to go to the desired state of consciousness at will. Our CDs are their 'training wheels.'

"When people ask me how one benefits from our program, I give them our 'Catnapper' CD. It gives the listener a deep 90-minute sleep in just thirty minutes. It gives them an experience that makes a believer out of them.

"Once people experience the 'shift,' they learn what a powerful tool sound is. Sound is life changing."

For more information, visit: www.MonroeInstitute.org.

www.JillsWingsOfLight.com – Art Gallery

Chapter Four

Sound and Light Machines

"Light and sound enabled me to grow up without getting older," Michael Stevens, co-owner of Theta Technologies, emphatically stated. "The light and sound technologies changed my whole belief system, my whole life."

"Now that is a big statement!" I said.

"Where do I even begin to tell Michael's story after a claim like this?" I mused. With a stroke of genius, I decided to start at the beginning.

"Michael," I ventured cautiously, "how did your adventure with sound and light begin?"

Michael started slowly, "At the grand old age of 35, I left the corporate world. No more managing carpet stores for me."

Michael continued, "One day my neighbor yelled across the fence for me to come over. He needed someone from 'mainstream business' to give him an opinion. I was unemployed. I had the time. So, into his house I went. He walked me to a dark closet with a chair in it. I was to shut myself in the dark and experience the effects of a machine."

"The scary music should start now," I imagined.

Michael was still talking slowly. "Thirty minutes later, I groped my way out of the closet, feeling rested and light. I asked my neighbor what he was going to do with that machine. He told me that he planned to sell them. I responded, 'Me, too!'"

My imagination went wild with the thoughts of what kind of machine helps someone know what he wants to do with his life? Did it have flashing colored lights that made it look like an eerie person? How did it give Michael a direction for his life that he believed had meaning? ...And why was it "in the closet?"

"What is this machine and who invented it?" I blurted out.

"Let's start with who invented it," Michael began. "Light and sound were used since the caveman days, creating altered states. After a caveman watched the fire for a while his brain vibrated in sync with the fire, about 8 – 10 cycles per second, a theta-functioning level of the brain. The flickering light of a campfire flows through the center of the brain to the visual cortex located in the back of the head.

"Approximately 40 percent of the caveman's brain was affected by light, but the rest of the brain could be indirectly affected, also. There may also have been a drummer in the corner of the cave," continued Michael, "creating shaman-like experiences with rhythms and pitches. Sound affects about 20 percent of the brain, so the combined impact is that almost 60 percent of the caveman's brain vibrated into a theta brain wave state. Given that the brain is the computer for the rest of your body, the theta brain wave affects the rest of the body. The caveman's whole body would groove with the fire and drumbeats."

"What happened to the caveman when he experienced theta brain waves?" I queried.

"Different brain waves allow us to have different experiences. The neurochemistry of restful sleep is found in the theta brain wave range. Theta is also the vibrational state of deep meditation. By accessing the theta state in a conscious manner we are able to connect with thoughts and feelings that we commonly only experience during our deep sleep cycles in a subconscious or unconscious state. Being able to access information hidden in our subconscious by experiencing theta brain waves has many benefits.

"Throughout history, many societies have cultivated meditation because of its benefits, except our culture. Western culture traditionally rejected meditation as 'voodoo.' However, meditation enables a person to connect to singularity of thought, rather than giving audience to the stream of babbling monkeys that constantly chatter in one's mind."

"I hope Michael is not referring to me," I wondered.

Michael continued, "Activity is the enemy of thought." Many people spend every minute being busy, to avoid being in touch with themselves. They work into a frenzy of motion, with constant activity becoming a habit. They don't even think which thoughts are their own, versus which thoughts come from others. In contrast, slowing brainwave activity allows us to be more conscious of who we really are, not who someone else said that we should be."

Michael's words flowed steadily. "With continued usage of the light and sound machines I managed repeated access to the theta brain state of this expanded consciousness. I questioned beliefs that I accepted as a child. In the past, people told me how to behave, what I should be doing, and what I needed to do to be successful in life. I believed these people, taking their words as reality. When I became what everyone else thought I should be, the good parts of me went by the wayside."

"At the age of 35 years, what I had turned into… had nothing to do with who I was. I certainly wasn't Mr. Mainstream Businessman. Not only did I not know who I was, but I wasn't even conscious that I didn't know."

"I believed only in things I could see and touch. I also believed I was afraid of nothing. After several years of experience using the light and sound machine I realized I had hidden fears and evasive behavior to avoid people or situations. I was afraid of life. Simply acknowledging this enabled me to let go of much fear. When I honored and understood who I was, life got easier. I got into the flow of things. I stopped being a victim. Before, I wasn't even conscious that I was choosing to be a victim.

"I was like a person who had stored junk in his garage for 35 years. It was too overwhelming to clean it up, so I just stashed more and more junk. (The garage is like negative emotions in my unconscious mind.) When I took a few boxes out of the garage to throw them away, my emotions kicked in - as I recalled unpleasant childhood memories. The garage was still full of junk I didn't want to face. It took me years to clear the wreckage of past emotional turmoil," Michael summarized.

"This sounded like the death of Mr. Carpet Man," I mumbled.

"People walk on the surfaces of themselves." Michael continued. "The irony is that we don't even know it. If we are going to improve ourselves we have to take that dive below the surface to engage our higher selves. It's that 'life unexamined thing.'

"There are two things that can happen to us in life. Either we get better or worse. There is no stasis, only change. Either we face our fears and improve, or we get worse, storing more negative energy as emotional baggage. There is no middle ground."

Michael continued:

- "The more *aware* a person is, the better he deals with life in general.
- The more *relaxed* a person is, the better he deals with life in general.
- The better *rested* a person is, the better he deals with life in general."

Michael's voice was growing louder. "The less cluttered our minds are, the more open we are to hearing our own inner voices.

"I then concluded that I was only afraid of myself. The good news is I am the one thing I can control and change. With this evolution in thought, peace came to me.

"My healthy relationships improved as I got in touch with myself. My unhealthy relationships disappeared, too.

"It could have taken me a lifetime to have this positive move forward, but I did it in a short time because of the light and sound machines." Michael's voice was at its peak.

"That's tremendous improvement in your life from light and sound machines!" I marveled.

"It happened over several years, as a result of me slowing down my brain waves," Michael clarified. "When your brain vibrates at certain frequencies, you change your experience and your consciousness. You change you. You become who you were meant to be. Sound and light machines do this easily and quickly.

"Meditation can produce the same benefits, but it can take a long time to learn. However, with light and sound machines, one can get results in twenty minutes. For example, one goes quickly to restful theta brain activity, gets energized or increases his learning speed."

"Perhaps our cells are like batteries. When we slow down, way down, they get a chance to reenergize?" I mused.

Michael continued, "As I used our light and sound machines, my world started to change. All of a sudden, I was achieving states of consciousness that a monk could spend years to learn. That is how I grew up without aging. My brain frequencies changed rapidly with sound and light.

"I wanted to share the gift of light and sound machines with the world. At first, we infiltrated the people known as the 'Woo-Woos,'" Michael explained.

"Whoa!" I halted the flow of conversation. "What's a 'Woo-Woo?"

Oh, yes, I wanted to know what is a "Woo-Woo!" Was it an extraterrestrial being?

"A 'Woo-Woo' is one of those people who wear purple T-shirts and crystals," Michael explained.

My breath stopped and in a knee jerk reaction as my hand went to my purple T-shirt, covering my crystal necklace. I didn't want to hear anymore about "Woo-Woos."

Michael reflected, "I feel good about what I do with my life now. People tell us that their lives change after experiencing frequencies from light and sound machines. The neat thing is that the machine is just a training tool. Once people use the machine for an extended period of time, they can create these brain states on their own. Accessing this state of brainwave activity is now a habit! They no longer need a machine as the catalyst!"

Michael continued on how his life changed when he used the light and sound machine. "When a person's pain is greater than his fear of change, then change occurs. Me? Since I altered my brain wave frequencies with the light and sound machine, I am able to change quicker. I use fear to mobilize me, not immobilize me. I have also noticed that I have lowered my threshold for pain, because I am able to change quickly when the situation calls for it."

"Can you describe a specific experience that resulted from the sound light machines?" I asked, looking for more details.

"After using the 'relax' frequency, I became conscious during sleep all night long." Michael smiled. "In this case, being a human is a detriment."

I wondered, "What would the alternative be?"

Michael was talking fast now, as his ideas flowed out of him. "The subconscious mind is more powerful than the conscious mind. When we sleep, the subconscious mind is free to process information. So, when I was conscious during sleep, my subconscious mind was not able to do its normal work," Michael clarified.

"It is like God took the most powerful thing in the universe, unconditional love (an energy - a soul), and shoved it into a physical form, similar to that of a monkey (a human body). Therein lies the rub, and much of the dilemma surrounding the 'human condition.' I call this 'God's little joke.'

"The experience of being conscious during sleep, out-of-body experiences and many other experiences pushed my thinking into bigger arenas. I could no longer contain myself to thinking about the material world," Michael concluded. "My world got a lot bigger."

"What a Woo-Woo!" I mused.

The Sound and Light Machines

"What do these amazing machines look like?" I asked, hoping the machines didn't need a dark closet to work.

My fears were relieved as Michael showed me the little hand held machine, with several buttons, earphones and dark glasses attached. One selected a program, such as relax, learn, change or energize. Then you put on the dark glasses that had little flickering lights, closed your eyes and listened with the earphones.

I know from my research, that when listening to tones in close proximity to the ear, the brain can only *"hear"* one tone. Different tones can be fed into each ear. The brain then combines the two frequencies and you perceive a pulsing sound, which is the difference between the two tones. This sound is called a binaural beat. Your brain waves match the frequency of the binaural beat in a matter of minutes.

When you put on the glasses with closed eyes, you see flickering colored lights. This light travels on neural pathways into your brain, affecting up to 40 percent of your brain.

Michael continued, "Between the light and sound, you flood your brain with frequencies that calm and focus your mind. The machine entrains your brain waves to a powerful state of mind... an 'altered state of consciousness.' Both sides of your brain are more equally in use, allowing what is known as 'whole brain function,' rather than the typical right or left brain dominant functions we use in our daily lives. Your awareness and ability to focus increases. Your speed of learning improves, too."

"Could this assist the elderly, who find themselves forgetting things all the time?" I asked.

"As we age, some brain cells lose their neural circuitry. The brain cells shrink and loose extensions to other cells, making information harder to retrieve. However, stimulating your brain with sound and light machines is exercising it. You can create new neural pathways at any point in your life. The flashing lights create new neural pathways in your brain. New neural pathways create new bridges to retrieve information," Michael answered. "So, yes, it helps the elderly with memory problems."

I read a study from UCLA in which Dr. Marion Diamond found that brains of stimulated rats weighed more than brains of rats that weren't stimulated. The stimulated rat brains also had more branching extensions to retrieve information. Diamond also discovered that stimulated rats developed a stronger immune defense response than those not stimulated. I was ready to volunteer to be "stimulated" with light and sound.

An article by Thomas Budzynski, Ph.D. flashed into my mind. The article was entitled, "Why is it so hard to be happy?" It related life-changing insights: "Some experts say that it is because we are burdened by negative, self-destructive, unconscious 'scripts' which are 'programmed' into us early in life. We start out as innocent, expressive, asking-for-what-we-want, loving, trusting little babies. How did we get to the point where we are fearful, distrusting, stressed, self-destructive adults? Our mothers, fathers, siblings, teachers, ministers, other children and other adults scared, punished, degraded, embarrassed, humiliated, and confused us, not to mention, acted as bad role models."

Dr. Budzynski suggested that frequently going into a theta brain wave state with a sound light machine could break loops of negative, habitual thinking that we have accumulated.

Michael added, "Our subconscious mind automatically repeats thoughts we believe. By repeating thoughts, we create ongoing inner dialogues at the core of our beings that are like a fountain of impulses and unconscious thoughts. These repeated thinking loops bolster our belief systems. Unfortunately, most of us think fearful thoughts, creating negative loops of thinking in our subconscious minds. For example, my daughter is deathly afraid of spiders. There is no apparent reason why she should be. She has never been bitten or otherwise traumatically affected by spiders. Somewhere in her subconscious she believes that she is supposed to be afraid of spiders whether it makes sense or not. It is just one of her negative thinking patterns.

"These subconscious negative thinking patterns are accessible when our brains are predominately vibrating in the theta brain waves or lower. Otherwise, these (often negative) thoughts are hidden from our conscious awareness. Using light and sound machines can make us aware of subconscious thinking patterns, allowing us to break the negative loop.

"When we experience theta brain wave activity consciously, rather than unconsciously, we become aware of previous subconscious thought. Next we can use the light sound machine, go to a theta brain state and imagine a better habit. For example, our automated thought regarding eating could be... 'Junk food is yummy.' We want to replace that automatic thought with this one... 'I feel great when I eat healthy foods.' To acquire this new habit we think this new thought many times. *The number of times we need to think this new healthy thought to create a new thinking habit is greatly reduced, if we are in a theta brainwave state.* In summary, we can use theta brain waves to make changes easier," Michael took a quick breath.

"Is this machine costly?" I peeped, hoping the answer to be "no." I learned that they could be obtained for as little as $339.

To check it out and get a sound and light machine? Visit http://www.jillswingsoflight.com/store.php?show=sound-light-machines

My feeling of anxiousness was growing as I tried the little hand-held sound-light machine (SL machine).

My first venture with the device wasn't life changing, but I felt like I was Frankenstein, with electricity zapping through my brain.

A friend grabbed the machine from me and tried the "relax" program. Within minutes, she was slumped over, in her chair. After her restful sojourn, she reported her chronic shoulder pain that was always present - was gone.

After I purchased a SL machine I got into a routine of waking up a half an hour earlier than usual in the morning, when I was not in a deep state of sleep. I then used the sound light machine to slip back into a deep state of relaxation (extending the amount of deep sleep that I got) and then afterwards I used an "energize" program. With this habit I did not need to take time out of my busy day to use the SL machine.

When I woke up for the day, I felt better rested than usual. I felt energized. Without the sound and light machine, I could barely shuffle into the bathroom in the morning.

I couldn't tell if my life changed from the SL machine alone, as I already meditated quite a bit and had experienced the benefits from stillness of mind. However, I feel peaceful and am more able to flow through the day without stress. My memory is better than when I was younger. I also have a full range of psychic skills, which require conscious control of theta brain waves.

While reviewing this manuscript, Michael told me of a near death experience he had. It gave me goose bumps. With Michael's permission, I'm sharing it with you.

Michael began, "After six days in Intensive Care with severe pneumonia, I suddenly found myself up in the corner of the ceiling looking down at my body.

"I felt like I went to sleep in the desert with my partner. When I woke up in the morning, not only was my partner gone, but all the water and supplies, too. My partner was my body, and it left me high and dry.

"Moments later, my body seemed like a discarded, empty water bottle," Michael said without any depression in his voice. "I had no emotional attachment to my body. It was just something I was done with.

"I was all alone. No, this was deeper than alone. There was nothing and no one to create an illusion of safety, control or reassuring comfort. I was all there was.

"Everything was brilliant beyond white, beyond light. Then I was 'beyond,' too. I was in a space that resembled a sphere, like being in the middle of a ball. Excepting that the walls of the ball were made up of brilliant white gaseous, glows-of-love. It was as if they had cleared this space to receive me and they went in all directions forever.

"Each glow was moving around me from right to left in a circular pattern and everything under and over me in a circular pattern as well. I could see in all directions forever. Everything was exactly as it was intended to be. In fact, I had no questions. All was clear to me and I understood all. At the time it seemed perfectly normal that such a thing could transpire. I was in a space of love inconceivable to the human parts of me. The best that I can describe it is that if I were to accumulate all the love that I have ever felt, given, and received in my time on earth and was to then multiply that by infinity, the total would not begin to approach the love that was here.

"Each of these "glows" somehow had an identity that belonged to them solely, but they were all far more a part of the whole than they were separate, *as was I*. The *oneness* was *all*.

"The spirits of the luminous-lights communicated, as one unified being. 'Michael, you can stay or you can go back.' My response was immediate. The first 35 years I never had fun. Only the last five years, I started to enjoy myself, and further, only in the last 2-3 years had I been able to give joy to others. I was not done with my work on earth. I had to go back.

"I returned as a human, but with a new understanding and view on life. In specific, I was back in my body with nurses getting ready to kick-start my heart. Four and one half minutes had passed since I had 'technically' died."

Michael believes that many people see loved ones that have already passed on when they die, as this scenario is a bridge to ease them into the strange and blissful "other side."

Michael got welcomed to the other side by the Stay-Puffed Marshmallow Man, who had been in a ferocious windstorm. Hmmmmm...I scratched my chin.

With pulsating wisdom Michael got back to the meaning of his story. Michael revealed: "We incarnate on Earth to:

- **Love one another.**
  The love we give comes back. We are not separate from our gifts of love.
- **Enjoy ourselves.**
  When we act with love, we radiate love to others. We are energy and not separate from others.

"Therefore, we should constantly fill ourselves with joyful, uplifting and positive feelings. These feelings become part of those around us as well. Without intending to hurt others, when we feel negativity, we give it to those nearby.

"These two rules are like two sides of one coin. To put in another way:

- Loving others brings love to ourselves.
- Loving ourselves brings love to others.

"Or another way of saying it is:

- When we deprive others, we deprive ourselves.

69

- When we deprive ourselves, we deprive others.

"Or yet another way of saying it is:
- When we enjoy ourselves, we enjoy others.
- When we enjoy others, we enjoy ourselves.

"For example, grandmothers love their grandchildren, but many mix their gift of love with guilt and shame when their grandchild 'misbehaves.' The grandmothers achieve partial success when they love their grandchildren, but they fall short on the 'enjoy yourself' part. When they pass the judgement on their grandchildren, both feel condemnation, instead of joy.

"I want to experience these truths in all ways and always," Michael confessed. "Some days I do and some days I don't. Some days I see a tree and feel its beauty, but some days I notice bugs hanging around it."

After being hugged by Michael's words, I felt uplifted, but I also saw Michael's tree bugs. And! The eternal sage, Michael's Stay-Puffed Marshmallow Man, left me with peace. "Everything is as it should be."

Chapter Five

The Magic of Sound

Let me introduce myself. I am Osborn Raticus, a rat. My left whisker is twitching. When I have a smirk on my face, my whiskers shake. And I'm smirking, because I see a wizard! You might not believe me, but I see an honest-to-God wizard. It's not Halloween and there is no masquerade party going on. This is the real thing. (The writing in italics in this chapter, represent the thoughts or words of Raticus.)

It's not every day you see a wizard. Generally speaking, wizards do magic behind closed doors or pretend to be scientists.

No, his name is not Merlin, it's Jack. Doesn't sound like a wizard name, but that is part of the disguise. He does have a pointed hat that flops down on his shoulders. And he puts magical spells in his hat.

Wizard Jack is a wizard specialist, a sound wizard. (I wish Wizard Jack were a cheese specialist.) Wizard Jack creates cauldrons of awesome musical spells, but I prefer the music of old time jazz, with the aged cheese crumbs flowing.

Wizard Jack studies the effects of tones, hoping to find more magic tricks to tuck away in his hat. Soon, he will need a bigger hat. I'd prefer that he store havarti cheese in there.

Surely with all that magic the wizard has crammed into his hat, there is a tasty crumpet and a smidgen of cheese for me? My whiskers twinge again, as I pretend I am sinking my teeth into tasty morsels, but the wizard hasn't noticed my hungry belly.

Wizard Jack doesn't have a wand, but magical earmuffs and occasional goggles with flashing lights that put spells on people's brains. At first we both cackled when people went under the spell, but for different reasons. He cackled when his spell worked and I cackled because I couldn't believe how ridiculous people looked with those earmuffs and flashing goggles!

Wizard Jack's earmuffs have magical streams of sound that twinkle and go into a person's ears." These magic streams alter people's brain waves, improve their health and change their personalities. *"I want to sneak the earmuffs on the wizard to encourage him to eat sloppier and drop a generous spread of crumbs for me.*

Me? I don't get near the earmuffs. I am afraid Wizard Jack will turn me into a toad, or worse yet, a nasty human.

Wizard Jack has been using binaural beats… oh, that is wizard talk." A binaural beat occurs when two different, low pitched frequencies are sounded into a person's ears through headphones. *Next, I help the Wizard Jack by saying the magical word, "Alakazam."*

The left side of our brain is used when we are using logic and processing analytic information. The right side of our brain is in use when we are being creative. Normally people use either their left or right brain, depending on the task they are doing. In this case however, each half of the brain receives a different sound that comes from a corresponding headphone. The brain can only hear one of the two tones at one time from the earphones, so both halves of the brain work together to subtract the smaller frequency from the larger one. Then you hear the difference of those frequencies. Both halves of the brain are up and running! The percentage of brain cells a person is using has just increased.

This pulsing tone, then, "hypnotizes" the brain. The brain is affected by the frequency of the combined tone. So when Wizard Jack uses binaural beats, he changes your brain wave frequencies.

Raticus thought to himself, here's one of Wizard Jack's notes on the floor. Hmmmm... Let me get my spectacles, so that I can read it. It says, Princeton Biofeedback researcher, Dr. Fehmi, says that the binaural beats get your whole brain to work, not just one of its hemispheres, so your intelligence improves. You also become less self-conscious and more intuitive. You don't feel separate from others or feel narrowly focused; your awareness widens.[10] Another researcher, Hiew, says the binaural beats create a relaxed, meditative and creative mental state. Binaural beats also aid sleeping.[11] *Sounds like magic to me! Only tasty cheese morsels falling from Jack's magical hat would be any better.*

Wizard Jack can change the pitch of the binaural beats in the earmuffs. Wizard Jack says that, "Different pitches induce different brain waves. Brain waves are categorized from fast to slow speeds, called beta, alpha, theta, and delta brain waves. Depending on the frequencies of the binaural beats used, selected states of consciousness can be produced."

Wizard Jack thinks the frequency of the tone causes the magic. I believe that the effect is due to the magic word, "Alakazam," that I speak when he uses the tones.

There are various ways that Wizard Jack uses his magical sound to change people's brain waves, but binaural beats is the fast track method.

Brainwaves are closely associated with certain mental states or states of consciousness. People enter magical adventure lands of consciousness by experiencing different brain waves. There is Alpha Land, Beta Country, Theta Experience, Delta Place, and beyond.

Here's the scoop on these vacation spots of consciousness that you can enjoy:

---

[10] "Dr. Lester Fehmi, Director of the Princeton Biofeedback Research Institute, Fehmi, Lester and Fritz, George. "Open Focus: The Attention Foundation of Health and Well Being," Somatics, Spring 1980, "The Scientific Research Behind Acoustic Brainwave Entrainment," Pgs. 4, 5, www.neuroacoustic.org

[11] Hiew, 1995 and Foster, 1990, "Acoustic Brainwave Entrainment with Binaural Beats," Pg. 3, www.neuroacoustic.org

Beta Country: Beta brain waves are produced in people's normal waking state. This is the normal state of consciousness that people spend most of their waking time in.

I wonder if people drop more crumbs in Beta Country or Alpha Land?

Alpha Beta Bridge: The magic at the Alpha Beta Bridge enables a person to be aware of what's going around him and within himself at the same time. The brain waves in the Alpha Beta Bridge slow down as does the heart beat, respiration and blood pressure, while the brain becomes more effective.

Alpha Land: Electrical charges of brain waves in Alpha Land become even slower and larger in amplitude, causing the brain waves to be more powerful. *Alakazam!* Magical power from alpha brain waves helps people become more creative, integrating many ideas.

The Alpha state ought to make studying for that calculus test easier. Wizard Jack has a note that says, "The Monroe Center reports people have increased concentration and mental alertness with Alpha frequencies."[12] Kennerly also reports that alpha brain waves improve memory.[13]

> Experience these brain waves with sound and light machines or special CD's with headphones that entrain the brain.

Wizard Jack's spell book tells us that Bulgarian psychiatrist Lozanov reports, "Students learned over five times as much information in less time per day, with greater retention… by using deep relaxation combined with synchronized rhythms in the brain that put students in the alpha wave state. In some cases, as much as 30 times as much was learned."[14] *Parents are going to want this magic for their kids!*

---

[12] Monrie, 1980. "Acoustic Brainwave Entrainment with Binaural Beats," Pg. 4. www.neuroacoustic.org

[13] Kennerly, 1994. "Acoustic Brainwave Entrainment with Binaural Beats," Pg. 3. www.neuroacoustic.org

[14] "Research Behind Acoustic Brain Entrainment," Pg. 5. www.neuroacoustic.org

Alpha Theta Bridge: On this mystic bridge you can observe your emotions and evaluate them. You can also increase your emotional intelligence and solve problems more effectively.

Theta Experience: While a person sleeps, the brain slows down and vibrates in the theta wave, facilitating emotional healing. Theta brain waves help us let go of painful emotions. *Good riddens!*

If a person is awake while creating theta brain waves, he can experience intense creativity, visualization, imagination, and out-of-body experiences.

Now, that's magic!

I don't want you to think that I, Osborn Raticus, have a problem from licking too much scotch off the floor, but you may want to know this. Dr. Peniston and Dr. Kulkosky, report that alcoholics have greater recovery and retention rates when using increased theta brain waves. In addition they have a "marked personality transformation including significant increases in qualities such as warmth, stability, conscientiousness, boldness, imaginativeness, self control along with decreases in depression and anxiety."[15]

Maybe with a smidgen of cheese cologne and Theta brain waves, I could attract more attention from the ladies, but I am still not sure I trust the magical earmuffs.

Hmmm... Here is a hidden note in Wizard Jack's spell book. It says that theta brain waves make people eager to learn. That report was from Suzanne Evans Morris, Ph.D., who also said that use of binaural beats can readily cause behavioral and belief system changes.[16] So people are more likely to grow and change when experiencing theta brain waves.

---

[15] Dr. Peniston and Dr. Kulkosky of University of Southern Colorado. "Research Behind Acoustic Brain Entrainment," Pg. 7. www.neuroacoustic.org
[16] Suzanne Evans Morris, Ph.D. (speech and language pathologist). "Research Behind Acoustic Brain Entrainment," Pg. 5. www.neuroacoustic.org

Suzanne continued to write that a person producing theta brain waves experiences expanded intuition and greater access to internal and external knowledge.[17]

Thomas Budzynski wrote that "Super Learning" occurs in the theta brain-state, quickening the time to learn a new language. One can also accept suggestions of change and memorize more information with theta brain waves. [18]

I found a secret message from McGaugh saying that the more the brain vibrates in the theta frequency, the greater one's memory is.[19] At MIT, Rosenzweig found that people in the theta brain wave state increased their IQ and learning abilities.[20]

Here's another entry in the spell book. "Those who produce theta brain waves are highly creative, have 'life altering' insights, are less rigid and conforming, are very healthy, and have improved relationships with other people as well as greater tolerance and understanding and love of one's self and of one's world."[21]

I think that Mrs. Raticus needs to use these earmuffs.

According to neurophysiologist Dr. Lynch, Theta brain waves help us form new memories and recall old ones.[22]

My Grampa needs these earmuffs!

Theta Delta Bridge: In this brain wave state, emotional difficulties heal. *Everyone can benefit from this!*

Delta Land: People adventure to Delta Land every night while they sleep. There are minimal mental or emotional processes, and no sense of time occurring while the brain

[17] "Research Behind Acoustic Brain Entrainment," Pgs. 5, 6. www.neuroacoustic.org

[18] Budzynski, Thomas. "Attuning in on the Twilight Zone," *Psychology Today*, Aug 1977 and "A Brain lateralization Model for REST." Paper delivered at the First International Conference on REST and Self Regulation, Denver, CO., March 18, 1983. "Research Behind Acoustic Brain Entrainment," Pg. 6. www.neuroacoustic.org

[19] "Research Behind Acoustic Brain Entrainment," Pg. 7. www.neuroacoustic.org

[20] "Research Behind Acoustic Brain Entrainment," Pg. 9. www.neuroacoustic.org

[21] Green, Elmer and Alyce. Beyond Biofeedback. NY, Delacourt, 1977. "Research Behind Acoustic Brain Entrainment," Pg. 7. www.neuroacoustic.org

[22] Dr. Lynch, neurophysiologist and associates form the University of CA. at Irvin. Lynch, Gary and Baudry, Michael. "The Biochemistry of Memory: A New and Specific Hypothesis," Science 224 (1984), 1057-63. "Research Behind Acoustic Brain Entrainment," Pg. 9. www.neuroacoustic.org

vibrates in the delta frequency. The body also recuperates and rebuilds while the brain vibrates in the delta wave lengths.

When a person is awake and experiencing Delta brain waves, he can access his long-term memory.

And Beyond: *Wizard Jack came up with more dreamy states. "Alakazam" and away we go!*

Gamma and Hyper Gamma: Gamma brain waves are higher frequency than Beta waves. *Wizard Jack says that a gamma spell helps one to see relationships between different pieces of information.* Gamma brain waves are associated with consciousness and "binding" information from all senses to a higher level of awareness of unity.[23] *Wizard talk! He is saying that in this extraordinary place, you get it all together!*

Lambda: This adventure comes from high cranking brain waves, faster than Hyper Gamma. *This sounds like a bigger rush than going on a rickety roller coaster!* Special effects include self-awareness, high insight, psychic abilities and out-of-body experiences.[24]

Epsilon: These brain waves are on the other end of the scale, slower than the deep waves of delta. Special effects include self-awareness, high insight, psychic abilities, and out-of-body experiences.[25]

Wizard Jack points out that the total opposite ends of the wave spectrum, Lambda and Epsilon, produce similar experiences.[26] They are the same cool vacation spot for brain waves! Wizard Jack thinks that brain waves create a circle. I know I am only a rat, but I think the cycles of brain waves create a spiral, similar to the one I see in the pretty stars at night and the same spiral I see in my cowlick in my fur.

I better hush. Listen! Wizard Jack is mumbling again. Hutchinson in *Megabrain Powers* says, "New scientists monitor brains ... rare individuals are able to enter peak

---

[23] "Epsilon, Gamma, Hyper-gamma and Lambda Brainwave Activity and Ecstatic States of Consciousness," Pg. 2. www.neuroacoustic.org
[24] "Sleeping/Waking/Awakening," Pg. 6. www.nueroacoustic.org
[25] "Sleeping/Waking/Awakening," Pg. 6. www.nueroacoustic.org
[26] "Epsilon, Gamma, Hyper-gamma and Lambda Brainwave Activity and Ecstatic States of Consciousness," Pgs. 2, 3. www.neuroacoustic.org

domains at will. Peak states are linked to special brain activity. Scientists found that by using precise combinations of pulsating sound waves, they could actually produce those peak states by producing those brain wave patterns in ordinary people."[27]

Out of those magical earmuffs, sound can create:

- Tranquility
- Pain control
- Creativity
- Euphoria
- Excitement
- Focused attention
- Relief from stress
- Enhanced learning abilities
- Enhanced problem-solving abilities
- Increased memory
- Accelerated healing
- Behavior modification
- Improvements in mental and emotional health[28]

With all the gifts he gives with his sounds, Wizard Jack must think it's Christmas, too! Perhaps, he's confusing his wizard hat with a Santa hat. Ho! Ho! Merry Christmas!

Certain uses of sound have a direct effect on:

- Heart/pulse rates
- Respiration
- Brain waves
- Stress reduction responses[29]

[27] Hutchison, Megabrain Power. NY: Hyperion, 1994, Pg. 31. "Research Behind Acoustic Brain Entrainment," Pg. 10. www.neuroacoustic.org
[28] "Research Behind Acoustic Brain Entrainment," Pg. 3. www.neuroacoustic.org
[29] "Acoustic Brainwave Entrainment Experiment, Group-Mind Linking," Pg. 1. www.neuroacoustic.org

Did you hear that pitter-patter? Oh, me, oh, my! It's the thumping of my own paws. I just got so excited; my hind leg just went thumping!

Chemical Spells for the Brain

Wizard Jack has magic spells written on the blackboard. Many researchers believe that brain waves are linked to the production of chemicals in our brains, such as beta-endorphins, vasopressin, acetylcholine, catecholamines and serotonin.

Why can't wizards talk in English! I wonder if any of these things are tasty? I can smell and taste the cheese! My tail is swishing around just thinking about it!

Dr. Bauer, one of the foremost experts in the field of electro-medicine, elaborates: "By sending out the proper frequency, proper waveform and proper current... we tend to change the configuration of the cell membrane... Cells that are at sub-optimal levels are stimulated to 'turn on' and produce what they are supposed to."[30]

"The increase of production of these neurochemicals greatly enhances memory and learning."[31]

Various researchers note that acetycholine is linked to memory.[32] U.C. Berkeley researcher Rosenzweig showed a direct connection between the presence of acetylcholine and intelligence.[33] Certain brain waves are linked with the production of this! So, that is why sound-light machines can make us smarter!

Endorphins improve mental focus.[34] Endorphins also release a sensation of pleasure. Vasopressin improves memory and stimulates the release of endorphins.[35] (Remember sound

---

[30] "Research Behind Acoustic Brain Entrainment," Pg. 9. www.neuroacoustic.org
[31] "Research Behind Acoustic Brain Entrainment," Pg. 9. www.neuroacoustic.org
[32] Studies by a research team at the Veterans Administrations Hospital in Palo Alto and studies at MIT, article by Douglas Starr, "Brain Drugs," Omni, Jan. 1983. Researcher Lester A. Henry. "The Response to Acetylcholine," Scientific American, Feb 1977.
[33] "Research Behind Acoustic Brain Entrainment," Pg. 9. www.neuroacoustic.org
[34] "Research Behind Acoustic Brain Entrainment," Pg. 9. www.neuroacoustic.org
[35] "Research Behind Acoustic Brain Entrainment," Pg. 9. www.neuroacoustic.org

and brain waves are linked to the production of these chemicals!)

"Different brain wave frequencies trigger the production of different brain chemicals.[36] For example, alpha frequencies boost serotonin that eases pain, while catecholamines, produced by theta frequencies, are vital for memory and learning," wrote Dr. Patterson.[37] "The brain's internal communication system, its language if you like, is based on frequency," [38] she continued.

Dr. Giampapa, of the Longevity Institute International, says that alpha, delta, and theta brain waves "dramatically affect the production of three most important hormones in relationship to increased longevity and well being: cortisol, DHEA and melatonin." DHEA increases one's resistance to disease. DHEA buffers against cortisol that we produce in response to stress. Cortisol increases the body's aging process.[39]

I believe I will look cool wearing those earmuffs and goggles. I must try them on and hear what comes out of the ear muffs!

In a before-and-after-study of people using headphones and listening to sounds that create specific brain waves, there was a 68 percent increase of DHEA in three days.[40]

DHEA increases one's resistance to disease! This magic is like the fountain of youth. Who wants to be sick? With this sound magic, I get more DHEA! Goodbye, ill health!

A study in the New England Journal of Medicine tells us, "An increase of DHEA in blood levels corresponded with a 48% reduction in mortality due to cardiovascular disease and a

---

[36] There is a correlation between sound waves that entrain your brain waves and brain waves activities, but not everyone's brain waves matches the sounds in the exact same way.

[37] Dr. Margaret Patterson in collaboration with biochemist Dr. Ifor Capel at the Marie Curie Cancer Memorial Foundation Research Dept. in Surrey, England. "Research Behind Acoustic Brain Entrainment," Pg. 8. www.neuroacoustic.org

[38] "Research Behind Acoustic Brain Entrainment," Pg. 8. www.neuroacoustic.org

[39] Dr. Vincent Giampapa, MD., of Longevity Institute International and vice president of the American Society of Anti Aging Medicine. "Research Behind Acoustic Brain Entrainment," Pg. 10, 11. www.neuroacoustic.org

[40] "Research Behind Acoustic Brain Entrainment," Pg. 11. www.neuroacoustic.org

36% reduction in mortality for any reason."[41] DHEA helps us live longer.

Do you think the Wizard Jack could transform me into Super Rat? Perhaps I could live forever with these magical earmuffs!

"Cortisol levels in the blood were down by an average of 46%, (with an increase of certain brain waves) with positive changes in 68% of the people." (Cortisol speeds up the body's aging mechanisms.) Keeping cortisol levels low helps us remain youthful.[42]

With decreased cortisol, I'd keep the lady rats winking at me and nuzzling me with their soft fur. Ooh la la! Where are those earmuffs with the magical sound?

Theta brain frequencies are linked to the production of melatonin, which helps us sleep. Theta brain waves increase melatonin levels on average 98%."[43] As people age, they fail to get enough sleep. The problem with getting less sleep is that the body needs sleep to regenerate and rebuild. Melatonin helps the body regenerate and rebuild.

Alakazam! Hold the cheese and pass the earmuffs!

Wizard Jack is writing again. "Slowing of brain waves pushes the brain to reorganize itself at higher, more complex levels of functioning," (predicted by Prigogine, 1977 Nobel Prize Winner).[44] *Has he been watching the Clymatic videos?*

With audio stimulus, the brain is pushed to reorganize, creating more neural pathways and increased communication between the right and left halves of the brain.[45]

Each time the brain reorganizes there are positive changes in learning ability, creativity, mental clarity, intelligence, intuition, and mental and emotional health.

[41] "Research Behind Acoustic Brain Entrainment," Pg. 11. www.neuroacoustic.org
[42] "Research Behind Acoustic Brain Entrainment," Pg. 11. www.neuroacoustic.org
[43] "Research Behind Acoustic Brain Entrainment," Pg. 11. www.neuroacoustic.org
[44] "Research Behind Acoustic Brain Entrainment," Pg. 11. www.neuroacoustic.org
[45] "Research Behind Acoustic Brain Entrainment," Pg. 12. www.neuroacoustic.org

Another benefit is that you can combine information that previously seemed unrelated.[46]

Wiz Jack left the room. The earmuffs are in my reach. Excuse me, will you? I have something important to do!

www.JillsWingsOfLight.com – Art Gallery

---

[46] "Research Behind Acoustic Brain Entrainment," Pg. 12. www.neuroacoustic.org

Chapter Six

The Wonderful World of Listening

"What an inviting voice Paul has," I mused as our conversation danced on about the power of sound - my favorite topic. I was relaxing in conversation with Paul Madaule and Morana Petrofski, co-directors of the Listening Centre in Toronto, Canada. The Listening Centre offers therapies based on the research of Paul's life long friend, the late Dr. Tomatis, of France. Dr. Tomatis was an ear, nose, and throat specialist. In the last half of the twentieth century Dr.Tomatis pioneered many discoveries regarding "listening" and fascinating healing processes.

"Dr. Tomatis gave the world an unorthodox view of listening. Specifically, he taught that listening and hearing are two different things. When we hear, we perceive sound. With listening, we zoom in only on what we want to hear. Our ears protect us to a degree against voices and sounds we don't want to recognize, and also loud sounds that can damage our ears." Paul continued in that rich voice.

"Listening should be spontaneous and easy. If paying attention requires a great effort, it means your listening skills are not working well. Listening is more than a receptive skill. We actively pick out sounds we want to hear over others. Listening is also actively involved in monitoring our voice."

Paul's harmonious voice, danced on, "Poor listening can cause:

- Speech and language impairment (For example, deaf people struggle to speak normally due to their hearing loss.)
- Learning disabilities
- Lack of concentration
- Lack of alertness
- Tendencies to interrupt
- Depression
- Withdrawal

"Sound affects more than our ears. Sound also impacts our whole body, coordination, space, posture, expression, energy, breathing, balance, focus, emotions, singing range and non-verbal communication. Think of a rabbit, his *entire body* standing erect and still, as he listens for sounds of a predator," Paul's story went on.

Paul reminded me of a white rabbit, standing tall and erect, as he is listening intently. Proper listening results in better posture he had said. My imagination was taking over as I saw Paul, the white rabbit, take out his pocket watch, murmuring, "I'm late!"

"Late for what?" I anxiously replied.

The white rabbit ran off and I hurried after him, watching him pop into a hidden hole in the center of a tree. Peeping down the hole, looking for the white rabbit, I felt dizzy. So dizzy that I tumbled right down into the rabbit hole. Deeper, deeper, and deeper and boom, I fell into a curious little house in Toronto with a cheery little sign that boasted, "The Listening Centre."

At the base of the sign I immediately saw two brightly colored pills, reminding me of the Alice in Wonderland story, in which eating one pill made you very tall and the other shrunk you.

I ate the hot pink pill and my hearing changed. I had acquired enhanced hearing abilities for high frequency sounds.

The sounds seemed to modulate as the emphasis or equalization setting (EQ) for the high frequencies varied. This must be the "filtered music" used in the Listening Centre!

Dr. Tomatis invented an "electronic ear" that enables us to hear more frequencies by strengthening the ear cilia (tiny ear hairs responsible for hearing specific frequencies). Dr. Tomatis discovered that we could tune out some (unwanted) sounds to such an extent that we become deaf in those frequencies. Even if we have "normal" hearing, the minute frequencies that we cannot hear have an impact of us! For starters, our voice cannot produce any tones that we cannot hear; so our voice can improve with better listening. I remembered that Paul had told me that our voice also stimulates our body, brain and consciousness.

Paul told me something else about frequencies: more cells are required to transport high frequencies than low frequencies to the brain. "High frequencies," he said, "carry more vibrations which give us sizzling, energizing power. Higher frequency is higher energy."

"Sound can be energizing, giving us feelings of stability, confidence, being at ease and a sense of well being," continued Paul.

"We get energy from many sources, just like we get energy from exercise and movement. Some sounds are as stimulating as two cups of coffee," I mused. "I have heard that Dr. Tomatis needed only four hours of sleep with his 'sound diet.'"

I remembered the lime green pill I still had in my hand. After gulping it down, the low frequencies I heard were amplified. Some low frequencies have high harmonics, sounding rich and lifting, but the low tones I was hearing were monotones, muffled, and flat. My headache started and I slumped down, feeling exhausted.

The lessons of the pills were clear to me. Some sounds are energizing and others take energy and clarity away.

I imagined that sounds were like food. We know the effects of fatty burgers, greasy fries, soft drinks and fresh fruits and vegetables. Too much fat, sugar and processed foods slow our bodies down. Some sounds are nourishing for us, just like healthy food.

I also wondered about the connection between sound and our body organs. Vibrations can enter the body and affect our organs. Do vibrations from sound waves travel to all areas of our body, giving us a tune up and harmonizing us?

I stopped my wondering when I saw it. A smile... only a smile. No, it was the Cheshire cat, playing tricks on me.

I asked the Cheshire cat, "Which way did the white rabbit go?"

The Cheshire cat smiled and pointed both ways at the same time.

"Stop teasing me," I protested.

"Did you know," the Cheshire cat hummed, "that the left ear is connected to the right brain. And the right ear is connected to the left brain?"

I focused on finding the white rabbit, I raised my voice to the Cheshire cat. "The white rabbit... which way is the shortest?"

With a sly smile, the Cheshire sang, "Why the shortest path is that of the right ear, which leads to the left brain. In the left ear, sounds jog around the heart and take longer to send and receive information from the brain."

I remembered Paul saying that Dr. Tomatis' methods can train people to have right ear dominance to improve their academic performance. The extensive research at www.Tomatis.com shows 85 to 95 percent improvement in many learning disabilities.

"But the rabbit! Where is the white rabbit?" I stammered.

Who should then appear, but the white rabbit, who was in the distance behind the Cheshire cat.

"Mr. Rabbit!" I yelled, but he was off again.

Then I saw her, the most cross woman you ever saw. Opps! She is the queen. She didn't look like what I thought a queen should look like. She looked more like a common pig with black hair and buckteeth.

I stopped dead in my tracks as I saw the white rabbit put headphones on the queen. The queen has a listening problem! Perhaps this is why she is so cross.

Not only was the queen listening to the rich high frequencies of the electronic ear, but to filtered sounds of her mother's voice – that she heard when she was in the womb and as a child.

Earlier, Paul joked that babies curl in the womb in the shape of an ear. Dr. Tomatis replicated the stages of listening-development, starting with sounds heard in the womb. Repeating the stages of listening from our inception presumes that our development is dependent on hearing certain sounds and vibrations for proper development, and a re-patterning or a "rerun" fills in lost gasps due to ear-infection-damage, stress and other factors.

Paul had told me that listening to filtered music from the "electronic ear" and the filtered sounds of your mother's voice resulted in:

- Enhanced vocalization
- Babbling
- Desire to communicate
- Increased nonverbal communication
- Increased affection
- Improved bonding
- More facial expressions
- Increased eye contact
- Greater sense of rhythm
- Improved spacial awareness
- Better motor skills
- Improved visual skills
- Enhanced motivation
- Better awareness of time and space
- Improved handwriting
- Increased organization.

This is a gift fit for a queen!"

"Are you listening?" queried Paul.
I popped out of my daydream. Oh, yes, I am in the Listening Centre in Toronto… for real… discussing their services. Paul's warm voice welcomed me back.
"Some of the people we helped include:"

- Pregnant women (good sounds for unborn babies)
- Incubator babies (In some hospitals in Europe, they filter Mom's voice into incubators.)
- Children with development issues
- People with language impediments
- Autistic people (open up communication)
- Hyperactive children (to calm down and focus)
- Those with learning disabilities (minimize dyslexia, improve academic performance)
- People with memory skills problems
- Those with academic challenges
- Athletes (improve motor coordination)
- Singers (those losing voice or to improve clarity, quality and range)
- Dancers (improve rhythm and timing)
- Business and Sales people (improve relationships and presentations)
- Artists (better appreciation of color and layout)
- Those learning a foreign language (introducing frequencies in a new language)
- People with Down's Syndrome (improve motor coordination)
- Those with head injuries (reprogram lost listening patterns)
- Anyone wanting their batteries recharged
- Elderly (maintain energy, balance and listening)
- People who had strokes (improve communication and motor coordination).

"Wow! Why don't they use filtered music in workplaces? Schools? Nursing homes?" I blurted out.

"We haven't realized that we do not hear all frequencies, because," I continued, "we perceive our listening is complete since we hear what others are saying. However, we can miss many frequencies and inflections. We have all tuned out frequencies associated with painful events. Ear infections, disease or genetic problems cause other deficiencies. We can benefit by restoring these vibrations to our hearing and bodies. In addition high-pitched sounds give us energy. Our ears are like gold mines that most of us haven't tapped."

"Yes, the ear does so much more than perceive sound. It harmonizes body functions and provides energy to the brain for a starter," Paul hummed.

"By sharpening our listening skills, people can live more fully," I added. "This listening stuff is so good, it sounds like magic!" I smiled as I felt a lump in my pocket. It was another hot pink pill. Hmmmmm..........

The Life of Alfred Tomatis

Dr. Alfred Tomatis' sixteen year old mother delivered him two and a half months early in France on New Year's Day 1920. The three pound boy was discarded in a basket, left to die by hospital staff. Alfred's paternal grandmother, who delivered twenty-four children herself, thought differently, rescued him and nursed him along. Thank goodness for the world that she did!

Alfred was a sickly, but bright child. His father Umberto Tomatis, an opera singer, rented an apartment for his son at the age of eleven, where he lived alone and went to school. At age nineteen he was a first year medical student and in the same year he was drafted into the French army. Alfred completed his studies in war hospitals.

Umberto Tomatis sent fellow musicians, who were losing their voices, to his son - the ear, nose and throat specialist. At that time the standard treatment was to give people strychnine to help their larynxes. Alfred tried this, but felt that it was useless.

He tested the hearing of the singers, as he had done with the munitions factory workers during the war. Both the workers who were exposed to loud explosions and the singers had the same range of hearing loss. With much testing, Alfred discovered that the longer a singer practiced, the quicker he lost hearing of some pitches. He measured that singing produced higher decibels of sound inside the human skull than a jet engine. Veering from tradition, he saw the singing problem - as one of hearing. In time he discovered that if you can't hear a frequency, you can't sing it. He summed it up, "One sings with one's ear."

Tomatis contributed many great discoveries to our world. He believed that the primary purpose of the ear is to convert sound waves to electrical impulses, to charge the neocortex of the brain. Sound is a vital nutrient for our nervous system. Tomatis listened for hours a day to sounds laden with only a shell of higher pitched components and reportedly slept only four hours a night. He pointed out that the number of nerve cells in the cochlea that respond to high frequencies is four times greater than those for lower sounds. Tomatis believed that listening to these sounds gave him far more energy than the average person.

Tomatis also discovered that we have ear dominance, in addition to being right or left handed. The sound from the right ear goes to the left brain hemisphere. The sound from the left ear goes to the right brain hemisphere. If one is right eared, then sound from the right ear goes to the left brain that houses language processing capabilities. In contrast, those people who are left ear dominant often exhibit symptoms of learning disabilities, as the sound goes to the right brain hemisphere with no language processing capabilities. Next the sound is rerouted to the left brain, but with a delay that causes learning impairment. Tomatis improved learning disabilities by increasing stimulation to the right ear - to make it the dominant one. At www.Tomatis.com, review scientific studies in which a high percentage of people overcame their learning disabilities with this treatment.

People have the ability, an unconscious one, to tune out certain sounds. Tomatis discovered this as he observed that Jewish people, who had survived WWII concentration camps, were deaf in the frequency spectrum of the sirens used to take Jews to the death camps. When we subconsciously dampen a sound enough, we lose our ability to hear that frequency. We unconsciously dampen sounds associated with unpleasant things. Joshua Leeds reported that he blocked out the sounds of his father's angry voice. However, when his father was not around, he still felt emotional problems with men who had the same voice range – including himself. Since he completed The Tomatis Ear Retraining Program, he built many meaningful relationships with men, including his father. Other benefits that he reported were: increased concentration, improved pitch in singing, better memory, improved language skills, and greater dexterity. Today Joshua Leeds has written extensively about the work of the man, who had such a powerful impact on his life, Alfred Tomatis.[47]

For more information: www.tomatis.com
Listening Centre 599 Markham St.
Toronto, ON M6G2L7
listen@idirect.com
416-588-4136
www.listeningcentre.com

[47] Leeds, Joshua. The Power of Sound: How to be Healthy and Productive Using Music and Sound, Healing Arts Press: Rochester, VT, 2010, Pgs. 58-59.

Chapter Seven

Music of the Spheres

"Everything is made of vibrating energy. How this energy vibrates and interacts affects everything," Harold Moses began. "The magical secret is that musical harmony governs vibrating energy.

"My son sent me an article[48] stating that a scientist lined the surface of an airplane wing with a conductive tape and played music through the wings. His experiments show that this music increases the lift of the wing, making the plane more efficient. In the future, sound will be used to enhance the performance of everything.

"The right use of harmony will transform everything on this planet." Harold smiled.

The Toy Box

I playfully imagined Harold sitting near a toy box, full of building blocks. The blocks aren't really blocks, but spheres or balls. (A sound wave looks like the humps on an inchworm on a piece of 2-D paper, but in our 3-D reality, think of the waves of the ocean going out in a circle in all directions, resembling a growing sphere.) The balls are brightly colored and are connected with Velcro strips. The balls represent different pitches.

Even though a tone appears to be one tone, it is not. What we consider one tone is in truth a mixture of tones. After a tone is sounded it immediately produces after-tones called harmonics.

---

[48] Macey, Richard. *"Page Tools,"* 8/05

When we drop a stone in water it creates a splash-circle that keeps getting bigger. Think of the stone as a musical note. As that circle, or sound wave, gets bigger, it creates harmonics. The harmonic waves constructively interfere and get progressively higher in pitch.

Water Ripples[49]

Have you ever been in a huge church and heard the echo of your voice? The circle of sound from your voice reflects off surfaces. The original sound waves and the rebounding sound waves interact, creating harmonics.

In my imagination, Harold plays with the toy spheres, building them into models. He starts with a big sphere representing a root note, and then the fun begins! Each little sphere that he adds represents a harmonic.

What is a harmonic? Just as we know that clear sunlight is composed of colors of the rainbow, a tone is composed of many different harmonic notes. Harmonics are geometrically related sounds. This was described earlier. Put a bit differently, if the fundamental frequency is f, the harmonics have frequencies $2f$, $3f$, $4f$.... There are 16 harmonics in a harmonic series.

Harmonic frequencies follow this ratio relationship continue onward and upward - potentially to infinity. Many universal principles of botany, chemistry and other sciences follow principles of the harmonics series.

---

[49] http://en.wikipedia.org/wiki/Ripple_effect

The diagram[50] below shows the relationship between the sequence of each harmonic (harmonics are called partial and upper partial tones in this diagram) and the frequencies of each harmonic. See the mathematical relationship between the two?

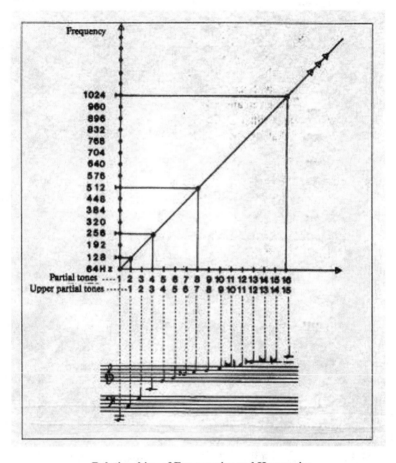

Relationships of Frequencies and Harmonics

Look at the elegant designs, formed by drawing the harmonics as sine curves!

[50] Reprinted with permission from Cousto's The Cosmic Octave.

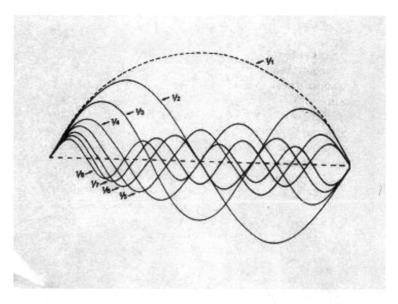

Sine Curves of the First Four Harmonics
Reprinted with permission from Cousto's <u>*The Cosmic Octave*</u>.

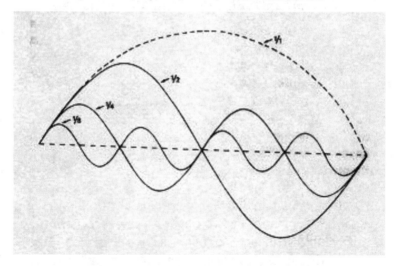

Sine Curves of the First Eight Harmonics
Reprinted with permission from Cousto's <u>*The Cosmic Octave*</u>.

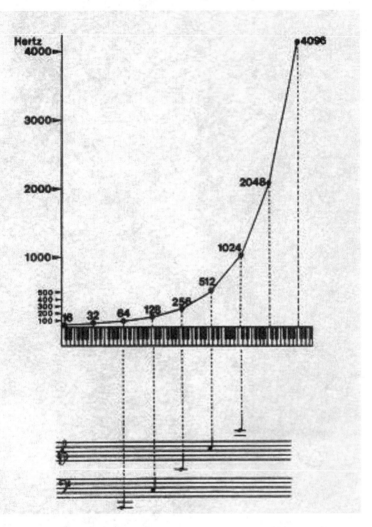

In the diagram above, the horizontal axis shows the keyboard of the piano. The vertical axis shows the corresponding frequencies of octaves.

Here's an interesting mathematical pattern. The frequencies of the octaves get exponentially higher with each additional octave.[51]

---

[51] Printed with permission from Hans Cousto, The Cosmic Octave.

Back to the Toy Box

Harold is playing with a big blue colored ball that represents the root note. (He uses different colored balls to represent different pitches.) Harold builds his toy model by using the formula to calculate the pitch of harmonics from a root tone.

This toy model gets complicated, because Harold is playing with several root notes at once. Sound waves in close proximity interact. The harmonics belonging to several root notes interact with each other, creating even more balls (new frequencies).

When the high parts (crests) of two sound waves overlap, they combine and create a new wave that is equal to the height of both the individual waves combined. Also, if the high and low part (troughs) of two waves overlap, they cancel each other out. When harmonic balls from different root notes combine, they create or cancel out pitches or energy. In physics some combinations of frequencies (balls) generate higher frequencies (energy), while others decrease energy. This is due to the way they interact or collide - constructively - adding their energy together - or destructively - canceling out each other's energy. (The waves can be said to be in-phase or out of phase.)

Harold marvels at the combined harmonic patterns from different root notes, noting which intervals of root notes create interacting harmonics with more or less colored balls.

Harold affectionately dubs the concentration of colored balls a "sweet spot." Certain intervals create more energy (colored balls) than others.

Harold is playing with intervals of harmonics in his mind, not really toy balls. He says, "Harmony is energy and energy is harmony. They manifest each other."

Have you ever sung in the shower? With the shower's highly reflective walls one frequency causes the shower to fill up with sound. You sing this special frequency and the shower seems to sing back to you. (Don't worry unless your shower talks to you first!)

When the sound waves bounce off the shower walls just right, your tone gets much louder. The harmonics of your voice bend off of the shape of your shower, and a certain root frequency will create harmonics that overlap and increase in strength. Sound is energy and you can use it to create even more energy.

Harold's CDs, "Drone" and the "Hyma Drone" are each composed of only two notes vibrating five notes apart (the fifth interval). The harmonics involved produce many sounds, harmonic interactions and energies from just these two notes. I suspect that Harold learned this by playing with his toys that represent harmonics. He discovered which note combination produces the most energy from interactions of harmonics.

I play Harold's "Drone" in the background when I am speaking, to keep my audience energized and alert. "The Drone" gives people energy without noticing they are listening to anything. However, my audience often complains when the "The Drone" ends.

In Harold's recording "The Drone," he used the interval of the fifth (two notes sounded at the same time, five notes apart) to produce unique wave interactions, that is, to create harmonic energy. This "secret formula" enables him to create energizing sounds for healing and transformation.

Lao Tzu (father of philosophy and Taoism, 6th century BC) says that the interval of the fifth is the harmony of the universe. Frequencies constructively interfere in the interval of a fifth, giving us energy freely.

Playtime is over and Harold puts the colored balls away, but he now better understand "secrets" about musical intervals and energy.

> "The fifth is an archetypal expression of harmony that demonstrates the 'fitting together' of the microcosm and the macrocosm in an inseparable whole. The fifth is a beautiful sound, because it demonstrates how the universe works."
> Stephen Ian McIntosh; The Harmonic Lyre. The Geometry of Sound Healing, www.aniwilliams.com

Everything Is Energy

Some scientists believe that the difference between different types of frequencies is just speed. Mystics and scientist, Keely[52] hypothesized that the speed of energy determines what form the energy takes. For example:

"Magnetism *slowed down yields*
  Electricity *which slowed down yields*
    Light *which slowed down yields*
      Heat *which slowed down yields*
        Sound *which slowed down yields*
          Physical vibration *slowed down yields*
            Matter."

Keely's mystical theory tells us that the difference between light, sound and matter is only frequency!

Keely's mystical ideas continue with the above idea:

"Love *slowed down yields*
  Thought *which slowed down yields*
    Feelings *which slowed down yields*
      Magnetism."

Form of Energy	Speed of Energy
Love	High
Thought	High
Feelings	High
Magnetism	Medium
Electricity	Medium
Light	Medium
Heat	Low
Sound	Low
Matter	Low

Dr. Bruce Lipton, a cellular biologist, reports that "Specific frequencies regulate:

- Cell division

---

[52] www.keelynet.com. John Keely (1827-1898) worked with sound and music and its effects on mechanics, chemistry, physics, mind, philosophy and spirituality.

- Gene regulation
- DNA
- RNA and protein syntheses
- Protein conformation and function
- Morphogenesis
- Regeneration
- Nerve conduction (structural arrangement) and growth."[53]

Dr. Lipton suggests that vibrating energy can heal us just like medicine.[54]

We Are All Energy and We Are All One!

Harold reports, "We exist entirely in a vibrating field of harmony."

"A field?" I asked.

"Yes. Some say the field is unity. Others say the field is the *all and the one,* the alpha and the omega."

"Albert Einstein said, 'Matter is constituted as regions of space in which the field is extremely intense.... There is no place ... for both the field and matter, for in the field there is only one reality.'"

When Harold says that nothing exists outside of the field, he reminded me of a passage in *Bible, John* 17:20-22.

- "I pray that... they may all be one, even as thou, Father are in me, and I in thee, that they may be also in us...
- The glory that thou has given me, I have given to them, that they may be one even as we are one...
- The love that thou has given me may also be in them, and I in them."

Harold brought me back from thinking about the *Bible* from a "sound" perspective when he said, "We are a harmonically unique vibrational signature of the Divine, a

---

[53] www.BruceLipton.com; "Electromagnetism and Energy Medicine," 2005. Pg. 3.
[54] www.BruceLipton.com; "Electromagnetism and Energy Medicine," 2005. Pg. 3.

chord in the cosmic symphony. We are composed of energy. We are energy, a *'sweet spot'* of vibrations in the field."

Music of the Heavens, Music of the Spheres

"When aligned, the field has a collection of 'sweet spots' (concentrations of colored balls) which are harmonic intersections in our cosmos," Harold began.

Harold's eyes twinkled as he continued, "Stars are regions in the field where waves are aligned and thus generate harmony due to the wave interaction. When the reflection of the waves interacts it can increase energy."

"Does wave interaction and harmony produce energy to create stars?" I questioned.

Pythagoras said that the Heavens played music to energize and create the universe. He called this the "Music of the Spheres."

Pythagoras also told us to study harmony to know the universe, but what can we learn about the universe from harmony?

Harold believes that the entirety of the Cosmos emanates from one central point. This point is the source of the fundamental tones of creation, the literal song of creation.

I like this imagery! Imagine someone singing a beautiful lullaby to create beautiful babies such as you and me. It is more personal than being created by a Big Bang!

Scientists have identified over ten million tones in the sun. The sun is a bell, ringing many tones. Hmmm, our sun is singing a song to us!

My CD, "Star Dust," has the tones of the stars twinkling in it. The tones of the planets moving in orbit are reproduced with special tuning forks. These tuning forks resonate in this CD, creating relaxing energy. I believe planetary tones are emotionally cathartic.

Our Personal Vibrations Affect Others

Harold's eyes twinkled as he continued, "People are composed of vibrating energy. Everyone has unique vibrations, which affect others."

I wondered how people energetically affect each other. I remember that lower pitches bend around corners, while higher pitches can shatter a glass. When you encounter someone with a high intense energy, could his energy pierce yours? Could his vibrations overtake yours? Or do your vibrations dominate? Harmonically speaking, other people change our frequencies.

The frequencies of people in close proximity interact. What is the sum total of a group's vibrations? This made me think of important quotes again.

• "We're all baptized by one Spirit into one body - all parts of the same Body." (*Bible, Cor*.12: 7-20)

• "You will know that I am in my Father, and you in me, and I in you." (*Bible, John* 14:20)

• Carl Jung's "Collective Conscious" is energy that we all tap into and share.

• "All is flow. All is in the flux." (ancient Greek philosopher, Heraclites)

We are all one, yet we are all different. It is as if we vibrate different notes, yet we all sing the cosmic melody.

We Have an Affinity for Harmony

Harold spoke, "Human beings seek out patterns. For example, people look at the Greek architecture and behold its great beauty. Greek architecture shares patterns that are found in music."

The golden section is a line segment sectioned into two according to the golden ratio. The total length, $a + b$, is to the longer segment a, as a is to the shorter segment b."[55] The golden ratio is approximately 1.618, phi.

---

[55] "Two quantities are in the golden ratio if the ratio between the sum of those quantities and the larger one, is the same as the ratio between the larger one and the smaller. At least since

Many artists and architects have proportioned their works to approximate the golden ratio. Many musicians use this pattern in their compositions.[56]

Goethe called architecture "frozen music," because architectural designs are often based on the same numerical patterns employed in musical compositions. Many harmonic mathematical patterns are also found in chemistry, biology, physics, astronomy, and in nature.

Our mind's wiring system subconsciously recognizes these patterns, these harmonies of energy. When the mind recognizes harmonic patterns, the human mind sees an innate beauty in harmonic patterns.

Leonardo Da Vinci used mathematical equations of musical harmony in the composition of his paintings. The result? People conclude his paintings have a transcending beauty, and they hang in museums.

---

the Renaissance, many artists and architects have proportioned their works to approximate the golden ratio. This proportion is aesthetically pleasing. " Wikipedia.

[56] Examples of music using numerical patterns found in architecture.

"James Tenney reconceived his piece *For Ann (rising)*, which consists of up to twelve computer-generated upwardly glissandoing as having each tone start so it is the golden mean.

Ernő Lendvai analyzes Béla Bartók's works as being based on two opposing systems, that of the golden ratio and the acoustic scale, though other music scholars reject that analysis. In Bartok's *Music for Strings, Percussion and Celesta* the xylophone progression occurs at the intervals 1:2:3:5:8:5:3:2:1."

"French composer Erik Satie used the golden ratio in several of his pieces, including *Sonneries de la Rose+Croix*. His use of the ratio gave his music an otherworldly symmetry.

The golden ratio is also apparent in the organization of the sections in the music of Debussy's *Image, Reflections in Water*, in which "the sequence of keys is marked out by the intervals 34, 21, 13 and 8, and the main climax sits at the phi position." The musicologist Roy Howat has observed that the formal boundaries of *La Mer* correspond exactly to the golden section. Trezise finds the intrinsic evidence "remarkable," but cautions that no written or reported evidence suggests that Debussy consciously sought such proportions.

Many works of Chopin, mainly Etudes (studies) and Nocturnes, are formally based on the golden ratio. This results in the biggest climax of both musical expression and technical difficulty after about 2/3 of the piece.

This Binary Universe, an experimental album by Brian Transeau, includes a track entitled "1.618" in homage to the golden ratio. The track features musical versions of the ratio and the accompanying video displays various animated versions of the golden mean.

Pearl Drums positions the air vents on its Masters Premium models based on the golden ratio. The company claims that this arrangement improves bass response and has applied for a patent on this innovation." Wikipedia

Leonardo was also fascinated with the Fibonacci numbers. What are these numbers? They are a result of a simple mathematical pattern. Any two numbers in the sequence when added together equals the next number. For example; 0, 1, 1, 2, 3, 5, 8, 13…

The Fibonacci numbers (or frequencies), when drawn, reveal a spiral. In contrast, the Western musical scale does not show this pattern. Some ancient people believed that listening to the "spiral" pattern in sound enabled one to "quicken" their soul, rising upward to God. (These numbers are found in solar systems, seashells, plants, and the human body.)

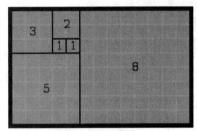

**Squares whose Sides are
Successive Fibonacci Numbers**

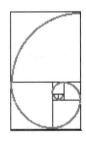 The pure Fibonacci numbers are not found in music today, because tuning to them would require a separate piano for each musical key. Our musical system has slightly altered these frequencies, making it easy for musicians to change keys, without changing instruments.

The Fibonacci series of numbers, converted to sound, are heard in my "Paint Your Soul" CD. These numbers are converted into corresponding cycles per second - sound waves.

The soothing and melodic "Paint Your Soul" CD uses tuning forks in the background that sound the pure tones of this spiral, Fibonacci pattern. These tones create sounds that some ancient cultures believed carved a pathway into the listener's consciousness, leading him closer to God - a literal spiral stairway to heaven! These tones also create patterns in people's brains for their consciousness to expand on.

Wired for Harmony

Scientists have discovered that a part of our brain recognizes harmony. Regardless of someone's musical education, everyone's brain has a switch that is turned on when harmony is played. Humans are wired for harmony.

Harold playfully reminded me that, "Humans and animals are set up to sing. Music is energy and songs affect things in close proximity to us. For example, bird songs have a positive effect on plant growth."

Caspra, who wrote *The Tao of Physics,* asks us, "Did you know that the sounds of frogs, crickets, and other insects and animals are necessary to maintaining the bio-acoustic matrix or sonic envelope of every ecosystem? If the crickets stopped singing, the ecosystem where they lived would die. Dolphin sounds are partly responsible for the growth patterns of coral in reefs. A bird chirping causes a flower to open."[57]

Harold remembered that in a friend's back yard two owls sang a "C" and "F" with perfect intonation. Of all the thousands of frequencies available, the owls chose two notes in perfect harmony, harmonizing the backyard.

Whales sing melodies with a range of seven octaves and also employ harmony.[58] The whales' songs can travel for miles. I wonder if whales are good at opera too?

Not only humans, but all living things are wired for harmony!

Harmony and Your Body

Harold sponsors "In-Chant," a weekly musical healing event.

"In-Chant is a singing experience that stimulates inner peace, encourages stress reduction and opens the mind to altered states of consciousness," Harold said.

---

[57] In the Afterword of the 4th edition of The Tao of Physics, Fritjof Capra says this.
[58] www.harmonicscience.org

"We are optimized harmonic alignments. We have been designed for harmony. Singing in harmony is a simple tool for spiritual transformation. In-Chant harmony flows between the singers' hearts, throats and minds. Music is an efficient method for distributing energy throughout the physical, spiritual and emotional body."

"When someone sings in harmony, his voice aligns in a harmonic, mathematical pattern. Suddenly there is increased energy, just like finding the right note when singing in the shower."

Harold uses the premise that we all affect each other in "In-Chant." People sing with rich and sonorous chords that produce energy. This mix and match of math, music and people produces a kaleidoscope of matrices and twinkling energy. People catapult their energy with Harold's carefully engineered harmonic intervals and music.

Harold continued that when a human being hears harmony, his heart and mind become synchronized. When someone sings, the effect of harmony is magnified. Singing can be a form of meditation.

When your brain vibrates in harmonic patterns, your subconscious mind reports pleasure to your conscious mind. No wonder people enjoy music!

Harold's web site reports that preliminary research indicates that "In-Chant" participants frequently experience one or more of the following:

- Stress reduction
- Improved attitude
- Greater breath control
- Improved respiratory function
- Effective pain management
- Improved mental clarity
- Increased energy
- Blood pressure regulation
- Strengthened immune system
- Spiritual awareness

- A sense of greater well being

"If in Phoenix, Arizona, come to 'In-Chant.' Singing can be a connection to the divine. When singing in a field of harmony, people are doing the same thing as the divine," Harold said with a smile.

What Our Songs Create

Harold reflects on societal problems and the lyrics of popular songs. One might think songs reflect the times, but could songs create reality?

We sing, "I can't live with out my loved one." Can this affect our health when we lose our loved one? With other melodies we doubt our personal value. Does this increase our insecurities?

I just listened to a song about whether or not to stay married. The song is entitled, "It is Cheaper to Keep Her." What type of vibration does that create?

Masuro Emoto photographed freezing, crystalline structures of water exposed to various words. The crystalline water structures exposed to kind words formed beautiful patterns, and those near negative words formed lopsided and distorted patterns.[59]

Without us consciously knowing what we are doing, can we impact our futures with our words and songs?

Music Changed an Entire Country!

In Estonia, a small Romanian country, I met Mara, who told me that a singing festival changed the course of the Estonians.

The people of Estonia had been slaves for thousands of years. Mara explained that her grandparents never had last names, because they were only slaves. Who wanted to bother with last names for slaves? Only when the Estonian people were free and the government wanted them to pay taxes, were

---

[59] Emoto, Masaru. The Hidden Messages in Water, Beyond Words Publishing Inc: Hillsboro, OR, 2004. Pgs.12 and 13.

they given last names to identify themselves. (Think people don't care about you? Try not paying your taxes.)

As slaves, the Estonian people were demoralized. At the time of the Russian revolt from the Czars, the Estonians saw their chance for freedom from Russia, but they did not have the courage to seize the opportunity.

In a country of a million people, half a million of them sang together for a week. According to Mara, the energy created from singing realigned the will, determination and spirit. Mara credited their country's courage and resulting freedom to the song festival.

Shortly after Hitler took control of Poland, Russia overpowered the Romanian countries, again. Under Stalin's ownership of the Estonian people, about a third of the Estonian people were randomly forced to work in Siberia. Many died. Later, Hitler as well as the Russians enslaved the Estonian men. The Estonians were forced to fight against each other, with brothers killing brothers. This painted the people with fear, shame, and horror, once again breaking the spirit of the people.

After World War II, the continued Russian occupation created harsh conditions, little food, no jobs, no places to live, but plenty of fear.

When the communist regime fell, the Estonian people found themselves again beaten down with no confidence to gain their freedom and no will to fight.

Once again the Estonian people came together with a song-festival for five days, with a half of million people attending. Mara was at this song festival, reporting that it changed her and she will never be the same. The Estonia people gained their freedom, crediting their courage to the energy created by their songs. To this day the Estonian people hold a song-festival every five years.

Harold's Advice
I asked Harold how people could utilize sound to transform their own lives.

"Find a reason to sing!" Harold's eyes were a twinkling of stars again.

"Listening to good music uplifts you, but nothing is as powerful as singing. Singing transforms your body, your mind, and your spirit."

Harold has learned secrets of harmonics and experiences heavenly vibrations by immersing himself in song and listening to beautiful music. He invites us to take the same transforming adventure.

Go to http://www.hgmoses.com/Music_Downloads.html for The "Drone" and other wonderful music!

www.JillsWingsOfLight.com – Art Gallery

109

Chapter Eight

Healing Sounds

Jonathan, a leading sound-healing authority, sang to the wound on his hand. "According to St. John's Hospital in London, wounds heal in two-thirds the normal time when we project sounds at them," he told me.

Singing to your "boo-boo" sounds crazy, unless you know about the power of sound. Sound also reduces the time it takes for bones to heal.[60] What a practical application of using sound to heal!

I was delighted to interview Jonathan Goldman, who is an expert on sound healing and a pioneer in the field of harmonics. Jonathan authored:

- *Healing Sounds: The Power of Harmonics*
- *Shifting Frequencies*
- *The Lost Chord*
- *Tantra of Sound*
(co-authored with his wife Andi)
- *The 7 Secrets of Sound Healing.*

I asked Jonathan to tell me about the power of

Jonathan has worked with masters of sound from the scientific and spiritual traditions, including the Dalai Lama's Chanting Gyuto and Gyume Monks and the Chant Master of the Drepung Loseling Monastery. Jonathan has a Master's Degree in the Independent Study on the Uses of Sound for Healing from Lesley University and lectures for the International Society for Music and Medicine.

He has appeared on national television and radio, including Art Bell's "Coast to Coast AM" and has been featured in national periodicals, including "USA Today." He was voted in the Top 7 Most Popular New Age Musicians by New Age Retailer magazine.

---

[60] Smith and Nephew's Exogen ™ system – ultrasound machine to accelerate bone healing

sound. It certainly was a force in his life.

Jonathan began...

"Sound is a wave energy that is measured in cycles per second. The number of cycles per second determines the frequency (pitch) of the sound. Slower waves create lower frequencies and faster waves create higher pitched sounds.

"We have the ability to hear vibrations whose wave speed varies from about 20 to 16,000 cycles per second, with young people being able to hear up to 20,000 cycles per second. However, just because we can't hear something does not mean there is no sound. Dolphins can receive and project frequencies up to 180,000 cycles per second. That is ten times greater than our range of hearing.

"Ancient mystics and some scientists believe that everything is sound. From stars in distant galaxies, to your chair, your body, or body organs, everything vibrates and creates sound."

I mused, "Sound produces subtle changes that may escape our observation. However, if everything is sound and sound waves in close proximity affect one another, then there is no end to the subtle changes that sound could make."

Jonathan responded, "*The New York Times*[61] said, 'Sound shape is a dazzling tool. It can make or break molecular structures and levitate objects.'"

"Sound is more than an energy that enters into our ears and brains, allowing us to

> Jonathan has over 30 recordings: many have been used in films and video games.
> His CDs include: "Ultimate Om" "Holy Harmony" "Dolphin Dreams" "Trance Tara" "Medicine Buddh," "Chakra Chants" "Ascension Harmonics" "The Divine Name" (co-created with Gregg Braden), Finalist for the 2004 "Best Healing-Meditation Album."
> His overtone chanting is on Kitaro's 2001 Grammy Award winning album.
> Jonathan's best selling release "Chakra Chants" won the 1999 Visionary Awards for "Best Healing-Meditation Album" and "Album of the Year." In 2001 "The Lost Chord" won runner up.

---

[61] "*NY Times*," science section, Feb. 1988.

experience the sensation of hearing. It can also go into our cellular structure and rearrange our molecules. I believe that it can change our DNA,"[62] Jonathan continued.

"I come from a family of physicians, and I respect the medical field. Today's doctors heal many people. Sound is a wonderful way to assist the healing process. It's a great complement to traditional medicine. Remember, we say that healthy people have *sound* health! One of the ancient meanings of the word 'sound' is to become whole or healed.[63]

"When we are healthy, we are like an orchestra playing this magnificent 'symphony of self,' with each part of the body being a player in this orchestra. When the second violin player loses his music, he plays out of tune. This out-of-tune note affects the other string players and eventually the whole orchestra. This is analogous to a part of our body vibrating out of its own natural frequency. It is vibrating out of ease or harmony. We call this out-of-tune condition dis-ease.

"Traditional medicine has two approaches to disease. They either give the string player enough drugs so that he passes out, or in the other approach it is analogous to the process of surgery, that is, cutting his head off. In both situations, this string player is no longer playing the wrong notes, but he is no longer part of the orchestra, either. Is it possible to simply give the violin player back his music, so he can play in tune? Is it possible to project the correct frequency to the part of the body that is vibrating out of tune? This is the basic principle of sound healing."

I injected that Royal Rife, a doctor in the early 1900s, used frequencies to heal. He measured the frequency of cancer cells and exposed them to the opposite frequency. To simplify the idea, think of this example, if the cancer cell was a +10 frequency, then he exposed the cell to a −10 frequency. The

---

[62] I thought this quote might be interesting. Change your DNA, Dr. Robert Gerard, 2002. Pg. 44. "DNA communicates by tones. Tones also are how the intent of the human mind is relayed to each DNA strand. The intent of the DNA strands is then communicated instantly. This alters the chromosomes, which, in turn, alters the cell."

[63] Change your DNA, Dr. Robert Gerard, 2002, Pg. 44.

two opposite frequencies canceled each other out when they combined. Dr. Rife attained outstanding results.[64]

Jonathan continued, "There are marvelous instruments, sound devices and CDs for healing. In fact, I produce CDs for healing that many people have had profound results with.

"Nevertheless, I believe that the most extraordinary instrument for healing is our own voice. Your voice can change the vibrations of your body, brain and chakras (major subtle energy centers in your body). Your voice is phenomenally powerful... and it requires no batteries, no electricity, it is easy to use, there are no complicated user manuals and it's free."

Toning, a Sound Healing Practice

Jonathan continued, "The method of using your voice for stress reduction and healing is called 'toning.' This term goes back to the 14th century, even the ancient Egyptians used the voice for healing.

"One tones when he sings extended vowel sounds, which has a profound affect on your body and chakras.

"These are the vowels I sing to chakras (start at the base of your spine and go towards the top of your head):

- **'Uh'** (as in the word "cup"). This is for the root chakra, the energy center at the base of the spine.
- **'Ooo'** (as in the word "you"). This is for the sacral chakra, the energy center about 3 inches below the navel.
- **'Oh'** (as in the word "go"). This is for the navel chakra, the energy center in the area of the navel.
- **'Ah'** (as in the word "ma"). This is for the heart chakra, the energy center in the center of the chest.
- **'Eye'** (as in the word "I"). This is for the throat chakra, the energy center at the base of the throat.

---

[64] See www.Rife.org for more information on Royal Rife.

- **'Aye'** (as in the word "say"). This is for the 3rd eye chakra, the energy center in-between and just above the two eyebrows.
- **'Eee'** (as in the word "see"). This is for the crown chakra, the energy center on the top of your head.

"Toning (singing vowels) enables anyone to experience profound shifts in health and consciousness. It also enhances balance and harmony.

"Toning is a nondenominational method of healing. Some methods of sound healing are based upon a particular system of beliefs. For example, some people might have difficulties toning a Hindu mantra, feeling it interferes with their religious belief. But the vowel sounds are found in every language. Vowel sounds are a common denominator for all languages.

"The 'Ah' sound is a universal sound that is associated with the heart, love and compassion. 'Ah' is a powerful sound that can help open your heart, assisting you to feel love, compassion and balance. This is an excellent vowel to 'tone' or sing. Most Gods and Goddesses have the 'ah' sound in their names, for example, Jesuah (Jesus), Buddha, Muhammad, Krishna, Wakantanka (Native American tradition), Yah, Tara and so on. 'Ah' is often the first sound we utter at birth and the last sound that accompanies our last dying breath.

"When I first researched sound healing nearly 30 years ago, different spiritual masters and scientists were in disagreement about the effects of different toned vowel sounds. They used different vowels to resonate the same organ or chakra successfully. At first I struggled with this, thinking there should be only one vowel sound to heal each organ or chakra.

"We are all unique vibratory beings and what works for one person will not necessarily work for another. For example, you may find 10 to 20 percent of people are allergic to penicillin. So penicillin heals about 80 to 90 percent and harms the rest. Some medicines work for you and not for me.

"The same thing is true for sound. Some sounds work for you and not for me. I have observed sound cure chronic illnesses. And at other times, the same sound will seemingly do nothing. For example, certain sounds improve headaches and asthma. And then again, I have also seen nothing happen with these same sounds," confided Goldman.

"I had a revelation: **Frequency + Intent = Healing.** Not only does the frequency of a sound affect someone, but also the intention of the person uttering the sound. Intention is the energy or the consciousness behind the sound.

"Our feelings, beliefs and motivations 'carry' on the sounds we make and affect people who receive them. When I do a recording I make sure that my intention is in total alignment with the purpose for the recording. I've applied this principle to every recording that I've made, such as my award winning CD 'Chakra Chants.' I not only used specific tones and sounds to resonate the chakra, but I also focused my *intention* and *attention* on balancing that chakra. That is one reason why 'Chakra Chants' is so powerful.

"My formula, Vocalization + Visualization = Manifestation, embraces the concept that consciousness can be encoded on sound. In other words, using your voice while imagining something, affects the outcome. For example, Tibetan monks chant mantras while evoking specific energies or deities and then they experience them. The power of this is undeniable.

"In Tibetan Medicine, there are three variables when attempting to heal another. The variables are:
- The healer's belief in his healing
- The recipient's belief in the healer
- The karma between the two.

"A person's belief system is a variable we can control. We can change or fortify our beliefs, thoughts and feelings. Thus, we play an active role in our own healing, even if someone else heals us.

"Another formula I recently created which employs this concept: Sound + Belief = Outcome."

Harmonics

Jonathan went on to say, "Harmonics have a powerful influence on people.[65] Simply listening to vocal harmonics spiritually uplifts many people. Such activity can reduce heart rate, respiration and brain wave activity.

"With regard to understanding harmonics, an intellectual discussion is not as powerful as the *experience* of feeling what harmonics can do for you. That's why I use exercises in workshops that help you resonate with harmonics. If you don't feel it, then it's not true for you. Until we experience something, it's mental gymnastics. By experiencing harmonics, you realize its power and then it becomes life changing.

"Listening to harmonics creates sacred space and vibrational shifts. Recordings with harmonics are available at www.healingsounds.com. We also teach people to sing harmonics, a powerful technique, especially when it is coupled with conscious intention.

"Listening to harmonics can be extremely profound. However, creating vocal harmonics can be a more extraordinary experience. You can vibrate different parts of your body, chakras and even project sounds to specific portions of your brain with self-created harmonics. It's amazing!"

Tuning Forks

Jonathan continued, "An easy way to experience sound healing is by listening to tuning forks. Pitches not found on our pianos nor in Western music can be created through tuning forks such as the ones we have at www.healingsounds.com. These are not the tuning forks you can buy at a music store to tune an instrument.

---

[65] Jonathan's book, Healing Sounds has more information on harmonics!

"Musical relationships of several pitches, called intervals, can have a powerful healing effect on our bodies and brains. For example, the Pythagorean interval of 3 to 2 is balancing and healing. The interval of a fifth (two notes that are five notes apart) has a ratio of 3 to 2.[66] When we hear this interval, our nervous and neuromuscular systems entrain to it. The same tuning forks balance the right and the left halves of our brains. People have listened to this ratio and it has cured headaches and popped vertebrae back into place. It's astounding. It's a wonderful tool for creating balance and enhancing relaxation.

"The 3 to 2 ratio is displayed in the proportions of the human body and natural forms, including leaf arrangements on stems, the spirals of the nautilus shell and the arrangements of billions of stars in galaxies. This ratio, the phi ratio, is found in the two adjacent numbers in the Fibonacci series.

"Our musical scale can use some of the Fibonacci numbers. The numbers 0, 1, 1, 2, 3, 5, and 8 are part of the Fibonacci series. Our scale approximates 1, 3, 5, and 8. The next number in this series is 13 and the interval of 8 and 13 has not been used in Western music or any other music I know of. I believe this 8:13 ratio represents an outer spiral of the phi ratio that had not yet manifested sonically upon this planet, until now.

"I was guided to create tuning forks that used this 8:13 ratio. When I first had the 8:13 ratio made into tuning forks, I heard angels singing and experienced a spiraling sensation. While researching the effects of these tuning forks, I brought them to a workshop where a well-known medical doctor and a psychic experimented with the 8:13 tuning forks. Both 'saw' this frequency bring light into DNA. The 8:13 ratio also seems to amplify intention and develop the higher chakras."

[66] Goldman, Jonathan. Healing Sounds, The Power of Harmonics. Healing Arts Press: VT, 2002, Pg. 28.

"The Lost Chord"

"My CD 'The Lost Chord,' uses the Fibonacci series of numbers converted into musical pitches. This recording is a journey through the chakras and the Kabalistic Tree of Life. 'The Lost Chord' features sacred mantras, harmonics and chants from the Hindu, Tibetan and Hebrew traditions. To my knowledge, it is the first recording that does this, using sacred chants from different traditions, all in the phi ratio."

Crystal Singing

"When you sing up and down with the pitch of your voice like a siren, into the base of a quartz crystal (the non pointy end) you will create an audible harmonic. The crystal will resonate with this harmonic. This powerful vibration can increase your energy and power. Crystal singing is a tool for transformation and healing.

"A group of people can stand, making a geometric pattern. For example, they can form a six-pointed star around a recipient. Each person then sings into the base of a crystal, pointing the crystal towards the recipient. Each person also projects his or her intent of healing to the recipient. The lines of sound go towards the recipient at meaningful angles, hitting the recipient at precise angles, which amplifies the healing."

The Healing Codes

Goldman continued, "My CD 'Holy Harmony,' contains the complete Healing Codes of the *Bible*, as described in Drs. Horowitz and Puleo's *Healing Codes for the Biological Apocalypse*. These nsix tuning forks are said to contain:

- The Divine frequencies of creation
- The fulfillment of certain Biblical prophesies
- Extraordinary healing and transformational energy.

"'Holy Harmony' also uses the chant of YHSHV (Yod Hey Shin Vav Hey), an ancient name of the Christ. The YHSVH Chant is composed of specific letters of the Hebrew alphabet, creating a sacred name for the Christ. The Chant can be used for protection, clearing, and resonating with Christ energy. I have pages of testimonials from people who experienced amazing healing and transformation from listening to this recording."

Jonathan's new creations include "Ascension Harmonics." This CD enhances altered states of consciousness and heightened awareness. Composed with overtone chanting, Tibetan bowls and bells, these undulating waves of Healing Sounds® transform. The sacred, multi-dimensional harmonic sounds are excellent for enhancing deep states of meditation as well as for shamanic journeys, rituals and the ascension process. This CD is a INAT's "Visionary" Award Winner for "Best Healing Music."

The "Chakra Chants" CD combines the Sacred Vowels with Bija Mantras from the Vedic traditions with Pythagorean tunings, Elemental & Shabd Yoga Sounds, Male and Female Choral Voices, Sound Current toning and more! This is an amazing hour long psycho-acoustic sacred sound experience. Designed for meditation and deep sound healing, it initiates a new level of the therapeutic uses of sound. It is a #1 New Age Best Seller and "Visionary" Award Winner for "Best Healing Music" and "Album of the Year."

"The Divine Name"

"I teamed up with Greg Bradden after he wrote the *God Code* and I created 'The Divine Name' CD. In the *Kabbalah*, the personal name of God is sacred. More than 2,300 years ago God's name was removed from the religious texts of over one half of the world's populations, to safeguard its use. Further, when it was written, this Divine Name had only consonants, which were not to be spoken freely.

"In my meditations, I discovered a way in which the Divine Name could be sounded using only vowel sounds!

"'The Divine Name' as it is sounded on this recording, uses no consonants, only vowel sounds. Therefore, it is nondenominational, transcending the barriers of cultures and traditions. It contains no delineation that is created through consonants, which create different languages. (Are consonants the Tower of Babel?)

"What if the 'divine name' was a universal sound (which of course, any sound created from vowels would be) that could be uttered to have a 'holy' experience of sound? 'The Divine Name' CD - with its specific combination of harmonically related vowel sounds - can create this experience.

"I have many testimonials from listeners who report life changing experiences. Some claim it gave them the most powerful spiritual experience of their lives. If hearing 'The Divine Name' CD can create this effect, imagine what it would be like to sound this name yourself.

"What would it be like if large groups of people sounded 'the divine name' together around the planet? It could be a sound that unites us all."

Tantra Of Sound

Jonathan continued, "My wife Andi and I have co-authored a book called *Tantra of Sound*. We use the term 'tantra' in its traditional way, meaning the interconnecting web that unites all of reality. Some call it 'the field.' Others call it 'Indra's net.' It is the unifying energy that connects us all. From our perspective, sound is the substance that makes up this force.

"*Tantra of Sound* tells us how to use sound to:
- Connect more deeply with yourself
- Connect more completely with others
- Manifest compassion
- Enhance self understanding
- Create more powerful connections with others
- Create inner harmony within your own being
- Generate harmonic energy for others."

Sounds for Planetary Healing

"I have been working in this field for 30 years," continued Jonathan." In the first 15 to 20 years, I helped people discover that sound can heal their bodies. Later, I taught that sound could help people enter deep meditation, quickly and easily. Then, I wondered, 'What is next?'

"In a deep meditation, I understood that sound could be used for 'planetary healing' to raise the consciousness of earth's people. This process generates compassion and kindness. In other words, we can consciously make our world a kinder and more loving place with sound.

"So how do we use sound to uplift the planet? Many people consider the Internet to be the neural network of our planet, our global mind. It's a great phenomenon, but we also need the energy of the global heart of the planet to balance this global mind.

"The energy of the heart is important. Spiritual masters throughout the ages have told us this, and science is validating this as well. Did you know that the electro-magnetic field generated by the heart is 60 times greater than the electro-magnetic field generated by the brain? The Heart Math Institute made this discovery. The heart is a powerful instrument, especially when it is manifesting the energy of love and appreciation.

"The question is: 'How do we activate the global heart of the planet?' The answer is simple. In Tibetan Buddhism the connective force that links the mind and body is sound! In order to activate the global heart of the planet and connect it to the global mind, we must make sounds together.

"On the Internet at my Sacred Sound Temple I ask people to tone the 'Ah' sound, which activates people's heart energy. People can't hear others on the Internet, but the effects are still measurable. Sound amplifies prayer. Further, as technology develops, we'll actually hear each other's sounds when singing from individual computers.

Sound, coupled with consciousness, can help 'awaken' people and assist in 'global harmonization,' that is, the creation of peace and harmony on earth.

"Sound enhances consciousness. With increased consciousness, we can be more compassionate with deeper understandings of one another. This loving kindness is an important element of consciousness that we need to evolve.

"A research project published in *The Journal of Conflict Resolution* showed that when a group of people meditated on peace for 24 hours, there was a decrease in violent activities within the city where the meditation occurred. This phenomenon was initially called 'The Maharshi Effect.' The Global Consciousness project at Princeton, New Jersey, conducted research showing that global meditations and prayers are elements of the consciousness of this planet."

"Further research on the power of group meditations showed that in order to affect a large group of people you only needed to have the square root of 1 percent of the population taking part in a meditation. Therefore, only about 8,000 people are needed to affect the entire planet. A small number of people can make a difference.

"Of course, I'd like to suggest that the people (the square root of 1 percent of the population) need to be skilled mediators in order to manifest change. They need to have mastered techniques to achieve inner peace before generating their energy outward."

"Www.templeofsacredsound.org, is the world's first interactive website dedicated to using 'intentionalized' sound to assist in global harmonization. This cyberspace, sacred sound temple enables people to enter three different toning chambers to sound along with others and to project these healing sounds to the planet. It is an awesome experience.

"Many people toning via the Internet using their sounds and conscious intent can change the vibration of our planet. Our sounds can bring peace not only to ourselves, but also to the earth itself. This is why I do this work," emphasized Jonathan.

Chapter Nine

A Revealing Encounter

The strangest thing happened in the parking lot of the site of the next interview. Out of an expensive car came, of all things, a rat!

Not any old rat, but one wearing an off-white, silk leisure suit. He sported rhinestone-studded, dark glasses, oversized gold jewelry and plentiful cheap cologne, enough to gag an army. Who could stand to be by his side and inhale his overbearing smell?

And look what else got out of the limousine: femme fatale, a la rat! For a rat, was she gorgeous... what a nice "piece of art" sauntering at his side!

Oh, look! This glitzy rat has a copy of my "Deep Wave Beauty" CD with soothing and transformative music sprinkled with frequencies linked to important vitamins and nutrients. These substances revitalize and renew the skin, musculature, tissues and collagen of the face and neck area. Frequencies related to collagen and facial/neck muscles are layered into the music. Sound intermingles with our energies and steadily provides alterations - as we absorb the sounds. The music and frequencies energize your face, while providing spiritual peace.

And this fashionable couple is going to the next interview at the SomaEnergetics Center. Hmmm, I wonder if they want to learn more about the mysterious Solfeggio tones.

Could this stylish rat could be Osborn Raticus, who spied on Wizard Jack and learned about all the marvelous gifts one can get from certain CDs and sound and light machines? Here's my chance. I'll try to interview this important-looking fellow and see who he is.

"Excuse me, sir," I opened. "May I have a word with you?"

The rat adjusted his ring finger so that the sun reflected on a facet of his oversized ring.

Slowly, the rat began, "Since I learned about the magic of tones, my life has a rags to riches story."

The rat's finger, with the big ruby ring, reached up and tipped down his rhinestone sunglasses, revealing deep brown eyes. In those eyes I saw the Raticus of old.

"Oh, my, Osborn Raticus!" I gulped. "Is that you? Osborn Raticus! What are you doing? Dressed up like this and where is Mrs. Raticus?" I couldn't help myself.

"Osborn, you used sound to feel and look younger. You used light and sound machines to increase your intelligence, you listened to Harold Moses' CDs to increase your energy, you attended the Swamiji's concerts to become healthier, but you forgot to use sound to lift your spirituality... unless you expect to be more spiritual by wearing gaudy jewelry. To become more spiritual you should be more loving and exhibit gifts of the spirit," I blurted out without thinking.

A sheepish Raticus waved my CD, "Paint Your Soul," slowly in front of my face. "I am just beginning to learn about this benefit of sound. I need to visit my friend, David Hulse and learn about the mysterious Solfeggio tones."

Raticus tipped his hat, looked down and turned his head. He disappeared into the SomaEnergetics Center. Like magic, the limousine was gone.

Chapter Ten

Secrets of the Ancient Solfeggio Tones

"Wahoo!" I exclaimed. I landed an interview with David Hulse, the founder of SomaEnergetics™ sound healing school.

David opened up our conversation with his view of music's place in modern physics. He expounded on Einstein and the equivalence of matter and energy.

"Matter is slowed-down vibration. Subatomic particles are not made of material stuff. They are patterns of energy," said David.

"Material forms are continually being created and dissolved. We are the observers who decide what is created and what is dissolved. Did you get that part? We (the observers) are a vital part of the process. Without us, there is no process."

David reminded me that music is energy, vibrating energy.

"Music is the key to unlock the universe. Certain tones and patterns of tones can improve our health, intelligence and consciousness," David offered.

David's eyes widened as he discussed the Solfeggio scale that he learned about in Horowitz and Puleo's *Healing Codes for Biological Apocalypse*. This book reveals a pattern of numbers encoded in *Numbers* 7:12 – 89 (in the *Bible*).

These numbers are converted into frequencies and are reported to have healing qualities.

The content of this seemingly unimportant text is divided into activities that occurred on different days. The Pythagorean skein[67] is then applied to the numbers of the associated verses of the different days. For example, the text describing the first day is on verse 12, which has a Pythagorean skein of 12, or 1 +2 = **3**. The second day starts on verse 18, or 1 +8 = **9**. The third day is located on verse 24, or 2 + 4 = **6**. The first set of numbers in this code is these three numbers or **396**. When you applying the same process to the rest of the chapter you get the following set of numbers:

Solfeggio Scale[68]

396

417

528

639

741

852

Horowitz and Puleo revealed that the Solfeggio tones were an ancient scale, which they claimed, "vibrates the exact frequencies required to transform spirit to matter, or matter to spirit." [69]

They also wrote that the Solfeggio tones are capable of "spiritually inspiring humankind to be more Godlike." [70]

In addition they told us that the removal of these frequencies from our musical scale "produced changes… in conceptual thought, further distancing humanity from God."[71]

---

[67] In the system of the Pythagorean skein, individual numbers are added up and ultimately reduced to the numbers 1 through 9. For example, with the number 245, 2+4+5 =11. With the number 11, 1+1 =2. The Pythagorean skein for the number 245 is 2.
[68] Notice the numerical pattern in the ones, tens and hundreds column.
[69] Joseph Puleo and Lenard Horowitz, Healing Codes for a Biological Apocalypse, Tetrahedron Publishing Co.: Idaho. 2001, Pg. 59.
[70] Joseph Puleo and Lenard Horowitz, Healing Codes for a Biological Apocalypse, Tetrahedron Publishing Co.: Idaho. 2001, Pg. 61.

Horowitz and Puleo pointed out that these ancient scales were Gregorian chants that have been removed from the records of the Catholic Church. In fact, they quote a professor Emeritus Willi Apel, who asserted that the origin of the Solgeggio tones arose from a medieval hymn about John the Baptist, and that the first six lines of the hymn corresponded to each note in the Solfeggio scale.

They believe that this healing scale was modified in two ways since medieval times:

- The frequencies were changed.
- The traditional musical scale has been assigned syllables that do not include all of the original syllables. When these changes occurred, the benefits of these special sounds were lost to mankind.

Benefits of Each Solfeggio Tone

David explained, "The original syllables were used as the notes of the musical scale. Since medieval times several of the vowel sounds have been changed. For example, the first note of the scale in our culture, 'do,' used to be called 'ut.'

"I looked at the definitions of the original syllables of the Solfeggio scale, using little-known entries from *Webster's Dictionary,* the original *Greek Apocrypha*, and *Healing Codes of the Biological Apocalypse.*[72]

"With this information and my own personal experience using the Solfeggio tones, I have determined the benefits of the six frequencies of the Solfeggio scale:

- **"Ut... Turn grief into joy** (396-hertz frequency). The first Solfeggio tone liberates energy, eliminating hidden blockages and subconscious negative beliefs.
- **"Re... Connect people to the Source** (417-hertz). The second tuning Solfeggio tone helps people to change.

[71] Joseph Puleo and Lenard Horowitz, Healing Codes for a Biological Apocalypse, Tetrahedron Publishing Co.: Idaho. 2001, Pg. 61.
[72] Horowitz and Puleo, Healing Codes of the Biological Apocalypse, Tetrahedron Publishing Co.: Idaho, 2001.

People say: 'I need another job;' or 'I need to move to a different place;' but they don't have the energy to do so. Harmonizing with this frequency can increase your energy beyond survival to creative modes."

David reflected, "A girl, who worked as a massage therapist, was hesitant to make changes in her life. After the tuning session with me, she called me. 'You won't believe where I am right now. I am in Sedona, Arizona!' After the tuning, I packed up everything I owned, put it in a truck and drove to Sedona. The dream of my life was to live in Sedona.

"Shortly after she moved to Sedona, the girl got a better job as head of all massage therapists at a resort. In summary, resonating with the Solfeggio tones can put us in touch with an inexhaustible source of energy that gives us power and ambition to make our dreams come true.

- **"Mi... Repair DNA** (528-hertz). The frequency of the third Solfeggio tone brings transformation and miracles into our life. The word 'Mi' derives from the phrase 'MI-ra gestorum' in Latin, meaning 'miracle.' Stunningly, this is the exact frequency used to repair broken DNA, the genetic blueprint upon which life is based![73]

- **"Fa... Connect people to spiritual family** (639-hertz). The frequency of the fourth Solfeggio tone helps us create harmony in relationships.

- **"Sol... Solve problems and increase intuition** (741-hertz). The frequency of the fifth Solfeggio tone gives us power of self-expression to be who we really are. Several women from my workshops would hardly make a sound without permission from a male or authority figure. Yet, after resonating with this frequency they assumed more control over themselves. For men, the fifth tuning fork enabled feminine energy *(representing our feelings)* to be expressed, balancing their masculine energy. Without this balance, men have difficulties managing their emotions.

---

[73] http://orgoneproducts.org/blog/2008/04/02/ancient-solfeggio-frequencies-528-hz-dna-repair/

- **"La... Return people to spiritual order** (852 hertz). The frequency of the sixth Solfeggio tone links the mind, body, insight, consciousness and spiritual evolution.

"By listening to the Solfeggio tones, people can open channels of energy within and receive life altering benefits." David continued.

Playing with Tuning Forks

"I had tuning forks constructed to produce the ancient Solfeggio tones," David continued.

David then told me how he developed SomaEnergetics, the technique to balance and restore energies using these ancient Solfeggio tones. "I began playing the ancient Solfeggio notes by using the tuning forks. The Solfeggio tones produced by tuning forks were alive in my hands! I wasn't using the tuning forks. The tuning forks were using me!

"These notes resonate with energy in our bodies. Believe me, these tones and our bodies know one another, like old friends! And I have developed a beneficial healing modality with these ancient tones.

"Over time, the tuning forks taught me many things that I combined with other healing methods," David continued.

"I 'mapped' the body with the tuning forks. For example, if I sounded a Solfeggio tuning fork on the right side of a person, the same frequency may sound entirely different on their left side. The side that sounded dissonant would be out of balance. I used the tuning fork's vibration to connect dissonant energy of the body to the heart and then the Solfeggio tone would return to a beautiful sound. Clients confirm this new balance brings about life changes that they claim result from the Solfeggio tuning forks.

"In another example, I used the tuning forks on a client, which revealed disharmony around his right hip. I combined this information with my knowledge of healing methods and I concluded:

- The left side of the brain controls the right side of the body.
- The left side of the brain represents masculine energy.
- The right hip is used to move us forward.

"Putting this together, I asked the client about moving forward with a man. The man revealed a personal struggle with his father and their business. This emotional situation was the cause of his energy blockage.

"With the Solfeggio tuning forks, I balanced the energy of a woman whose father had molested her as a child. She had never told a soul about this. But the tuning fork found that trapped, negative energy that had controlled her, creating a life based in fear and limitation.

"With the Solfeggio tuning forks, I found a flat zone in a woman whose daughter had just been killed. I didn't know that had happened. See? The tuning forks found the dissonance, released it and then restored harmony and balance.

"The tuning forks revealed the problems symbolically; then people discussed issues weighing them down, which helped them release negative emotional energy quickly.

"Later, I had the tuning forks created with weights on the two long prongs - that together form a 'U' shape. These transferred the Solfeggio frequencies into the body via the stem of the tuning fork. When the base of the tuning fork touched the body on acupressure points, these frequencies then traveled in the body on subtle energy meridians and loosened subtle energy blockages within the physical body.

"Tuning forks without the weights balance the subtle bodies of energy around a person. The subtle energy is where emotional stress is recorded, and if accumulated, will transfer to the physical body causing illness. We need to release this energy and be proactive in our lives. The Solfeggio tones can do this!

"My SomaEnergetic workshops teach how to use all six tuning forks together to produce the frequencies which open people to divine inspiration, revelation, wisdom and knowledge."

David teaches three courses of healing techniques using the Solfeggio tuning forks. For more information, go to www.SomaEnergetics.com.

More on Solfeggio Tunings

"When applying the sound vibration of the Solfeggio forks to myself, it has healed my chronic sinus and upper respiratory infections, relieved lower back pain, lessened headaches/migraines, diminished an enlarged lymph node behind my ear …assisted in relieving emotional trauma, reduced the swollen area…in my ear." *Mary LoPiccalo*

"The most common remarks I hear after a SomaEnergetics session is 'I don't understand why, but my mind and body just seems to be asking for more.' I encourage you all to give it a try. It is part of a universal language; we are all energy, we are light, we are all vibration. We are living in pretty dense times right now and anything we could do to heal ourselves and raise our own sense of love and mastery in this world, we should use." *Margarete Brandenburgh*

www.JillsWingsOfLight.com – Art Gallery

David performed a 20 minute SomaEnergetics™ Tuning Session on this woman who he had never met before the session. The pictures are taken using Kirlian[74] Photography.

BEFORE~1.JPG
Before Tuning Session

AFTER_~1.JPG
After Tuning Session

Applications of the Solfeggio Tones

Now that we know of the solfeggio tones, what do we do with this knowledge? The most obvious application of the solfeggio frequencies mimics their use from medieval times - as notes of a musical scale. Pianos and instruments can be tuned to these frequencies as opposed to the scale that we currently use, the equal temperament scale. Composers can write songs using these tones, just as once was done with the "Hymn for John the Baptist."

Some people altered the standard musical scale that we listen to by detuning concert A. They still applied the formula of the equal temperament scale, but created very different feelings from the adjustment. One would not assume that a song sounds different by altering the tuning pitch, but it does. The difference is subtle, but discernible. For example, Led

[74] Electromagnetic Kirlian photography records electromagnetic fields. Photos are compliments of Laura Kaye!

Zeppelin's "Stairway to Heaven" reportedly tuned to an equal temperament scale that includes the 4th solfeggio tone, 417 hertz. The song has a special feeling of its own. The song still uses the equal temperament scale so it only includes one solfeggio tone.

The solfeggio tones are most powerful when sung. Increase the impact of these frequencies by using your own body as an instrument. If you own the solfeggio tuning forks, you can mimic their pitch or vocally accompany *YouTube* videos featuring these tones. When singing, these vibrations go up and down your spine, belly, chest, head and vocal chords. Singing creates internal waves that interface with your central nervous system and engage in cell to cell vibrational transfer - resonating into the far reaches of your body.

Many people report receiving beneficial energy after hearing the solfeggio tones. These mysterious frequencies that slip in-between the notes on our pianos are embedded on my "Paint Your Soul" CD,[75] which features an expanded set of 18 Solfeggio Tones. Reflections and testimonials on the music in "Paint Your Soul" are extraordinary, perhaps due to the solfeggio tones in the background:

"The CD brought tears to my eyes at first, and weeks later, still leaves me in a state of contemplative quietude after listening." *J. Stitt*

"As I listened to your music for the very first time, I felt it immediately begin to minister love, peace and well-being to every cell in my body. Frankly, that hasn't happened EVER in my life. I felt every cell coming into perfection as I closed my eyes to breathe in this amazing music." *M. Murphy*

"I found in your music a hidden secret, the unconfused part of myself that I know to be the truest, most precious and the most sacred part, which I have steadfastly ignored." *Dr. Michael Lagan*

---

[75] Download free Sound healing music at www.jillshealingmusic.com and at the bottom of the home page at www.jillswingsoflight.com, including a selection, *My Soul*, from the *Paint Your Soul* CD.

"When I listen to your beautiful CD my cares melt away and I feel the illusion of fear dissolve as I experience the truth of light and love." *Anne L*

Paint Your Soul

Solfeggio, Reverse Solfeggio, and
Fibonacci Tones

"Paint Your Soul" CD

Load the solfeggio tones into an iPod, so each tone can radiate out of the ear buds. Try placing an ear bud on various parts of the body. For example one could sit on an ear bud - with his posterior receiving the first tone - to balance the root chakra. In another application, place the ear bud on an injury such as a bruise or cut to determine the impact of the frequency.

The frequencies coming from an ear bud are digital, which have a different impact on the body than analog waves produced from a live instrument or a tuning fork. Generally analog frequencies have more healing benefits, but digital is especially good at killing pathogens or certain other unwanted frequencies. Digital frequencies do not create a precise representation of the note's harmonics, but can transfer large amounts of information at one time.

Solfeggio Frequencies and Water

Jacques Benveniste[76] published a paper supporting the principles of homeopathy and the ability of water to copy information. An original substance was poured into water, but diluted so much that virtually no molecules of the original substance remained. Benveniste discovered that the diluted water showed qualities of the original solution. Benveniste even asserted that this "memory" could be digitized, transmitted and reinserted into another sample of water, which would then contain the same active qualities as the first sample. A journalist coined the term "water memory" to describe this attribute of water.

Our bodies are about 75 percent water and our brains contain up to 85 percent water. What does listening to the solfeggio frequencies do to the water in our bodies?

The ancient Egyptians wrote healing symbols on papyri and submersed it into water, creating "healing potions." Seems silly at first glance, but modern day Masuro Emoto published numerous books with photographs of freezing water crystals exposed to sound and written words. Words of love and positive sentiments produced frozen crystals that were symmetrical and resembled beautiful snowflakes. Words of hatred produced the opposite - distorted and lopsided crystalline structures. Did the ancient Egyptians create healing water by exposing drinking water to shapes and symbols?

Dr. Emoto exposed water to the solfeggio tones and the following beautiful crystalline structures were formed.

---

[76]Jacques Benveniste (1935–2004) was a French immunologist.

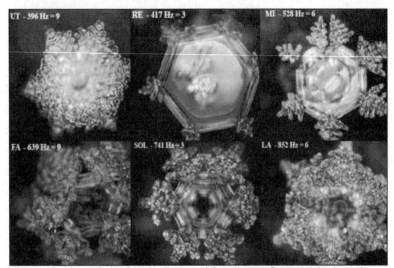

Photos used with permission from Jay Emmanuel: http://powerofharmony.tripod.com Jay Emmanuel produced a CD using these tones called, "The Healing Forces of Harmonic Sounds and Vibration."

Drumming has also been known to give "structure" to water and blood, creating appropriate shapes within water molecules. Dr. Pollack reported that if you don't have properly structured water in your cells, it can negatively impact the functioning of many larger protein molecules (and others) that are interfacing with it.[77]

A logical application, using water and the solfeggio tones, mimics the ancient Egyptian method of transferring the energy of symbols and words to drinking water. Write the numbers of the solfeggio tones and fasten them to the bottom of a drinking glass or a pitcher of water. Fill the container with pure water and sit it in a peaceful location. Drink the water thoughtfully and enjoy the experience as you are fully in the moment. I exposed drinking water to the solfeggio sounds. I tasted water exposed to the solfeggio frequencies and a test sample of water without this sound exposure. I found the solfeggio water to be sweeter tasting.

---

[77] http://articles.mercola.com/sites/articles/archive/2011/01/29/dr-pollack-on-structured-water.aspx

Wouldn't it be fun to swim in a pool with cymatic images of the solfeggio tones on pool tiles or panels sporting the written solfeggio frequencies? How about a hot tub that "listened" to the solfeggio frequencies? Could we buy ice cube trays with the numbers of the solfeggio frequencies embossed on it?

The pictures of the solfeggio shapes can be inserted in air tight baggies and placed in your bath water. Play the solfeggio tones when you shower or bathe. We absorb many frequencies through our skin. Humans have about four million skin pores. A region the size of a quarter has about 600 pores. Dr. Alfred Tomatis referred to the skin as a different type of ear. The skin has hundreds of thousands of receptors for temperature and tactile vibrations. Submerge your skin and relax in a solfeggio-treated-bath.[78]

An interesting experiment would be to expose plants to the solfeggio tones. Remember from earlier that Physicist Joel Sternheimer measured the frequencies of amino acids, the protein builders, in plants. When the frequencies were sequenced in the same order as the amino acids and played back to the plant, he reported up to 250 percent plant growth and resilience to disease. Frequencies interact with our wonderful friends in the plant kingdom. Wouldn't it be interesting to taste the difference between a regular carrot and solfeggio carrot?

Play creatively with the solfeggio tones and enjoy their magic!

---

[78] Water is an excellent conductor. Keep ear buds and sound devises powered by electric away from water.

Chapter Eleven

The Stars are Singing to You.

I recently learned that the lovely Ani Williams played her harp in Egyptian temples to great effect. She learned secret ways that music was used in ancient Egyptian temples. I had the chance to meet Ani and immediately asked how she gained that opportunity!

Ani took a big breath, "I had been hired as one of three musicians to accompany a group pilgrimage into the Egyptian temples during the Harmonic Convergence. The Harmonic Convergence refers to the system of keeping time used by the ancient Mayans. They measured time in terms of the earth's cycles around the galaxy, an orbit of roughly 26,000 years.

"According to the Mayan and other ancient systems of time, the earth entered a new orbit around the galaxy in the year 2012. Ancient knowledge tells us that each age brings new lessons for mankind to evolve our consciousness. (An age is a period of 2,160 years, the time it takes the earth to observe a new constellation on the Vernal Equinox.[79] For example, we

---

[79] Astrological age exists due to precession of the equinoxes. Basically the stars and constellations appear to slowly rotate around the Earth independent of the movements of the Earth on its own axis and around the Sun. This slow movement takes slightly less than 26,000 years to complete one cycle. Traditionally this rotation is calibrated for the purposes of the astrological ages by the location of the zodiacal constellations at the Vernal Equinox around the 21st of March each year. Approximately every 2,160 years a new zodiacal constellation appears at the Vernal Equinox. However zodiacal constellations are not uniform in size and so some astrologers believe that the corresponding ages should also vary in time - this however is a contentious issue amongst astrologers.

are now entering the Age of Aquarius.[80]) And! In the year 2012 we entered a new 26,000 - year era of growth for the consciousness of mankind.[81] The year 1987 marked the astrological countdown to this important time and was called the Harmonic Convergence."

Ani continued, "That journey to Egypt on the Harmonic Convergence changed me forever. When I played my music, the temple stones chanted back."

There was so much information in Ani's words. I felt I was reeling in an Egyptian pyramid!

"Whoa," I begged Ani. "You were changed forever by the music in the Egyptian temples?"

"Yes, the Egyptian knowledge of music and its effects is powerful stuff," Ani assured me.

Eager to get Ani talking about the secrets of music in the Egyptian temples, I pushed on. "How did the temples chant to you?"

Ani continued. "In the temple of Abyddos, the stones answered our music. The temple stones and space responded to the resonance of the music and the harmonics sang back to us. The length, width and height of the smooth stones, produced the dominant resonance of the temple. The temple's stones sang together with us! Not only did the stones affect our music, but they affected the singers as well. After we listened to the harmonics, we all felt uplifted.

"I later returned to the temples to study how they interacted with sound. I traveled with a colleague who was a mathematician and explored acoustic design. He created mathematical calculations of the building dimensions and applied laws of harmony to find the proposed dominant tones (tones that are the loudest) in each temple. I experimented with sound by using the audible responses and my intuition. We worked independently and both came up with the similar

---

[80] Ani tells me that the Age of Aquarius relates to the pitch, A#, corresponding to our nervous and electrical fields.

[81] "Every epoch, especially a grand one such as this, requires rethinking our reality. Sound, as a creative force, comes forward as a primary tool for change and healing." Ani Williams.

conclusions of the hidden, musical gifts available in Egyptian temples.

"For example, we discovered musical scales formed by the layout of the temples."

"What do you mean by musical scales?" I replied. "Each temple formed a different musical scale?"

Ani responded, "In each temple I could hear the timber or the quality of sound changing with different notes that I played on my harp. I was able to tell which notes were richer, louder and enhanced in each temple chamber. The group of richer, harmonic notes, I am calling the 'musical scale of the temple.'"

"That is what the Hindi call a mode," I replied. "You describe a group of notes that create a feeling and energy for a specific purpose."

"Yes," Ani replied. "When I play the temple's 'musical scale,' it transports listeners to a specific state of consciousness."

"Why is that?" I queried.

"The best way to explain this is to relate an experience I had with Michael Helios, in a workshop about the music of the five platonic solids.[82] With his knowledge of mathematics, ancient history, astrology and astronomy, Michael calculated the pitches of the five platonic solids. As he played these pitches to our group, each one of us clearly 'saw' the shape he played. So, music had transmitted a mental, visual image. Music can also transmit emotions, states of consciousness that correlates to shapes!"

"Wow!" I murmured. "Can you tell me about different transmissions that the various temples produced?"

"As I walked from end to end of the Abyddos temple, while playing a small harp, the lower tones sounded stronger. As I walked towards the other side of the temple the dominant

---

[82] In geometry, a Platonic solid is a convex regular polyhedron. These are the three-dimensional analogs of convex regular polygons. There are precisely five such figures, Tetrahedron, Hexahedron, Octahedron, Dodecahedron, Icosahedron, or Cube. They are unique in that the faces, edges and angles are all congruent. Wikipedia

harmonics became more refined and got higher in pitch. I could feel the energy stirring in the major chakras of my body, starting with the root chakra and working up my body's energy centers. As I continued to play my small harp I walked towards the part of the temple that stimulates the Crown chakra, the harmonics got so refined and high pitched that I had to stop playing. I was overwhelmed by the state of consciousness I had entered.

"Dr. Jim Hurtak,[83] author and scholar of ancient texts, calls the Egyptian pyramids 'voice activated, geophysical computers.'" Ani continued.

Ani went on to tell me that the position of the stars influenced the location of the temples. For example,

- "The three Egyptian pyramids of the Giza Plateau mirror the three stars in the belt of the Orion.
- "Temple builders recorded where the star light fell on the ground throughout the year. Starlight was important to the Egyptians. Temples were built so that at certain times of the year (such as the first day of summer, fall, winter and spring) the starlight would fall at important spots in the temple.
- "The Great Pyramid is aligned to true North-South (as opposed to magnetic north – south).
- "The shafts inside the queen's and king's chambers faced important stars, such as Sirius, Orion or the Pole star.
- "The Sphinx faces east, gazing at the point where the constellation Leo arose."

---

[83] Dr. James Hurtak is a scholar, author, and founder of the Academy for Future Science. He authored The Book of Knowledge: The Keys of Enoch® and has written over 15 books, including commentaries on ancient mystical and Gnostic texts including the Pistis Sophia. Former professor at California State University and California State University, with two Ph.D.'s. Hurtak has spoken throughout the world. He has been featured in numerous film documentaries, and has appeared on television programs throughout the world. In the early 1970s he published the relationship of the star shafts in the Great Pyramid with the "Belt" of Orion. Dr. Hurtak is Research Director at the Great Pyramid of Giza Research Association. He is also co-author of the book entitled The End of Suffering, which he wrote with physicist Russell Targ. Wikipedia

Ani concluded, "The temples mirror the movements of the stars and the planets. Astronomical considerations were important in the design of the temples worldwide."

"Ani," I whispered, "Does the architecture of the building create energy?"

Ani replied, "According to Gyorgy Doczi,[84] many temple proportions express the Golden Mean (.618) harmonic ratio, which is also the musical interval of a sixth. Goethe, the German mystic and poet, called sacred architecture 'frozen music' and structures based on musical proportions have a powerful harmonizing effect on the human energy system.

"The most common proportions found in the ancient Egyptian temples correspond to harmonious musical intervals, such as octaves, fifths, fourths, thirds and sixths. For example, in the temple of Horus, the ratio of one chamber's width to height is 2:3, which is the ratio in a musical fifth. And the ratio of another chamber's height to width is 3:4, which is the ratio of a musical fourth.[85]

"In the temple of Denderah, the temple dedicated to the Goddess Hathor (Goddess of Music and Fertility), there are drawings of many musicians. Hieroglyphics on the wall translated 'The sky and its stars are singing in you.'

"Ancient scientists from the Sumerians, Babylonians, Egyptians, Greeks and as late as the 16th century scientist Kepler have studied how music may be applied to the cosmos."

Music of the Stars in our Daily Lives

"Ani, do you use the secrets of music of the ancient Egyptians and the stars in your daily life?" I asked.

---

[84] Gyorgy Doczi is an author and architect, who studied nature's harmonic shapes. He rediscovered the designs revealed by slicing through a head of cabbage or an orange, the forms of shells and butterfly wings. These images suggest an order underlying their growth, a harmony existing in nature. The book, Power of Limits, was inspired by this harmony. Gyorgy noticed certain proportions occur over and over again in nature. Patterns are also repeated in how things grow and are made - by the dynamic union of opposites - as demonstrated by the spirals, which move in opposite directions in the growth of a plant. Wikipedia

[85] Antoine Seronde. Rediscovering Music in Architecture of the Ancient Egyptian Temples, Quoted from www.aniwilliams.com

Ani replied, "Yes, the information I learned from the pyramids helped me come up with a system I call 'Songaia Sound Medicine.' I combine an analysis of the harmonics and tones in your voice with the ancient art of medical astrology."

"Whoa! I am lost again! What's medical astrology?"

Ani laughed. "Medical astrology charts the positions of the stars at one's birth, noting where the planets' energies interacted because of their position in the sky. The unique planetary pattern also creates a sound pattern of influence that is distinct for each individual. The heavenly patterns can influence a person's talents, abilities or health. These patterns can also provide a challenge for one's personal growth, or cause tendencies towards certain mental, nervous or physical illnesses. One's genetics and stress levels affect whether or not these tendencies develop.

"I calculate, based on one's birth time, what combinations of planets were present and the energetic influence of the stars that were "blueprinted" into someone's energy field at the moment of birth.

"I also analyze one's voice. A voice analysis tells me what harmonics are strong, weak or missing in your voice. I use a computer software program to analyze the voice, or alternatively a digital tuner and a microphone. I have done thousands of these readings.

"The voice analysis records physical, emotional and spiritual tendencies. This closely matches information that I gather when I use medical astrology to note a person's tendencies. Harmonic tones in your voice correspond to one's astrology sign. The song of the stars at the time of your birth is the blueprint of your speaking voice, revealing influences and tendencies affecting you.

"Both systems tell me the same things. I learn where one's physical, mental or emotional health is vulnerable and where there is potential for healing and growth. I use both systems to cross-check my work."

"Ani," I asked, "This is interesting, but why is the information about tones in our voice and the positions of stars at our birth important?"

She replied, "The energy of the stars provides an energetic map for our health, opportunities and challenges. This information pinpoints health issues. For example, my brother recently had a $7,000 medical evaluation completed. Shortly thereafter, I provided him with information based on medical astrology and his voice tones. He laughed! I gave him the same information as the medical evaluation, with less trouble and cost. I am not suggesting that you should not follow medical options, but why not incorporate some of the many alternative health modalities that are available?

"With this information, I am able to recommend helpful exercises and diet to support certain organs along with the sound therapy.

"I also recommend specific tones to create tonal integrity! By singing your missing tones or just listening to them, a state of harmonic balance is achieved, bringing you greater health and consciousness.

"When people sing their missing frequencies, they connect with their true feelings and with their soul's purpose. People can give a voice to emotional or physical pain, which is incredibly liberating. We may have to go to a private spot to voice painful feelings, but part of eliminating the invisible burdens of pain is to acknowledge it. After we get this out of our system, we can then use our voice to expand our consciousness."

"Does the absence of a specific note, such as 'D' in a voice's harmonics mean something different than the absence of another harmonic, let's say, 'C?'" I asked.

Ani replied, "There is significance to each frequency that is present in and absent from your voice. For example, the 'D#' missing in your voice, may show a tendency towards weight, respiratory and digestion problems.

"In another example, the 'C' and the 'C#' relate to the base chakra and issues of power, control and sexuality. It's interesting that for hundreds of years, the 'C' string on harps was always colored red. The color of red is associated with power, control, being grounded, survival and sexuality.

"If you are missing the tone of 'C' you have the potential to be ungrounded, and have issues with the circulation of blood, the heart of systemic conditions like Candida, fibro-myalgia or viruses.

"By bringing in the 'C' harmonic into your speaking voice, you feel more powerful, grounded and in control of your life. Sound vibration affects the energy level at first and later influences your physical body as well, with the reduction of pain and stress. Heart, pulse and oxygenation rates can change instantly. Headaches or pain in any area of the body may go away. Emotions can be cleared and stress dissolves.

"To get best results, one needs to use these tones every day. With extensive use, some people have reduced tumors and pushed cancer into remission," Ani finished.

"How did you discover the helpful correlation with each note?" I inquired.

"I worked with a group of teachers. We compared and documented our collective experiences with these frequencies, and many case studies. We then reached these conclusions.

Our Hidden Creative Abilities

"Did I hear you say that one can discover his creative potential from star and musical information?" I queried.

Ani replied, "As children, most of us were told that we couldn't sing, or do this or that. We were also taught not to voice our true emotions. We got to music class and were told that we sing out of tune. And we believed that these judgements about us were true.

"We are greater than we believe. We have greater energy, wisdom and creativity available to us. For example, we only use about ten percent of our brain. We only use about half of the potential harmonics in our voice.

"If tones are missing in our voice, we can add back these same tones to increase our health and creative potential.

Astrology and voice analysis enables us to hone in on the exact missing frequencies in our potential harmony."

"Is the idea to have all harmonics sounding in your voice, in order to be complete?" I asked.

Ani answered, "Yes. That's it. One wants tonal integrity and a harmonic balance. We grow stronger through our imperfections and yet by finding the missing tones in our harmonics we can speed up the healing process. Singing these tones facilitates our growth in life on many levels.

"One's voice energy and harmonic frequencies suggest areas in which one has potential. As one talks about different subjects, the harmonics in his voice change, indicating potentials.

> "The voice is a barometer of the soul. By listening to someone's voice you can tell the state of physical, spiritual and mental being."
> Hazrat Inyat Khan

"For example, a 'D' harmonic comes up when a woman talks about travel or writing. She mentions that she always wanted to do these things, but hasn't. When she tones the 'D' and listens to this tone, she is energized to travel and write," Ani continued.

"Dr. Alfred Tomatis, the French ear nose throat specialist, found that when missing frequencies in a person's hearing were played back to him, there were astonishing improvements in many disabilities.[86] We conducted tests with the Tomatis Center in Mexico City and found that frequencies missing a person's voice and hearing- were similar. These same missing frequencies played back to the person can help overcome many conditions.

"When people do not express themselves through their voices, they lose the connection between their spiritual and physical selves. Their voices become thinner, lacking depth and resonance.

---

[86] www.tomatis.com

"People must sing again! Singing brings harmonic resonance into their voices, which affects their mental, emotional and physical bodies. Integrating all tones is inspiring and healing. It creates movement, literally, and helps us attain our life's purpose."

> Listening to sacred sound is the quickest path to conscious awaking.
> *Hindu Manhabharata*

"In 5000 BC, the Chinese used music to control aspects of their society. Later, the druids had 'perpetual choirs' in which they fed harmony into their realm to maintain natural order. Today, some Tibetans use perpetual chanting of mantras to channel peace and other desired states of being into our world.

"Can you imagine a world in which people sing more? We can bring harmony into our personal lives and to the rest of the world as well!" Ani beamed!

For more information, go to www.aniwilliams.com. Ani offers voice analysis, CDs of the sacred music from ancient cultures, healing music and pilgrimages to sacred sites!

www.JillsWingsOfLight.com – Art Gallery

Chapter Twelve

A Star Is Born

A lone Osborn Raticus sits by himself, nestled next to an old tennis shoe. His body appears to have magnets in it, pulling him down towards the floor. He's more than physically tired; he's confused about everything, even what he wants in life and what is right and wrong. His thinking is dizzy. What's up and what's down? Even that's confusing.

It was the light beaming off his dazzling ring that first caught my eye.

"Osborn, is that you?" I spoke softly, sensing his confusion that bordered on depression.

A soft "mmmmm..." was his only reply. It was as if he heard me and could only respond in slow motion.

"Is that snazzy girl of yours gone?" I queried.

"Mmmmm... She wanted a flashy life with star-studded parties and buckets of money to throw around," Osborn whispered.

"But Osborn, didn't you give that to her?"

"Mmmmmm, but I am not sure that is what I wanted."

"Mmmmmm," I replied.

Osborn's deep dark eyes looked up. I could see his confusion and insecurity about not knowing what to do or who he wanted to be.

"There's more to life than money and popularity, and even health isn't that valuable if you don't know what to live for... mmmmm," sighed Osborn.

"Osborn, your confusion isn't a bad thing," I added. "It's just a stage in which your old world crumbles because you are forming more beautiful and intricate patterns of thinking. Remember the Cymatics pictures that Jeff Volk shared with us? The rising pitches of sound caused ever-changing patterns in the sand."

Osborn cocked his head. That thought perked him up.

"So I am not a disappointment? I am just evolving!" questioned Osborn. "Mmmmm…"

Osborn began breathing deeper and I think his fur looked fluffier.

"Mmmm, tell me more about the Fibonacci numbers and how they help us evolve," Osborn asked meekly as the pitch of his voice rose a bit.

Before I could answer, Osborn continued, speaking faster, "I overheard people talking about your CD, 'Paint Your Soul.'" His spine straightened a little. "Let me tell you what I heard."

"While listening to the 'Paint Your Soul' CD, I was taken by the haunting beauty of the vocals and the cascading effect of the music. It seemed to create rhythmic surges of consciousness as if my attention was being swept in and out, like the waves of the ocean that were also part of the music." *Jeff C.*

"Your music is as close to the sounds I experienced in a near death experience, near heaven, than anything I've ever heard." *Judy Fitzgerald.*

"While listening to 'Paint your Soul,' I felt a sensation of extreme well-being that manifested emotionally as a quiet effortless peace that had displaced old fears and seemed to seep into my whole being, and mentally I had a picture of Mother Earth coddling me in her arms as if I were a small child being rocked to sleep. It was an extraordinary experience." *Keith Henry*

"When listening to 'Paint your Soul' CD, I felt like I was rising out of body. I felt like I was doing a Sema ritual and actually rose closer to heaven. I felt pressure on the top of my head as if I was trying to burst out of myself." *Rebecca Gonzales*

"The tones of the Fibonacci numbers, converted to music, in the 'Paint Your Soul' CD are enticing." I suggested to Osborn.

I began my story about the Fibonacci numbers, relieved to see my old friend's spirits rising.

"Leonardo De Pisa (who lived approximately 1180 – 1240 AD), better known as Fibonacci, observed that branching, flowering and spiraling patterns in nature were organized according to principles found in musical harmony. The numerical pattern he observed was the Fibonacci series of numbers: 0, 1, 1, 2, 3, 5, 8, 13, 21, 34, 55… unto infinity. (Adding any two adjacent numbers will give you the next number in the series.)

"The ratio of neighboring Fibonacci numbers approaches phi (1.618).[87] These ratios are found in our bodies,

---

[87] Phi is the symbol for the golden ratio. "The golden ratio has fascinated intellectuals for at least 2,400 years. Some of the greatest mathematical minds of all ages, from Pythagoras and Euclid in ancient Greece, through the medieval Italian mathematician Leonardo of Pisa and the Renaissance astronomer Johannes Kepler, to present-day scientific figures such as Oxford physicist Roger Penrose, have spent endless hours over this simple ratio and its properties. The fascination with the Golden Ratio is not confined just to mathematicians, biologists, artists, musicians, historians, architects, psychologists, and mystics have pondered and debated the basis of its ubiquity and appeal. The Golden Ratio has inspired thinkers of all disciplines like no other number in the history of mathematics.—*Mario Livio,*
  The Golden Ratio: The Story of Phi, The World's Most Astonishing Number
- Luca Pacioli (1445–1517) defines the golden ratio as the "divine proportion" in his *Divina Proportione*.
- Johannes Kepler (1571–1630) describes the golden ratio as a "precious jewel." "Geometry has two great treasures: one is the Theorem of Pythagoras, and the other the division of a line into extreme and mean ratio; the first we may compare to a measure of gold, the second we may name a precious jewel." These two treasures are combined in the Kepler triangle.
- Charles Bonnet (1720–1793) points out that in the spiral phyllotaxis of plants going clockwise and counter-clockwise were frequently two successive Fibonacci series. (Continued in the next page's footnotes)
- Martin Ohm (1792–1872) is believed to be the first to use the term *goldener Schnitt* (golden section) to describe this ratio, in 1835.
- Edouard Lucas (1842–1891) gives the numerical sequence now known as the Fibonacci sequence its present name.
- Mark Barr (20th century) suggests the Greek letter phi (φ), the initial letter of Greek sculptor Phidias's name, as a symbol for the golden ratio.

the spiral of a seashell and in billions of stars in distant galaxies.

"Major chords approximate the Fibonacci numbers 1, 3, 5 and 8. The next number in the Fibonacci series is 13. When the 8th and 13th tones are played together, they create the 8/13th interval. The 8/13th interval is believed by some to harmonize and thereby raise our consciousness as if we were continuing up the Fibonacci spiral, and precipitate mankind's next evolutionary step.[88]

"Mmmmm..." murmured Osborn. "Oh, I over heard other people, who had impressive results from listening to your 'Paint Your Soul' CD." Here is what they said:

"After listening to 'Paint your Soul,' I found myself rising so high, making my heart happy. I immediately felt the energies dancing in both crown and third eye areas," *Margarete P.*

"Every time I listen to the melodies I go into a deep trance and pop out of it when the music is over. I am always looking for new ways to meditate and listening to this is a most efficient way of achieving a higher energy." *by Rick H.*

"With your music I feel divine mother energy surround me in a large dose of unconditional love." *by Sarah L.*

"While listening to your music I felt a deep healing, profound peace and lightness. The music resonated right into my being, healing my spirit and soul." *by Ane L.*

"Jill's music is peaceful and heavenly. You feel a healing, wanting to cry and releasing pain. If stress sums up ill

---

- Roger Penrose (b.1931) discovered a symmetrical pattern that uses the golden ratio in the field of aperiodic tilings, which led to new discoveries about quasicrystals." Wikipedia

[88] Consciousness defies simple definition. It has been defined loosely as a constellation of attributes of mind such as subjectivity, self-awareness, sentience and the ability to perceive a relationship between oneself and one's environment. It has been defined from a more biological and causal perspective as the act of autonomously modulating attentional and computational effort, usually with the goal of obtaining, retaining, or maximizing specific parameters (food, a safe environment, family, mates). Consciousness may involve thoughts, sensations, perceptions, moods, emotions, dreams, and an awareness of self. Wikipedia

health, get rid of this baggage daily Try listening to this divine music." *Raelon, owner Rumor Mill News*

"The 'Paint your Soul CD is just the vehicle to carry us higher and higher. Resonating with the chakras, the body's energy centers, this music frees us from worldly concerns and takes the spirit to the next step up!!" *Susan G.*

"My son gave me a bouquet of flowers for Mother's day, but several tulips were drooping. After playing the 'Paint your Soul' CD, the tulips stood upright and they still are." *Karen R.*

After thanking Osborn, I continued on with my story. "The Fibonacci ratios, if drawn, reveal a spiral, similar to the one found in a nautilus shell. In contrast, Western music creates a circle when drawn (The original pitches have been modified in the just-intonation scale that we use today). Many ancient traditions believed that listening to the 'spiral' pattern in sound enabled one to 'quicken' his soul and rise closer to God.

"You don't hear the exact Fibonacci frequencies in our music today, because they are frequencies in-between the musical notes in our musical scale. "The 'Paint Your Soul' CD uses the pure tones of this spiral pattern from Fibonacci tuning forks."

"The 'Paint Your Soul' CD also has twelve additional Solfeggio tones, not including the six tones that David Hulse discussed in chapter ten," I revealed.

I felt that I had lifted Osborn's spirits with these thoughts, but his depression was not completely gone. He looked away, into the corner, nervously twisting the old dirty shoelace of the faded tennis shoe.

"But I was going to be a star." The pitch in Osborn's voice dropped so low that it became an eternal whisper.

"Osborn, you are a star." My voice was firm.

"Mmmmm?" queried Osborn.

"Osborn, what are stars made of?"

No answer, not even a "…Mmmmm."

"The universe shares common elements. Some elements in the stars are carbon, hydrogen, oxygen, and nitrogen," I stated, proud of my knowledge.

"Osborn, what are you made of?"

No answer.

"You have material in your body that was forged from in a star, such elements including carbon, hydrogen, oxygen, and nitrogen,"[89] I replied. (We have different proportions of these elements than the stars do.)

"Many compounds in our bodies can only be made out of trace elements that come from stars.

"Sounds associated with carbon, hydrogen, nitrogen and oxygen twinkle in the background of the 'Star Dust' CD."

Osborn nodded silently and then reminded me of comments he overheard about the music on the "Star Dust" CD.

"When I listened to 'Star Dust' while I wrote it, tears where streaming my face. Thank you for such beautiful, moving music. Your music just flows through you, perhaps more through you than of you. It reminds me of what Jesus said, "It is

---

[89] **Carbon (C)** The element carbon is perhaps the single most important element to life. Virtually every part of our bodies is made with large amounts of this element. The carbon atom is ideal to build big biological molecules. Virtually every part of your body is made up of these big molecules that are based around chains of carbon atoms. Hence, we are known as "carbon based life forms." Without carbon, our bodies would just be a big pile of loose atoms with no way to be built into a person.

Hydrogen (H) It would be virtually impossible to overstate the importance of this element to human life. First of all, water is a compound of hydrogen and oxygen. We can survive years, or at least months without getting most of the other elements that we need to survive. We can survive weeks without food, but we would die after only a few days without water. Almost 50 % of our bodies are made of water. It dissolves other life-supporting substances and transports them to fluids in and around our cells.

Nitrogen (N) Nitrogen plays an important role in digestion of food and growth. Almost 80% of the air we breathe is made up of nitrogen. But it is in the wrong form for humans to breathe. We get nitrogen, in a different form, from the food that we eat. Fortunately, there is plenty of nitrogen in food to nourish our bodies. While our body is busy digesting the rest of this food and making it into energy, these nitrogen atoms are already being used to help us grow.

Oxygen (O) It may seem obvious that people need to breathe oxygen to survive, but plants need this element, too. Many people think plants "breathe" carbon dioxide and "exhale" oxygen. But in reality, plants also "breathe" oxygen at certain times. Without oxygen, plants could not survive. Without plants, we wouldn't have food to eat. It is also worth mentioning that water is a compound of hydrogen and oxygen and that water is absolutely necessary for virtually all life as we know it. http://www.mii.org/periodic/LifeElement.html#n

not I, but the Father who acts through me." *Mike Conner*

"While walking in nature I played the 'Star Dust' CD and birds started chirping a lot more, even the winds picked up! The trees and cicadas came out to play - the cicadas hovered around my head. Nature absolutely reacts to the frequencies in this music! We have the power to infuse all around us when we are resonating with these frequencies." *David Fine*

"When I listen to the 'Star Dust' CD my air purifier goes crazy and the air smells really fresh. How did the music improve the air?" *by Scott K.*

I thanked Osborn and continued.

"All matter consists of vibrating particles. On the smallest scale the matter making up our bodies is comprised of quanta packets possessing particle and wave properties. These fundamental particles make their own music. The elements in our bodies sing the same frequencies - as their counterparts in the stars.

"A French physicist, Joel Sternheimer, investigated sound frequencies of elemental molecules. Joel has a formula to convert atomic mass for any element on our Periodic Table to frequency.[90] Everything has a frequency... a song, if you will. The stars sing a song and so do we!"

> "Whosoever shall make a copy (of the cosmos) and shall know it upon earth, it shall act as a protector for him, both in heaven and upon earth."
> Heaven's Mirror by Graham Hancock.

"As we already learned, Pythagoras believed that musical scales were based on planetary tones. He also believed that the same mathematical proportions used to create musical intervals also predicted the movement of the planets in our solar system.

In the 1600s scientist Johannes Kepler sought evidence for a harmony in the universe as described by Pythagoras and

---

[90] Maman, Fabien. The Role of Music in the Twenty-First Century, Tama-Do Press: Boulder, CO, 1997. Pg. 15, footnote.

others from antiquity. In antiquity, musical intervals were inseparably linked to simple, whole numeric ratios.[91]

In his book, *Hermonices Mundi, the Five Books on Musical Harmony*, Kepler compares the values of the angles of the planets (as measured from the sun) formed by their extreme positions in elliptical orbits during a twenty four-hour period. A system of simple intervals emerges, sixteen in all, *(two exceptions)* that are musical consonances or intervals with whole number ratios.[92] He offers this as proof of harmonic laws in the cosmos."

I stopped talking about Kepler and addressed Osborn's desire to be a "star."

"People's bodies produce musical tones that our ears cannot hear. Our bodies hum together with the planets and the stars! Our tones are either harmonious with the heavenly spheres or not!"

The silence between us began to resonate.

"Can I sing the song of the stars?" Osborn replied.

"You certainly can," I answered, and began to explain about the songs laced with the star tones found in the CD 'Star Dust.'

"Star Dust" CD

---

[91] Godwin, Joscelyn. Cosmic Music: Musical Keys to the Interpretation of the Universe, Rochester, VT: Inner Traditions, 1989, Pgs. 111 and 112.
[92] Godwin, Joscelyn. Cosmic Music: Musical Keys to the Interpretation of the Universe, Rochester, VT: Inner Traditions, 1989, Pg. 117.

Sounds of Planets, Sun and Galaxy

In antiquity the ancient Chinese "musically played the stars. The tone system of ancient China, the 'Lu' scale, consisted of twelve notes obtained by successive musical fifths[93] (five notes apart). Each of the twelve Lu was assigned a month or constellation of the zodiac... During a given month, it was only permitted to play music based on ... a scale stemming from the corresponding Lu."[94] In the ancient cultures the musical system and the calendar were often intimately connected.

I discovered more information on cosmic tones from my studies of Hans Cousto. We share a belief that there is a deep spiritual harmony in the design and flow of the universe. Music literally is an expression of this harmony. Hans Cousto's life work has been to apply his scientific training in unlocking the deeper link between the stars, and musical octaves and pitches.

In his book *The Cosmic Octave*, Cousto shares his revelations, "It was the result of a way of seeing things which moved me to combine the old teachings of harmonics with new findings in physics and other sciences. The result is an all-encompassing system of measurements with which it is possible to transpose the movements of the planets into audible rhythms, sounds and colors. This basic system of measurement clearly demonstrates the harmonic relationship that exists between different kinds of natural phenomena in the fields of astronomy, meteorology and microbiology."[95]

Cousto explains his system of measurement, which, "like the harmony of music, is inherent in the general structure of all beings."[96]

---

[93] "Naturally for the sake of practical music making they are transposed into a narrower compass." Godwin, Joscelyn edits Hans Lauer. Cosmic Music, Inner Traditions: VT. 1989. Pg. 185.
[94] Godwin, Joscelyn edits Hans Lauer. Cosmic Music, Inner Traditions: VT. 1989. Pg. 185.
[95] Cousto, Hans. The Cosmic Octave, Origin of Harmony, LifeRhythm: Mendocino CA, 2000. Pg. 10.
[96] Cousto, Hans. The Cosmic Octave, Origin of Harmony, LifeRhythm: Mendocino CA, 2000. Pg. 10.

Cousto links the orbital and rotational motions of the stars and planets to specific frequencies for each celestial body. He then translates the celestial frequencies into audible pitches through the principal of octaves. In this way, Cousto lets us listen to the harmonic rhythms of the cosmos.

The time it takes for a planet to complete an orbit is equal to 1/ the frequency of the planet in motion.[97] With this formula Cousto calculated the frequencies of our moon, sun, earth and the other planets in our solar system.

> Hans Cousto explained that the orbit time and the frequency the planet makes in its orbit are inverse proportions.
> Time of rotation = 1/frequency.
> Frequency =1/time of rotation.
> For example, the earth takes 365.24 days to orbit around the sun. Therefore, the corresponding frequency the earth makes in its rotation is 1/365.24. By doubling this frequency (increasing the pitch by octaves), we hear this pitch, which is a "G."
> Cousto, Hans. The Cosmic Octave, the Origin of Harmony

The Harmony of Colors

Sounds and colors are wavelengths that we *perceive* as sound or color. Our ears and eyes distinguish between different wavelengths or frequencies, transforming waves into signals that are sent to our brains. We then see colors or hear sounds.

From science, we know that there are differences between waves of light and sound. For example, sound needs something like air or water to carry waves on and light waves do not. Light has properties like sound waves as well as particle-like properties. Sound does not act like particles do. Despite the differences, sound healing scientists insist that the laws of musical harmony also apply to wavelengths of light.

> The colors we see (red, orange, yellow, green, blue, indigo and violet) correspond to notes in the musical scale.

---

[97] Cousto, Hans. The Cosmic Octave, the Origin of Harmony, LifeRhythm: Mendocino, CA, 2000. Pg.18.

Just as we have learned that music can heal, so can colors. Professor Max Luscher[98] proved that the growth of testicles in drakes could be impacted by the use of color. He used two groups of drakes under identical conditions, except one group of drakes lived under orange-red lights and the other group lived under pale-blue-lights. The testicles of the drakes that lived under the orange-red colored lights grew to be twice as large as the drakes that lived under the blue lights. Clearly color impacts us, just as sound does.

According to Hans Cousto, the phenomenon that determines color and the timber of a tone is mathematically described by the formula for harmonics (that we discussed with Harold Moses).[99]

> The ancient monks of India and Tibet wore orange-red robes. I wonder if they desired to absorb the vitalizing effect of this color.

The Harmony of the Earth

Hans Cousto calculated the frequency of the earth's rotation as the tone "G." Cousto called this the "earth day" tone.[100]

Two different scientists discovered with different methods, that DNA and RNA have resonance maximums[101] the same as an octave of the earth's rotation.[102]

If you raise the frequency of an earth-day 65 octaves, the math equals the frequency of the color orange-red. The maximum resonance of DNA is the 66th octave of the earth-

---

[98] Luscher, Max. Der Klinishe Luscher test.

[99] Cousto, Hans. The Cosmic Octave, the Origin of Harmony, LifeRhythm: Mendocino, CA, 2000. Pg. 18.

[100] Cousto, Hans. The Cosmic Octave, the Origin of Harmony, LifeRhythm: Mendocino, CA, 2000. Pg. 38.

[101] In physics, resonance is the tendency of a system to oscillate at maximum amplitude at certain frequencies, known as the system's *resonant frequencies*. At these frequencies, even small periodic driving forces can produce large amplitude vibrations, because the system stores vibrational energy. Resonant phenomena occur with all type of vibrations or waves: there is mechanical resonance, acoustic resonance, electromagnetic resonance, and resonance of quantum wave functions. Wikipedia.

[102] Cousto, Hans. The Cosmic Octave, the Origin of Harmony, LifeRhythm: Mendocino, CA, 2000. Pg. 35.

day tone, *linking the resonance of DNA and the color orange-red.*[103]

Also, listening to the earth-day tone and its associated octaves gives you energy, according to Cousto.[104] (I wondered if Osborn would benefit from an orange-red robe, like the monks in India and Tibet wear.)

Hans Cousto recommended placing an earth-day tuning fork on various meridian points on your body to experience invigorating effects.[105] He also suggested placing an earth-day tone tuning fork on the lower part of your breastbone to reverberate this sound within you.

Cousto tells us when you harmonize with the earth-tone that you simultaneously tune into the energy of beings such as the Indian and Tibetan monks, who are in harmony with the earth.

By tuning into their energy, you resonate with their peaceful presence, and you "become part of the morphogenetic field" of those already in harmony due to their regular meditation.[106]

Cousto reminded us of the phenomenon of the hundredth monkey. When a certain percentage of a monkey population learned a new trick, the entire population of the monkeys - even those on other islands who had never seen the activity - could then easily perform the trick. The British biologist, Rupert Shaldrake, tells us that information belonging to a species is available to other members of that species when a certain percentage of the species learns the information - even if a different member is around the world.

If enough people tuned into the earth-day frequency, what do you suppose would happen?

---

[103] Cousto, Hans. The Cosmic Octave, the Origin of Harmony, LifeRhythm: Mendocino, CA, 2000. Pg. 42.

[104] Cousto, Hans. The Cosmic Octave, the Origin of Harmony, LifeRhythm: Mendocino, CA, 2000. Pg. 35.

[105] To purchase The Cosmic Octave, go to www.LifeRhythms.com or call 707-937-1825.

[106] Cousto, Hans. The Cosmic Octave, the Origin of Harmony, LifeRhythm: Mendocino, CA, 2000. Pg. 62.

> "Happy are those familiar with the tone of our planet, attuning themselves to the basic rhythm and movement of the earth."
> Cousto, Hans.

Tones and the Weather

Cousto reflected on an interesting comparison between electromagnetic impulses from the earth's atmosphere *(called spherics)* and the earth-day tone. The earth's rotation continuously creates spherics. Spherics are octaves of the earth-tone.[107] The spherics have a determining effect on our weather.[108] Spherics can also modify the structure of protein molecules. Does the earth's tone affect weather and proteins?

Cousto reflected, "The Schumann Resonance theory suggests that the entire (human) body vibrates at the fundamental frequency of approximately 8 cycles per second in a relaxed state. As one of the ramifications of the earth's rotation and electromagnetic radiation, the earth also vibrates at this frequency. As a result, a synergistic relationship develops between the charged layers of the earth's atmosphere and the human body.[109]

"Similarly, the energy fields around a tree change in advance of weather patterns and other atmospheric conditions. If weather disturbances affect the earth's atmosphere, perhaps the phenomena also accounts for the behavioral changes seen in some learning disabled children prior to certain types of storms."[110]

The Frequency of the Moon

Cousto calculated the frequency of the moon by using the length of time it takes to pass from one full moon to

---

[107] Cousto, Hans. The Cosmic Octave, the Origin of Harmony, LifeRhythm: Mendocino, CA, 2000, Pg. 13.
[108] Cousto, Hans. The Cosmic Octave, the Origin of Harmony, LifeRhythm: Mendocino, CA, 2000, Pg. 33.
[109] Davis, Dorinne. Sound Bodies through Sound Therapy, Kalco Publishing: Landing, NJ, 2004, Pg. 228.
[110] Davis, Dorinne. Sound Bodies through Sound Therapy, Kalco Publishing: Landing, NJ, 2004, Pg. 228.

another.[111] This frequency is a "G#." The moon affects the tides and our body fluids. Cousto suggested that tuning with the moon, to "G #," can help stabilize fluid imbalances.[112] Cousto cautions us to not use tuning forks to replace traditional medicine.

The Harmony of the Sun

In India, musicians tune to a "C#," the exact frequency of the movement of the earth around the sun! (In the West, musicians tune to an "A.") Indian tuning practices take longer than in Western civilization, because they include harmonizing the audience to the frequency of "C#." This is done by continually playing the "C#" so the audience will entrain with this frequency.

Attuning to a "C#," the sun-tone, has a calming and stimulating effect on one's being.[113] Harmonizing with the sun-tone helps those who are stressed, and need fortifying and calming energy.[114]

Cousto summed up: "Meditation music attuned to sun-tone is beyond all imagination and leads the listener into new dimensions. It is for people whose souls are full of joy and whose spirits are clear - for those who are prepared to leave everything behind them without regret."

Meditation carried out to the sun-tone takes the listener to a state beyond:

- Good and bad
- Shame and guilt
- Space and time
- Knowledge and wisdom
- Action and rest

> Kepler wrote about musical harmony of planetary movement. "Four kinds of voices are expressed in the planets: soprano, alto, tenor and bass."
> Stephen Hawking: On the Shadow of Giants

---

[111] Cousto, Hans. The Cosmic Octave, the Origin of Harmony, LifeRhythm: Mendocino, CA, 2000, Pg. 78.

[112] Cousto, Hans. The Cosmic Octave, the Origin of Harmony, LifeRhythm: Mendocino, CA, 2000, Pg. 79.

[113] Cousto, Hans. The Cosmic Octave, the Origin of Harmony, LifeRhythm: Mendocino, CA, 2000, Pg. 62.

[114] Cousto, Hans. The Cosmic Octave, the Origin of Harmony, LifeRhythm: Mendocino, CA, 2000, Pg. 62.

- Being and non-being.

"It leads to a state where a being has no name - where the all-in-one and the all-encompassing are not separate entities, but reunited at their tone, their common origin - the origin that is also you."[115]

Tuning with the Galaxy and the Stars

The earth completes a full rotation in our sky every 25,920 years, a platonic year. When we use Cousto's formula to calculate the pitch or wave of this movement, we get an "F."

Cousto explained that this pitch stimulates our spirit, which is a higher consciousness than our soul.

Many traditions believe that our soul gives us divine guidance. Our soul is closer to our consciousness and personality than our spirit is.

In contrast, our spirit is not affected by our emotions, because it is beyond all good and bad, and resulting emotions.

For example, our spirit wouldn't understand the concept of forgiveness, good and bad, or duality. It only understands unconditional love. Therefore, nothing needs forgiveness. In contrast, our soul understands the concepts of duality, good and bad, and hence, forgiveness, just like we do.

Cousto relates the vibration of a "C#" with our soul and an "F" to our spirit.

Cousto attributed the great wisdom of the ancient Chinese to their extreme emphasis of the spirit. Cousto believed that their concert tuning practices based on the frequency of the platonic year, an "F,"[116] enhanced their focus on the spirit.

[115] Cousto, Hans. The Cosmic Octave, the Origin of Harmony, LifeRhythm: Mendocino, CA, 2000, Pg. 95.
[116] Cousto, Hans. The Cosmic Octave, the Origin of Harmony, LifeRhythm: Mendocino, CA, 2000, Pg. 73.

According to Cousto the emotion one resonates with after attuning to the frequency of F," a platonic year, is cheerfulness above suffering and desire.

Hans Cousto associated the Crown chakra with the platonic frequency. He quoted Hans David: (The Crown chakra or this resonance) "…represents the highest stage of spiritual development… where all problems, tensions and conflicts have been resolved or overcome and transcended."[117]

Summary of Planetary Rotation Frequencies

Cousto compared the different earth, sun and galaxy frequencies to stages in our lives.

Tuning to "G," the **earth-day**: We activate our neural and genetic equipment. We are a receptor for many levels of consciousness. This is beneficial to the young in spirit or those interested in starting families.

Tuning to "C#," the **earth-year**: In this stage, we harmonically integrate with people and our environment. We learn new perspectives as we resolve issues.

Tuning to "F," the **platonic year**: We no longer participate in unconscious activities. We divert our reliance from the outside world to rely on ourselves, as we make new choices.

Further Benefits of Planetary Tones

BioSonic Repatterning, developed by John Beaulieu, N.D., Ph.D., is a natural method of healing using tuning forks based on the sonic ratios inherent in nature. At the BioSonic website,[118] I found further benefits of **planetary tones** listed:

---

[117] David, Hans. "Die Welt des Yoga. Alpha," Verlag: Berlin, 1986, Pg. 243.
[118] www.biosonics.com. John Beaulieu, N.D., Ph.D., founded a Sound School in 1985 to promote artistic, healing, and scientific dialogue on sound as well as the relationship of sound to energy medicine and consciousness.

"**Sun-tone**: Enhances a sense of strength, motivation, self-identity, vitality and radiance. It promotes enthusiasm, assertiveness and determination.

"**Moon-tone**: Promotes emotional tranquility, softness and intuition. It enhances feelings, the feminine energy and a flowing flexibility with life.

"**Earth-tone**: Enhances the deep security and safety of Mother Earth. It is the cosmic sound of 'om.' It grounds and centers us.

"**Mercury-tone**: Strengthens cooperation and understanding. It sharpens communication skills through reason, writing and speaking with confidence.

"**Venus-tone**: Enhances an ability to feel, love, receive and share, and have close relationships. It enhances creativity. It also increases our love of pleasure, harmony and self-appreciation.

"**Mars-tone**: Builds strength, desire, motivation and action. It brings out decision-making abilities and assertiveness, while strengthening our courage and sexual nature.

"**Jupiter-tone**: Promotes openness, trust, optimism, good fortune and brings a jovial sense of laughter. It helps one to be receptive to grace and adventure in life.

"**Saturn-tone**: Develops discipline and setting limits with others and ourselves. It helps us to be structured, organized and take responsibility.

"**Uranus-tone**: Enhances ability to make life changes through inspiration, insight and freedom of expression without self-imposed limitations.

"**Neptune-tone**: Creates spiritual experiences and emphasizes compassion. It supports our dream life, artistic nature, music, art, dance and creativity.

"**Pluto-tone**: Helps us face our deepest secrets and rings light to the darkness. The energetic forces of Pluto help us let go of old patterns, bringing a rebirth in consciousness."[119]

I ended my story and turned my attention to Osborn.

"The tones that Cousto calculated for the planets and the sun are played on tuning forks and twinkle in the background of this deeply sonorous and fluid 'Star Dust' CD."

I didn't think Osborn's eyes could open any wider, but they did. He loosened his grip on the old shoelace that he was nervously twisting. Gracefully, the shoelace danced in the air as it slid onto the floor.

"Mmmmm…" came Osborn's reply.

"The stars sing gently to us," I murmured. "Just as you see the gorgeous 'starscape' at night, you can let the songs of the stars twinkle in you," I gently continued.

A strong vibration, in close proximity, will cause a lesser vibration to match itself. So when you hear the sounds of the stars (raised up octaves into your hearing range) your smaller vibrations can entrain to the star tones.

"As you hear a star's vibration, you vibrate in harmony with it. You can sing the "song of the stars" - the stars sing in you! **We are in the choir of the uni-verse, meaning one song."**

A twinkle of a distant star flashed in Osborn's eye, just for a moment.

Osborn nodded his head and abruptly scampered off.

Then I noticed it. A red twinkle of light flashed where Osborn had been. I looked closer towards the dirty old tennis shoe and then I saw the oversized, gaudy ring that had once graced Osborn's finger. Perhaps he no longer needed flashy jewelry to feel important.

Visit www.JillsWingsOfLight.com & www.Ancient-Music.com to hear music combined with the Fibonacci, Solfeggio and Star Tones.

---

[119] BioSonics.com Planetary Tuners

Chapter Thirteen

Taming Emotions

Before the next interview, I dashed into a garden nursery, to pick up some daisies to add a few splashes of color for my kitchen table. With my happy daisies in tow, I noticed a wiggling cord near the cash register. Upon a deeper investigation, I noticed that the cord was attached to a cute, furry little rat. Hmmm... could this be my friend, Osborn Raticus?

"Osborn, what in the world are you doing in a flower shop?" I opened.

After recognizing me, Osborn's eyes cast down and away from me. "I am looking for peace and spirituality in my life. First I discovered that looking youthful, sporting a pretty dame and being intelligent was great, but then I wanted things that had a deeper significance. As I searched for inner peace, I decided to mend the fences with my wife and re-establish our relationship, but I failed." Osborn's face changed and he set his jaw. "It doesn't bother me. I am just fine without her," scowled a sorrowful Osborn.

"You don't sound fine, Osborn."

Osborn's little mouth started quivering... "Well, my wife did give me a second chance, but... I blew it." The quivering got more noticeable. "She said that I wasn't sincere, just nice when I wanted something."

Osborn's eyebrows tipped up near his nose, but his shaking mouth pulled down. Moisture formed in the corners of his eyes, as he nervously played with his paws.

Osborn choked out, "She threw names at me, like impatient, demanding and insincere."

The moisture, now tears, was running down his cheeks, taking away all the softness of his fur as the salty tears matted his fur.

"I came here to be alone, because it feels good to be near flowers. They don't call me nasty names."

"Osborn," I called softly. "You have good instincts, being around flowers does make people feel good. You ingest their positive energy. Don't give up on Mrs. Raticus as I have a plan."

Osborn's quivering mouth slowed to a halt. Time seemed to stop and he focused on me.

"A plan?" he whimpered.

"Osborn, have you ever heard of the Bach Flower Remedies and the 'Healing Flower Symphonies'?"

He shook his head sideways.

Healing Flower Vibrations

"A flower shop is a great place to learn about the secrets of the flowers, Osborn.

"A flower, like anything else, is in its simplest form, energy. Some indigenous tribes of South America believed that the energy of a flower is a gift to mankind, a unique gift, in that a person can receive a specific healing energy from a flower. For example, one can feel the energy of cheerfulness from a daisy or beauty from a rose," I said as I looked Osborn straight in the eye.

"The indigenous tribes have an ancient, time-tested process that captures the essence or energy of a flower in liquid form. The process includes soaking the flower in pure water and bathing both in sunlight. The water absorbs the flower's essence. If one drinks the water, then they receive the flower's signature energy.

"The energy of flowers and our emotions interact. For example a fearful person drinks the rock-rose flower water, so the flowers' energy transforms his emotional energy from fear into trust. No wonder you want to be with flowers to help you heal, Osborn," I said softly.

Categories of Emotional Baggage

I continued with my story, "Noting personality patterns in people, a man named Edward Bach classified 12 common human conflicts that people can experience throughout their lives. They can master negative emotion and in the process turn it into a virtue. Examples are:

- Turning Doubt into Trust
- Turning Indecisiveness into Inner-Certainty
- Turning Escaping-Reality into Living-in-Reality
- Turning Fear-of-the-World into Trust-of-the-World
- Turning Impatience into Patience
- Turning World-Savior into Light-Bearer
- Turning Isolation into Togetherness
- Turning Inner-Conflict into Inner-Equilibrium
- Turning Panic into Heroic-Courage
- Turning Passive-Service into Active-Service
- Turning Pretend-Harmony into Inner-Peace
- Turning Demanding-Love into Giving-Love-Freely[120]

"Bach observed that virtues, such as the ones listed above, could be classified by specific emotional states. For example, we know what being 'trusting' or 'patient' feels like. We can also recognize the feelings of 'isolation' versus 'togetherness.'

"Bach found 12 flowers throughout the world, which had energy similar to common virtues. He called them ' soul-flowers.' Bach claimed that the right flower vibration could raise the energy of one's difficult emotion and transform it into a virtue,"[121] I continued.

---

[120] Mechthild and Scheffer. Encyclopedia of Bach Flower Remedies, Healing Arts Press: Rochester, VT, 2001. Pgs. 44, 58, 62, 76, 81, 95, 120, 128, 152, 172, and 185.
[121] Adapted from: Barnard, Julian. Bach Flower Remedies: Form and Function, Lindisfarne Books: Great Barrington, MA, 2004. Pg. 139.

"Bach also taught that we could find our essential nature in one of these flower descriptions. We advance our soul by perfecting the corresponding virtue.[122]

"Bach believed that a soul accepts the lifetime challenge of *one* of these paths, but I have experienced struggles in most categories."

"Me, too," piped in Osborn.

"Further, Bach claimed that each group of people overcoming a common emotional challenge, created an essential virtue on earth... necessary for the evolution of our societies. As we transmute our own life difficulty into a virtue, we increase these essential essences on earth.[123]

"Bach then used the methods of the indigenous tribes and created liquid essences to enable people to ingest the soul flower essences. This allowed them to achieve emotional success over these emotional challenges," I finished.

Healing Musical Vibrations

"I had an experience, in which, I observed the emotional gifts of music lessons peoples' stored emotional baggage."

I continued, "After playing violin in a home for the elderly for over a year, I perceived that people benefited from musical selections that expressed sorrow and self pity, as well as joyful music.

"At first I thought that sad music would increase people's sorrow, and it did for a bit. However, later I detected it had a long term beneficial effect.

"After times of pain, people are hesitant to be vulnerable and open, lest they be hurt again. When asked about something painful, people brush a painful situation off with a statement like, 'It doesn't bother me,' but in truth, it

---

[122] Adapted from: Barnard, Julian. Bach Flower Remedies: Form and Function, Lindsisfarne Books: Great Barrington, MA, 2004. Pg. 139.
[123] Adapted from: Barnard, Julian. Bach Flower Remedies: Form and Function, Lindsisfarne Books: Great Barrington, MA, 2004. Pg. 139.

does. Just like earlier you said that it didn't bother you that Mrs. Raticus wouldn't have you back, but it does.

"Invisible, yet insidious pain gathers after years of life's trials, weighing people and rats down, and eventually freezing their emotional bodies.

"As I played music for the elderly in a nursing home, I observed my audience, who appeared frozen, sit in cradled positions with never a glance or word to anyone.

"I believed that my captive audience allowed the sorrowful music to loosen their stored emotional baggage, and allowed them to release it. After this happened their emotional strength improved and they were able to improve relationships with other people.

"All the troubles you felt in your life can be released from your mind, body and feelings, so this energy doesn't poison you and those around you.

"Pretending that you don't have negative feelings doesn't make them go away. This just pushes them into your subconscious mind. Similarly, you don't get rid of a bad habit by ignoring it. First acknowledge it, and then consciously choose a better habit. Likewise, after you feel and let go of negative emotions, you can practice and strengthen healthier feelings," I insisted.

"Music vibrated their pain until it was loosened, enabling them to let go of it."

"After six months of giving their full attention to live, cathartic music (no phone-calls, interruptions or places to go), the elderly began talking and interacting normally. What a change!

"I believe that emotions, such as happiness or sorrow, are energies and that we accumulate them. I also theorize that music rekindles old emotional baggage.

"Music (not the words of songs) is processed in the right brain, which doesn't utilize language. Music helps people feel an emotion (such as sorrow or pity), and avoid details about how they experienced that negative emotion. Such music stirs old emotional memories, so they can be released. It is easier to do this if people don't have to remember specifics of what made them sad," I concluded.

Osborn's breath was still shallow, but there was a tone of hope in his voice. "Maybe if I could get rid of my negative feelings that weigh me down, I could deal with my emotions easier," Osborn whispered as I continued.

Musical Vibrations of Flowers

"'The Healing Flower Symphonies' are the music of the twelve " soul-flowers" that I composed, after learning secrets about music and emotional healing.

"A friend of mine showed me how to measure frequencies of an object, such as a rose petal with a sound oscilloscope. He then graciously gave me frequencies for the Bach soul flowers, which I recreated with a sound generator, and imbedded in the musical tracks of 'The Healing Flower Symphonies.'

"Whether you listen to the frequency associated with a pill or take a pill, your body vibrates at that same frequency. (All things, pills and flowers included, have a composite frequency!) A frequency associated with a flower has healing benefits, just like vibrating in resonance with a mineral or a vitamin.

"The frequency of the soul-flowers can be captured in a sound vibration! The frequency associated with each flower is embedded in the corresponding 'Healing Flower Symphony.'

"'The Healing Flower Symphonies' musically weave in and out of sounds that resemble typical types of pain (such as fear, distrust and insecurity). Each 'Healing Flower Symphony' allows the listener to re-live emotions. Just as the elderly home residents felt a painful emotion before they could release it, the listener gives the energy of an old emotional struggle its due attention to loosen and then releases it.

"After loosening negativity, the 'Healing Flower Symphony' then evolves into triumph, giving the listener the experience of transmuting stored, negative feelings into the corresponding emotional virtue. Listen intensely, be conscious to let the negative feelings go, and then be open to receive the vibrational feeling of positive emotions.

"Use the flower songs and corresponding feelings to improve your emotions, behaviors and hence, how people respond to you. For example, Mrs. Raticus accused you of pretending to be nice when you wanted something from her. One flower's music helps the 'pleaser' personality, one who is nice, but not sincere. This person approves of another's actions in order to appear pleasant. At first the 'Agrimony Healing Flower Symphony's harmonies are pretty, appearing pleasant. After the initial tones are sounded, the tones bend out of tune. It is barely noticeable, but the sour 'after-vibration' leaves one with a bitter feeling.

"Later the 'sounds-like-harmony-but-isn't' music transitions into deep, calm and pure harmony, allowing the listener to practice feeling true inner harmony. He can feel the contrast between pretentious harmony and the real thing. When we oscillate between sincerity and pretending to be sincere, we clearly recognize how each different state of consciousness feels.

"We are being insincere when we voice a nice message that we don't mean. Often we are not aware of the negative feeling we attach to our nice comments and we act insincerely without thinking.

"We may not be aware that we have an underlying negative emotion, because we are trying to be positive. For example, we think we have forgiven someone, when we really are still angry. Since we don't want to see ourselves as being angry, we don't allow this idea to surface in our consciousness. We try so hard to be good that we don't acknowledge what we are feeling. Unfortunately, the anger doesn't go away.

172

"When we stop burying our pain, we increase our well being. With emotional integrity we acknowledge our feelings and this releases negative emotional build up, which cripples our emotional health.

"We forget what it feels like to be free of negative emotional baggage or to express sincerity (even though we may not be conscious of this). In order to be sincere, we must know what it feels like to be free of (often hidden) insincerity. We must acknowledge and stand true to feelings of disapproval. Emotional honesty is 'such a relief.'

"Are you telling me that I can practice feeling sincere by listening to the 'Agrimony Healing Flower Symphony'?" Osborn sounded doubtful.

I was not. "By listening to music to feel a specific positive emotion, like joy, you are practicing being joyful.

"Let me back up. Our subconscious mind stores repeated thoughts and feelings, passing them to our conscious mind for quick decisions. For example, if one lies often, his subconscious mind suggests lies to his conscious mind, because he is in the habit of lying.

"Your feelings are powerful energies. Virtues or attributes are feelings. For example, patience feels different than impatience. The energy of a virtue grows when you feel it over and over again. Feeling things many times creates a habit.

"How do you change habits? You repeat a new behavior many times until it becomes a new habit. Your subconscious mind will store and pass this new behavior into your conscious mind. Later, you will use this emotional habit without even thinking. Now, people associate this emotional habit with you. For example, they may conclude, 'you are a joyful person.'

"You don't have to be at the mercy of habitual, negative emotions. Put yourself in the driver's seat by choosing and feeling good emotions repeatedly. The flower essences and the 'Healing Flower Symphonies' aid in this process.

"Your feelings also affect your physical body. For example, worry creates ulcers in your body. Your body interacts with your feelings, and you can become ill.

"Physical illness was thought by Bach to be a symptom. Accumulated negative emotions (such as our fears, cares and anxieties) are the root cause of physical illness."[124] Therefore, medicine treats the results, but not the root cause of physical illness.

"To maintain health, we need to maintain emotions like peace, joy and happiness. By cultivating positive emotions we reap better health." I couldn't stop talking.

"To sum it up, 'The Healing Flower Symphonies' allows you to feel negative feelings, release them and, then, let the music prompt feelings that create beauty, strength and a bountiful basket of emotional gifts."

"Music can help me control my feelings?" Osborn queried.

Raticus, My dear friend, listen to what other people have said, "

"Listening to the 'Healing Flower Symphonies' taught my body about feeling, thinking and releasing that which no longer serves my highest good. After listening I felt glorious - radiating beauty deep from my soul. I desired to do healthier activities, like connecting with people which is new for me, going out rather than staying in and being less affected by life's unpleasant moments." *Susan C.*

"I had a deep lingering sadness that lasted almost six years. I unsuccessfully tried many energy healing modalities. I then listened to the 'Healing Flower Symphonies' for about three months. I shifted from being sad and helpless all of the time to being joyful and empowered. This is huge!" *Kris Mitlas*

"My little autistic daughter spent most of her time cutting paper. She is low functioning. We found Jill's music and to our surprise our little daughter put down her scissors.

---

[124] Bach, Edward. The Bach Flower Remedies, Keats Publishing: New Canaan, CT, 1979, Pg. IX.

She ran to the CD player, smiling, humming and singing. Usually she was sullen and downtrodden. We have never seen her like this before – full of joy." *Debbie Frazen*

"Music always has influenced people's feelings." I continued. "Marches have been used to encourage people to go to war and fight. Some songs encourage pity or anger, while others make you want to dance. Why do you think love songs are so popular? It helps people feel this wonderful emotion!

"Part of enjoying life is not just harnessing your mind, as you already do with sound, Osborn, but also by cultivating consistent, wonderful feelings. Further many feelings, such as determination, persistence and confidence, give us great strength."

My speech finally slowed down. Speaking of feelings, I began to feel peace in Osborn.

"Tell me more," murmured Osborn.

"I will describe emotional struggles and how 'The Healing Flower Symphonies' assist in overcoming them, and develop virtues."

The Chicory Flower: The Motherliness Flower
Demanding Love to Giving Love Freely[125]

The chicory-flower-song helps those who are overly cautious for children, relatives and friends. These people smugly correct what they consider wrong. They also require that their loved ones be near them.[126]

The chicory-melody crescendos from a seductive and demanding beat, as if it was singing, "This is what I'll do for you, when you do what I want you to!" The chicory personality seeks to control someone, to insure he does what the chicory person perceives is right.

The seductive and rigid beat in this song endures while the melody frees itself from the controlling chains of the

---

[125] Mechthild and Scheffer. Encyclopedia of Bach Flower Remedies, Healing Arts Press: Rochester, VT, 2001, Pg. 76.

[126] A quote from Edward Bach by Mechthild and Scheffer. Encyclopedia of Bach Flower Remedies, Healing Arts Press: Rochester, VT, 2001, Pg. 76.

rhythm. Demanding energy is replaced by the feeling of enjoyment. The continuos seductive beat surprises us, similar to the wonderful feeling one gets when he stops controlling people and loves them unconditionally. This new type of love produces a beautiful peace, not possible with the energy of control.

The Cerato Flower: The Intuition Flower
Indecisiveness to Inner Certainty[127]

The cerato flower helps those who lack confidence in making decisions. Constantly seeking advice, these people are often misguided.[128]

The symphony builds to a peak that is never culminated… as the melodic line changes its direction and rethinks the melody line again and again without any conclusions. This lack of "knowing what to do" and decisiveness builds pressure. Worry clouds the music until it discovers a simple and happy "knowing" of what to do.

Agrimony: The Honesty Flower
Pretended Harmony to Inner Peace[129]

The vibration of the agrimony flower uplifts people who love peace and are distressed by argument. To avoid confrontation, these people sacrifice too much. They feel tormented, compromised, restless and worried, while they hide their negative feelings.[130]

A beautiful harmony is presented in the agrimony music, but the after-vibes of the notes are slightly bent out of tune. The lovely melody leaves a bad taste in the mouth, just as inner turmoil builds with lack of emotional integrity. The soul-flower symphony then raises its vibration into pure and absolute harmony, creating the transparent and deep emotions of peace.

---

[127] Mechthild and Scheffer. Encyclopedia of Bach Flower Remedies, Healing Arts Press: Rochester, VT, 2001, Pg. 62.

[128] A quote from Edward Bach by Mechthild and Scheffer. Encyclopedia of Bach Flower Remedies, Healing Arts Press: Rochester, VT, 2001, Pg. 62.

[129] Mechthild and Scheffer. Encyclopedia of Bach Flower Remedies, Healing Arts Press: Rochester, VT. 2001, Pg. 44.

[130] A quote from Edward Bach by Mechthild and Scheffer. Encyclopedia of Bach Flower Remedies, Healing Arts Press: Rochester, VT, 2001, Pg. 44.

Centaury: The Service Flower
Passive Service to Active Service[131]

The centaury song blesses those who are kind, quiet and gentle, but over anxious to serve others. People on this path overtax themselves, becoming more like servants than willing helpers. Due to their good nature they do more than their share of work, neglecting their own mission in life.[132]

The centaury-melody sounds like a music box with a dancing ballerina. She twirls and delights people as she goes round and round in her prescribed path. She is beautiful, yet mechanical, repeating what movements are expected. The dance of the music-box-ballerina then unravels and freely flows, as if the chords ascend into sounds, resembling dazzling light.

Vervian: The Enthusiasm Flower
World Savior to Light Bearer[133]

The vervian-flower-music uplifts inflexible people with fixed principles who are confident they are right. People, who benefit from this melody, try to convert others to their views. They are strong willed due to their convictions.[134]

The symphony dances to a fixed rhythm; its melodies relentlessly following the established drum beat. Diverting from rigid and stylistic music, the melody breaks free. Eventually each note becomes diffuse, like colors swirling into a translucent white light. With no desire to control or be controlled, the melody sings itself free.

---

[131] Mechthild and Scheffer. Encyclopedia of Bach Flower Remedies, Healing Arts Press: Rochester, VT, 2001, Pg. 58.

[132] A quote from Edward Bach by Mechthild and Scheffer. Encyclopedia of Bach Flower Remedies, Healing Arts Press: Rochester, VT. 2001, Pg. 58.

[133] Mechthild and Scheffer. Encyclopedia of Bach Flower Remedies, Healing Arts Press: Rochester, VT, 2001. Pg. 172.

[134] A quote form Edward Bach by Mechthild and Scheffer. Encyclopedia of Bach Flower Remedies, Healing Arts Press: Rochester, VT. 2001. Pg. 172.

Water Violet: The Communication Flower
Isolation to Togetherness[135]
The energy of the water violet caresses people that like to be alone, even if they are ill. People learning the lesson of the water violet speak gently and move little. Being independent, clever, capable and self reliant, they are almost free of the opinion of others. However, being aloof, they go their own way without the benefits of rich relationships. This is unfortunate, as their peace and calmness are blessings to those around them.[136]

Delicate and isolated tones paint a translucent color-wash on a canvas. As the song progresses the single melody finds companions that it softly intertwines with. The melodies dance together, but don't exert control. The feeling of isolation becomes lessened and transposes into an ethereal sound as it glistens and swirls into bliss with the companion of other tones.

Impatiens: The Time Flower
Impatience to Patience[137]
The energy of the impatiens-flower soothes those who want things done immediately. They push slower people to make them quicker or they work alone.[138]

The melody tosses and turns, while it searches for quick resolutions. Invariably, obstacles in the melody provide delay and frustration. Likewise, the negative energy of impatience surfaces when one wants everything done right now. In the music the feeling of impatience is transformed into peace, acceptance and a calm rhythm of breath.

---

[135] Mechthild and Scheffer. Encyclopedia of Bach Flower Remedies, Healing Arts Press: Rochester, VT, 2001. Pg. 185.

[136] A quote from Edward Bach by Mechthild and Scheffer. Encyclopedia of Bach Flower Remedies, Healing Arts Press: Rochester, VT, 2001. Pg. 185.

[137] Mechthild and Scheffer. Encyclopedia of Bach Flower Remedies, Healing Arts Press: Rochester, VT. 2001. Pg. 120.

[138] A quote from Edward Bach by Mechthild and Scheffer. Encyclopedia of Bach Flower Remedies, Healing Arts Press. Rochester, VT, 2001. Pg. 120.

Mimulus: The Bravery Flower
Fear of the World to Trust in the World[139]

This song is for those with fears of illness, pain, accidents, poverty, loneliness and misfortunes. Fear haunts people with mimulus-flower-energy, as they quietly bear their dread.[140]

Creepy and overwhelming fear rips through the music with a scary hiss. The nasty music finds an unexpected sense of knowing… a sense of well being that lies beneath a feeling of trust. Knowing, a foundation that supports the feeling of trust, is represented by the literal sound of a heartbeat. Trust and the melody are built upon the consistent and enduring beat of the heart.

Clematis: The Reality Flower
Escaping Reality to Living in Reality[141]

This "Healing Flower Symphony" gives relief to those who are dreamy, drowsy, "not-fully-awake" and who show no interest in life. These quiet people are dissatisfied, living more in the future than in the present.[142]

A breath becomes the percussion beat, combines with diffuse tones to create a state of dreaminess. Foggy tones and echoes muffle clarity. As the song continues, the warmth of the sun beckons the soul to awaken, to see more clearly and dance in the glory of the fully awakened light and with clear melodic tones.

Gentian: The Belief Flower
Doubt to Trust[143]

The gentian flower has special gifts for easily discouraged people. Any small delay causes doubt and

---

[139] Mechthild and Scheffer. Encyclopedia of Bach Flower Remedies, Healing Arts Press: Rochester, VT, 2001. Pg. 128.

[140] A quote from Edward Bach by Mechthild and Scheffer. Encyclopedia of Bach Flower Remedies, Healing Arts Press: Rochester, VT, 2001. Pg. 128.

[141] Mechthild and Scheffer. Encyclopedia of Bach Flower Remedies, Healing Arts Press: Rochester, VT. 2001. Pg. 81.

[142] A quote from Edward Bach by Mechthild and Scheffer. Encyclopedia of Bach Flower Remedies, Healing Arts Press: Rochester, VT, 2001. Pg. 81.

[143] Mechthild and Scheffer. Encyclopedia of Bach Flower Remedies, Healing Arts Press: Rochester, VT, 2001. Pg. 95.

disheartens them. Doubt transforms into the energy of faith and overcomes obstacles.[144]

The frantic struggle and scurry of the music anticipates Murphy's Law: "Anything that can go wrong will!" By focusing on potential problems, the melody worries, as it is never satisfied with any answers. The steady frustration from struggles and the emotion of doubt are later replaced by a sense of "knowing" that things will work out for the best.

A steady "ah" sound underlines the conclusion of the Gentian melody. The "ah" sound is said to be associated with the heart, love and compassion. The "ah" sound is found in the words "Ma" and "Pa." The same sound is in the name of many gods and goddesses, such as Jesuah (Jesus), Muhammad, Buddha and Krishna. An open heart easily allows the energy of trust to enter in.

Scleranthus: The Balance Flower
Inner Conflict to Inner Equilibrium[145]

Those who can't make up their minds are relieved with the energetic power of the scleranthus flower. These indecisive people are usually quiet and bear their difficulties alone.[146]

The music goes this way and that, mulling over the negative sides of options. Despair and tension arise from the lack of confidence that any decision will not produce the desired results. The song eases into the feeling of confidence, like the feeling you get when you know you are doing the right thing. Repeated experiences of "knowing" create feelings of peace and inner balance, leaving the feelings of isolation and dread behind.

---

[144] A quote from Edward Bach by Mechthild and Scheffer. Encyclopedia of Bach Flower Remedies, Healing Arts Press. Rochester, VT, 2001. Pg. 95.

[145] Mechthild and Scheffer. Encyclopedia of Bach Flower Remedies, Healing Arts Press: Rochester, VT, 2001. Pg. 161.

[146] A quote from Edward Bach by Mechthild and Scheffer. Encyclopedia of Bach Flower Remedies, Healing Arts Press: Rochester, VT, 2001. Pg. 161.

Rock Rose: The Liberation Flower
Panic to Heroic Courage[147]

The rock-rose-soul-type lives "mutely under intense pressure of fear."[148]

In the rock-rose-symphony gloom and fear drip onto the listener, as the sound of a heart beat struggles with terror. Eventually, a sobering resolve is birthed; one can overcome any obstacle. Determination and power increase as the momentum of energy builds and lifts the listener into the emotional space of courage.

"Well, Osborn, what do you think now?" I queried.

"I have a wonderful bouquet of flowers for you!" he beamed!

Sample "The Healing Flower Symphonies" at www.JillsWingsOfLight.com.

www.JillsWingsOfLight.com – Art Gallery

---

[147] Mechthild and Scheffer. Encyclopedia of Bach Flower Remedies, Healing Arts Press: Rochester, VT, 2001. Pg. 152.

[148] Barnard, Julian. Bach Flower Remedies: Form and Function, Lindisfarne Books; Great Barrington, MA, 2004. Pg. 132.

Chapter Fourteen

Awakening Our Note in the Cosmic Symphony

Each person has a "signature" fundamental tone that harmonizes his body systems. Dr. Jeffrey Thompson has advanced the understanding of the benefits of fundamental tones.

Before we go into detail, let me introduce Dr. Jeffrey Thompson to you. The vision for his sound healing and research center, the Center for Neuroacoustic Research, is to heal individuals, and eventually the world; Thompson aims to help people be healthy and to live their highest purpose. The motto "Healing the Body, Heart, Mind and Spirit through Sound" states the mission clearly.

The Center for Neuroacoustic Research has worked for over two decades doing scientific research with thousands of people.

Dr. Jeffrey Thompson, DC, BFA, physician, scientist, musician and composer, is the founder and director of the Center for Neuroacoustic Research.

Fundamental Frequency

Dr. Jeffrey Thompson started his interview with a reminder that our world is full of energy, including the energy of sound.

"Elements, which are the building blocks of everything in our world, are simply energies that vibrate," Dr. Jeff began.

"The elements in the Periodic Table have unique densities and each element has its own vibration!"

Dr. Thompson is recognized as a worldwide expert in sound healing. He has:
- Produced over 90 sound healing CDs
- Produced 1000s of custom CDs
- Invented about 14 sound healing techniques
- Designed and produced acoustic-visual healing equipment
- Written many publications, see www.neuroacoustic.com
- Lectured widely on the benefits of sound
- Worked with Deepak Chopra, Loiuse Hay, Bernie Siegel, Barbara Max Hubbard, Bru Joy, Susan Jeffers, NASA
- Been interviewed on national television (20 times in 2005 alone)
- Featured in many international magazines and newspapers (such as the Wall Street Journal).

"Hmmm," I mused. "If each element sings its own note, then our world is a symphony."

Dr. Jeff continued, "The atomic periodic chart is organized according to musical harmony." He offered this concept to illustrate his point. "The numbers of electrons that can fill an electron orbit follow the mathematical formula for harmonics. Also, the number of elements in a group (on the Periodic Table) is the same number of the notes between octaves. It's as if each 'octave' of elements forms a group that has similar characteristics."

Dr. Jeff continued, "If you expose a wineglass to various frequencies of sound, you will find one, and only one, tone that makes the wineglass shake. The wineglass 'resonates' with that particular tone and vibrates at the same frequency. That particular frequency is the fundamental frequency of the wineglass. One can find the fundamental frequency for all things.

"I came up with a system to measure the fundamental frequency of each vertebra in one's back," Dr. Jeff explained.

"If someone's vertebra was pushed to the right, and I pushed it even more out of place, my action triggered an alarm in his brain - that produced increased pain, heart rate, pulse rate, respiration, blood pressure, electromyography (EMG) rate, brain waves (EEG) and changes in galvanic skin response. We can measure this," Dr. Jeff added.

"When I pushed the vertebra out of place, I simultaneously played different tones. One tone made the vertebra move into place, despite my pushing it in the opposite direction. All stress responses stopped. This tone was the fundamental frequency of that vertebra.

"Each vertebra is connected to another part of the body, such as an organ or a gland. By tuning a vertebra, you can also affect the part of the body connected to the vertebra. When an organ vibrates in harmony with its fundamental frequency, the organ becomes healthy.

"Blood tests before and after a vertebra is put into place with the fundamental frequency reveal improvements in areas of the body connected with the vertebra!

"However, when the vertebra was put into place without the tone by my hand, and then pre and post tests were conducted, there were no improvements in the corresponding body part.

"For example, the 9th thorax, a vertebra, supplies the adrenal glands. Putting the 9th thorax vertebra into place with its fundamental frequency has a positive effect on the adrenal glands. However, putting the 9th thorax vertebra in place with your hands does not have the same positive effect on your adrenal glands.

"Is there a relationship between the fundamental frequencies of the organs and the fundamental frequencies of the vertebrae in the back?" I asked Dr. Jeff.

"Yes. For example the 9th thorax, a vertebra, supplies the adrenal glands. The fundamental frequency of the adrenal gland is either the third or the fifth harmonic of the fundamental frequency of the 9th thorax. So the 9th thorax and the adrenal glands have a physical working relationship and also a harmonic one. Your body is a harmonic web of frequencies," Dr. Jeff replied.

"Every organ and vertebra has its own unique fundamental frequency, which remains constant. So, if I document a person's overall fundamental frequency then I can use that calculation again and again to give that person a body tune up.

"Fundamental frequencies vary among different people, however. We are unique vibratory beings," Dr. Jeff concluded.

"I explored which fundamental frequency in the body was most significant," Dr. Jeff continued.

"If an organ or a vertebra is not functioning properly, it is not its fault. The organ or vertebra gets instructions from the brain. The brain will tell as many as five muscles how much to relax to keep a vertebra in place.

Ancient wise Masters established conscious control of their physical bodies, specifically the organs. When they detected disharmony within an organ, they tuned it to harmony, which they associated with the health of the organ. In the Deep Wave Body Healing CD, establish healing connection and tuning of organs, with the help of frequencies associated with healthy body organs.

Jill Mattson's "Deep Wave Body Healing" CD uses ancient techniques with vibrational energy and frequencies that invigorates and tunes your body's organs. Its meditative techniques instruct you to become conscious of your body organs and maintain their harmony (associated with health).

"A chiropractor puts a vertebra back into place, hoping to get the brain to change its faulty directions. However, it takes 21 days for the brain to 'reprogram,' so the patient has to see the chiropractor for 21 days before the correction is permanent. In contrast, if sound is used to put the vertebra in place, not only is the healing complete, but you see improvements in corresponding parts of the body.

"Therefore, I correct the fundamental frequency

in the portion of the brain that directs the organs and vertebrae. When the brain works perfectly, it instructs the body perfectly and health is restored," related Dr. Jeff.

Octaves, Harmonics and Resonance

"Let's pretend that you are a wineglass and a certain frequency makes you shake, just like it could make a wineglass shake," Dr. Jeff continued. "This is a fundamental frequency of your body. Related frequencies will also impact you as follows:"

"**Sympathetic resonance** occurs when your fundamental frequency vibrates your body. Your body naturally matches this frequency. This is the strongest resonant vibration in music and in your body.

- "**Octave resonance** occurs when you hear any octave of your fundamental note. Your body naturally matches this frequency.
- "**Harmonic resonance** occurs when an interval of a third (or three notes apart), or a fifth (or five notes apart) of your fundamental frequency vibrates your body. Your body naturally matches this frequency. This is the weakest resonance vibration.
- "**No resonance** is a tone that has no relationship with the fundamental frequencies or its harmonics. A tone with no resonance causes harmful stress. Your body will not noticeably match a frequency of no resonance."

Dr. Jeff continued, "Different octaves of your fundamental frequency resonate different parts of your body. This is because different organs in your body have different densities. Slower or lower frequencies penetrate denser matter. For example:

- "Your *fundamental frequency* affects your skin.
- *"One octave below* your fundamental frequency, vibrations affect your muscles.
- *"Two octaves below* your fundamental frequency, vibrations impact your joints, tendons and ligaments.

- *"Three octaves below* your fundamental frequency, vibrations affects your bones.[149] A note that is three octaves below your fundamental frequency is in the range of a bass guitar.
- *"Four octaves below* your fundamental frequency, vibration impacts your body fluids and cells.
- "All of the octaves of your fundamental frequency take you into homeostasis (or a state of perfect rest),"[150] concluded Dr. Jeff as his eyes danced with excitement.

I never considered that different pitches of the fundamental frequency would affect different parts of me, but it does make sense when you consider the different densities of body parts.

"At a rock concert stand near the bass guitar player, you'll feel the bass notes vibrating your bones. I started slowing down the fundamental frequencies by octaves, to lower frequencies to vibrate your bones.

"I learned that you can't recognize your voice when you take it down several octaves, but your body recognizes it on a deeper level.

"A deeper part of your consciousness is awakened through the recognition of patterns that make up almost everything we see. An integral part of you (that you are not aware of) is the intelligence that made you. This part of you recognizes the patterns and frequencies that it used so many times." Dr. Jeff

---

"Hear" With Your Body

Dr. Thompson reported, "I invented a 'sound table' to transmit sound into the body. This puts the fundamental tone not only into one's ears, but also into one's body."

Dr. Tomatis, a French ear, nose and throat specialist, wrote that sound takes a different path into the brain when it

---

[149] Research has shown that bone has electrical properties. The bone matrix is a biphasic (two-part) semiconductor, i.e. a crystalline solid with an electrical conductivity. http://www.affs.org/html/biomagnetism.html

[150] Homeostasis is a property of an open or closed system, especially a living organism that regulates its internal environment so as to maintain a stable, constant condition. Wikipedia

travels via the bones, as opposed to through the ears. The nerves that take sound from the bones to the brain travel through the subconscious portion of the brain, while sound coming from our ears is hard wired to our right and left brain hemispheres. Therefore, sound has a different impact on us depending on whether we hear sound through our ears or body.

Dr. Jeff barely paused, "When our body receives direct stimulation through sound, our whole body is stimulated, especially at a cellular level. We can measure this.

"Sound travels through water five times faster than through air. Our body is mostly water. Therefore, the body is a great transmitter of sound, allowing sound to deeply stimulate our cells.

"It is extremely healthy to stimulate our cells. Sound resonates our cells just like sound resonates a wineglass. When you boost a cell's frequency with sound, it takes in food and rebuilds tissues faster, while eliminating waste faster. With a frequency boost, a cell gets its work done quickly and then has time to rest, which is healthy.

"In addition, your nervous system has bundles of nerve tracks going up your spine. Sound vibrations can travel on these as they go to your brain. So not only your cells, but also your brain benefits from the frequency boost."

Sound, Emotions, and Consciousness

Dr. Jeff continued, "There is a relationship between emotions and fundamental frequencies. Each emotion has a fundamental frequency and is tied into an organ. For example, angry people tend to have liver problems. Their anger leads to liver problems. After a while, a liver problem makes a person angry. It becomes difficult to discern the root cause of the problem. Is the problem the liver or the anger?

"In Louise Hayes' book, *You Can Heal Your Life*, she uses analogies of physical and emotional problems. For example, a person with a shoulder problem feels he can't 'shoulder' responsibility. His emotional problems are too much to bear 'on his shoulders.' The energy of his emotional discomfort collects in his shoulder area, because of the connection between the harmonics of emotions and the physical body. Pain in the shoulder occurs, because the emotional problem lowered the fundamental frequency of the shoulder. Likewise, an injury to the shoulder can also trigger the feeling of not being able to 'shoulder' responsibilities."

"Fascinating!" I thought. I asked Dr. Jeff, "Do sounds and corresponding emotions affect anything else?"

Dr. Jeff began, "In our last example of the shoulder pain:

- "The shoulder is not the problem, as the problem has been caused by a signal from the brain.

- "The brain is not the problem, because it is affected by an emotional problem.

- "The emotional system is not the problem because it has been caused by a faulty belief system. This person doesn't have self-confidence to handle issues in life. However, if I tune the frequency to his shoulder (which has a harmonic relationship with the emotions), this person believes that he can handle things in a shorter time frame. The emotions and the physical problem are related.

- "The faulty belief system is impacted by a lack of consciousness. A person's reality is that he is not who he thinks he is. He is much more than a chemist, or an athlete, or Bob. He uses these labels to describe himself when he fills out income tax forms or introduces himself at a party. The problem is that he forgets that these labels are not who he is. He is a cosmic being whose purpose is to evolve. Our life is a journey of the soul, learning while we are in our body."

"Hmmm," I thought, "He needs to be conscious that he can be more than he thinks he is. He needs to be all he can be."

"Dr. Jeff," I asked. "Some people in ancient societies believed that sound and music could evolve one's soul. Do you think that?"

"Yes," Dr. Jeff continued. "We are born as children who perceive the world as magic and a wonderful adventure. We aren't afraid and don't have emotional baggage, but that changes.

"Children innocently follow their feelings and don't blame themselves for behaving like a child. As they grow, they forget their innocence and bury their feelings. They add insecurity and other negative emotions to their consciousness.

"As we grow older, we eventually ask ourselves: 'What am I to do with my talents and life?' Most people don't know the answer to this question, because they have buried their feelings. Their feelings reveal what they enjoy and what should be their life's work. Rather than search for a path in life that is uplifting, most people give up and get a job instead.

> "If you follow what makes you happy, uplifted and energetic, then your energy bodies sing in harmony and health!"
> Dr. Jeff

"When someone gets a mundane job that doesn't help his soul evolve, his soul cries out with the only tools it has: physical, mental and emotional energies. These are fire alarms of the soul, to help us get back on track.

"To soul-search, one addresses his feelings, but many have buried too many painful memories. Rather than tackle the unseen and scary monster of one's accumulated painful past, people ignore their feelings. When their soul sets off the fire alarm with a physical or emotional problem, many people disconnect the fire alarm. Instead, they should nurture their feelings in order to recognize and release their painful memories.

"However, if people soul-search, gain a deeper understanding of hidden emotions and discover their path in life, their consciousness is raised. This makes them feel good, which can make their physical, emotional and mental symptoms disappear." Dr. Jeff continued.

"Sound has been used for thousands of years to raise people's consciousness, that is, to wake up a person at the deepest level. Part of being awake is to know what makes you happy. With this knowledge people can pursue goals or jobs that can lead to fulfillment."

"Raising my consciousness by listening to beautiful music, what could be better?" I marveled.

> "Sound was used in ancient times, not so much as to heal the physical body, but to raise consciousness, which in turn, healed the physical, mental and feeling bodies."
> Jeff Thompson

How Our Fundamental Frequency
Affects Our Consciousness

Dr. Jeff gently continued, "There are relationships between states of consciousness and your fundamental frequency.

"Let's say your fundamental frequency is 100 cycles per second;

- If you create a tone an octave below your fundamental frequency, the frequency is cut by half and is now 50 cycles per second.
- Create a tone down another octave; the frequency is 25 cycles per second.
- If you create a tone down another octave lower, the frequency is 12.5 cycles per second.
- Take a tone down another octave, still lower, the frequency is 6.25 cycles per second.
- If you create a tone down another octave again, the frequency is 3.125 cycles per second."

"The human ear can't hear below 20 cycles a second. However, a frequency below 20 cycles per second is associated with brain waves, which can cause specific states of consciousness.

"Our brain experiences the frequencies below 20 cycles per second when we sleep. The specific frequencies that heal our mind, body and feelings in deep sleep are lower octaves of our overall fundamental frequency. We can calculate and produce exactly which brain frequencies enable you to receive these beneficial gifts. You don't have to be in deep sleep to receive these benefits!" smiled Dr. Jeff.

"Let's go the other way and raise your fundamental frequency by octaves. Let's start at 20,000 cycles per second (the highest sounds that people hear) and raise this pitch by an octave, which means we double the frequency to create each new octave," Dr. Jeff offered.

"The new octave is above our hearing range. As we increase the frequency by octaves, the speed of the wave increases to the speed of radio waves, TV waves, microwaves and then to X - rays. When we increase the frequency 40 octaves, frequencies are now measured in angstroms, that is, millions of cycles per second. These high octaves above your fundamental frequency are as fast as light!

> "Musicians can go into an altered *emotional* state to write their music. Anyone who listens is then teleported to the same emotional state."
> Dr. Jeff

www.JillsWingsOfLight.com – Art Gallery

Brain Wave States:
- **Beta** (30 - 13 cycles per second)
- **Alpha** (13 - 7 cycles per second)
- **Theta** (7 - 3.5 cycles per second)
- **Delta** (3.5 - .5 cycles per second)

Dr. Jeff discovered and named the lowest and highest brain states:
- **Epsilon** (below .5 cycles per second)
- **Lambda** (higher than 200 cycles per second).

The benefits of epsilon and lambda brain wave states are the same:
- Create a consciousness similar to being in an extraordinary meditation state.
- Electricity is created and synchronized between the right and left halves of the brain.
- You experience deep levels of insight, personal problem solving and high degrees of self-awareness.

"In fact, your fundamental frequency is a specific color. If we were to shine this color of light on you, you would go into homeostasis or 'perfect rest,' Dr. Jeff added.

"When you sufficiently excite elements in a compound, they emit light characteristic of distinct color frequencies for each element.

"We can also measure the frequency of the color of an element, let's say lead, and then calculate the tone of lead."

Dr. Jeff added, "An oil painting could be another octave of a symphony." My mind danced with this idea.

Harmonics in the Voice

Dr. Thompson continued, "After several years of creating fundamental sounds with an electric keyboard, I then used the human voice to find people's fundamental frequency.

"Everyone's voice contains harmonics. However, in each specific voice, the volume of various harmonics differs. When a different harmonic is louder, then the voice creates a different sound. The human voice is an acoustic fingerprint!

"A spectrum analysis of each person's voice reveals the harmonics created by his vocal chords. The peaks in his voice are harmonically related. There are even mathematical patterns in the harmonics of your voice!" Dr. Jeff smiled.

"I read a study that presented people with a variety of pictures of faces and bodies. People were asked to choose which faces and bodies were beautiful. Close to 97% of the people chose the faces and bodies with the proportions that are also found in music and in nature. We are wired to perceive these proportions as beautiful.

"Everything is harmonically related. For example, the major chord in music is perceived by the brain to be pleasing or 'harmonic.' This is because the brain recognizes patterns in music that are the same patterns used to create other things in the universe, such as the elements in the Periodic Table, food you eat, and the proportions of your body." Dr. Jeff smiled even bigger, his eyes looking gentle and wise.

Bio-Tuning®

Dr. Jeff was speaking with a smile and a little faster. "We can monitor the autonomic nervous system, which controls involuntary functions in our body, like the function of our liver and other organs," Dr. Jeff told me. "The autonomic nervous system directs energy to where it is needed.

"The central nervous system monitors voluntary systems, such as moving your arm.

"The autonomic nervous system sends signals through either of two opposing nerve branches:

- The sympathetic nervous system, which is your 'fight or flight' response.
- The parasympathetic nervous system, which maintains and rebuilds organs and tissues.

"When a person is in a 'fight or flight' situation, his sympathetic nervous system receives energy. The person experiences an increased heart rate, galvanic skin response and blood pressure. A 'fight or flight' situation takes energy from the parasympathetic system, which then stops rebuilding organs and tissues.

"Many people are so stressed they live in the 'fight or flight' stage all of the time, with symptoms such as high blood pressure or blood sugar. They also have difficulties sleeping, as if they have 'one eye open,' waiting for the predator to come. Lack of sleep makes their problems worse," Dr. Jeff continued.

"When the autonomic nervous system is not channeling energy into the parasympathetic or the sympathetic system, the person is in a state of homeostasis or perfect rest. This is an excellent state of being. A test of a person's degree of health is shown by how fast he can go from the parasympathetic or the sympathetic system into homeostasis!" Dr. Jeff stated.

I imagined that without rest our body gets tired, overworked and ages quickly. The autonomic nervous system needs rest, too!

"We have machines that measure one's heart rate, which in turn analyze the parasympathetic and sympathetic nervous system. We monitor how long it takes for a person to go into homeostasis, to measure his degree of health," Dr. Jeff continued.

"Since we can monitor the autonomic nervous system, we can watch the body's response to frequencies. We can calculate which one frequency will take a person into homeostasis! In homeostasis the autonomic nervous system, which controls the rebuilding of all the automated systems and organs, gets a rest!

"I call this process Bio-Tuning," Dr. Jeff revealed.

"Hmmmm," I concluded with a smile. "Your unique frequency tunes your autonomic nervous system, which creates harmony in the body!"

Primordial Sounds

Dr. Jeff continued, "Primordial sounds are space sounds, sounds of nature, sounds of our bodies, and one's own voice - changed so that our left brain doesn't recognize it.

"Primordial sounds give people a visceral response, like getting goose bumps.

"A visceral response can be caused by a signal in the brain as a response to primordial sounds. The primordial sounds also stimulate the production of beneficial chemicals in our body. Therefore, primordial sounds can be beneficial for your body."

"I used primordial sounds in my CDs, to awaken deep levels of recognition in the subconscious mind. In psychoanalysis, people awaken deep levels of their subconscious. Listening to primordial sounds does the same beneficial thing.

"Primordial sounds can create a deep and lasting healing in one's subconscious mind, while expanding consciousness," Dr. Jeff continued.

"I use an electronic keyboard that takes a voice and recalibrates the piano so that all its notes contain this voice, in different pitches.

"I tape people speaking affirmations of things they want to change in their life. I then take the person's voice down two to four octaves so the voice is not recognizable to the human ear. In this way a person recognizes this sound on a deep subconscious level when it is played. Listening to his affirmations in his own voice that only his subconscious recognizes, affects his behavior. Easily he takes steps to realize his affirmations, quickly and permanently!

Predictions based on Musical Harmony

"The California Institute for Human Science studied noble gases. The outer electron shell is completely filled in Nobel gases. Other elements combine to complete their outer shell of electrons and that achieves balance.

"Noble gases are associated with each chakra. Pretend that atoms are people. In the Periodic Table there are only six 'enlightened' atoms (the noble gases) or people in our analogy. These six atoms are complete and their electrons do not require joining with other atoms to be complete. The Noble gases' energy is balanced and perfect as it is. All the other atoms in the Periodic Table have to get 'married' or join with other elements to be energetically complete and balanced. When the chakras are working perfectly, they are complete and balanced, just like the Noble gases.

"There are seven chakras, but only six noble gases. One could accurately predict the discovery of the seventh Noble gas from the laws of musical harmony. In fact, the last several noble gases were predicted using the laws of harmony and later discovered.

"The California Institute for Human Science created a copper room, closed the door and turned out the lights. This room shielded you from electromagnetic energy. Being in this room was as dark as being in a cave 1,000 feet underground," Dr. Jeff told me.

"In utter darkness, with a photon counter (an instrument that precisely measures the tiniest units of light), scientists measured their infrared body heat, which is a frequency of light. Our body generates about one photon of light a second, except at the seven major chakras from which about 100 photons were measured. This is the first scientific proof of the existence of chakras."

How Do We Decide What to Listen to?

Dr. Jeff has so many healing CDs and sound therapy methods, I asked him for advice. How do we find the "right" music to heal ourselves?

"People know on a deep level what music feels good. They have a visceral response to music that is uniquely healing to them. Their brain recognizes and enjoys the underlying patterns in the music as the same patterns that are the building blocks of our bodies and the universe." Dr. Jeff explained. "So, listen to music that feels good to you."

I asked Dr. Jeff if he could recommend a "sound" product or a "sound" therapy. Jeff reminded me that we each have a sophisticated tone generator, our voice. The voice has been used throughout the ages for healing at the deepest levels. Different forms of chanting, toning, mantras, and group chanting are powerful healing tools available to people and they are free.

Dr. Jeff recommended sampling his audio programs in the CNR Sound Store at his web site. Feel which CDs give you pleasure or a visceral response. You can read about which CDs help you sleep, meditate, heal, grow, relax, learn, remember more easily or perform at peak states. A custom made CD plays your fundamental frequency.

With more investment, Dr. Jeff highlighted the sound tables and chairs. The CDs and the sound table or sound chair will "play" your body with the music, creating a greater body response.

The Center for Neuroacoustic Research offers seminars on sound healing. You can train to be a Neuroacoustic Sound Practitioner or a Neuroacoustic Sound Therapist. Upcoming seminars, workshops, and internships are listed on www.neuroacoustic.org.

www.JillsWingsOfLight.com – Art Gallery

Chapter Fifteen

Music of the Earth and Stars

Fabien's Story

I asked Fabien Maman to tell me his story. I wondered how he came to create musical instruments that connect with the stars and harmonize with the heavens!

Fabien told me that he was a musician in a jazz band, giving concerts in Japan, Mexico, New York and Germany.

"People responded to our music differently depending on where we played. It was more than just cultural differences, because people had different reactions to our music within the same country, but at different times of the year. The musicians and the music were the same, but the time and place changed," Fabien said.

Fabien continued, "I felt the crowd's emotional response to our music and I also saw their energy fields" (auras). At one concert Fabien saw the audience's auras light up and flood the stage, hugging the musicians with iridescent colors.

In 1974 Fabien's band was giving a concert in Japan. The Japanese do not clap after each song. Without clapping, the subtle energy built up faster and formed waves that cycled from the audience to the stage. "These experiences deeply affected me. I wanted to know more how music affected people's mind, body and soul," Fabien recalled.

Acupuncture and Energy Systems

Before one concert, Fabien's band was exhausted. Fabien asked an acupuncturist in the hotel to rejuvenate their energy. The acupuncturist tuned and played their bodies like a harp. They were all astounded at the magnificent changes that they felt.

"That was a life changing experience for me, as I realized that in the room of musicians, the acupuncturist was the 'real' musician. I wanted to be a 'real' musician, too. I took what I thought would be a three-month break from music to learn acupuncture, and then extended my study of this art for the next seven years," Fabien continued.

Fabien summed up his thoughts:
- The location and time music is played, affect how people respond.
- Music can affect people's auras.
- Subtle energy travels on musical sound waves.
- Clapping breaks up the subtle energy that music creates.

Ancient Musical Methods to Improve Energy

"I have been on a life-long journey to discover the impact music has on physical and subtle energy fields (the auras)," Fabien softly recounted.

During his quest for knowledge, Fabien researched ancient Chinese tones that resonated with the five elements (fire, water, earth, wood and metal). In fact, he went to China three times to find people who still used this ancient method of balancing subtle energy fields with the tones of the five elements. He found no one.

Fabien studied with a Hindu Brahman, Sri Marcos Hanuman, who taught him the Hindu art of healing music. He learned many modes. (A mode is a group of notes that are exclusively used in a song.)

Hindu modes change depending on the time of the year and day. As the earth rotates on her axis and around the sun, the energies from stars change so Hindu music changes to harmonize the changing energy of our environment every two hours.

Fabien also studied the ancient musical systems of Bali, Egypt, Greece, Plato (who taught special modes change mental and emotional energies) and even the *Old Testament*. Fabien then mentioned that the trumpets that caused the walls of Jericho to fall must have played a fifth interval in the key of 'G.'

"Hmmm," I mused. "Miracles (like taking down the walls of Jericho) are simply scientific phenomena that we don't yet understand."

Fabien studied Kototama, the ancient "Science of Pure Sound" (toning vowels and consonants) to stimulate each of the five elements, which in turn stimulates a specific organ, harmonizing and increasing the organ's vitality. Fabien learned that we are linked to the five elements through our internal organs.

After an exhaustive study of ancient sound healing systems, collaboration with physicians and scientists - all taken together with his intuition, Fabien formulated a system of toning and harmonizing with the elements, that is healthy for our organs.

Based on the Chinese five notes of the five elements, Fabien created a system linking the twelve acupuncture meridians as well as the organs with twelve notes. This task required seven years of research.

Earth and Star Energies

Fabien delved into how the energy from the earth and the stars affect people and music. "Is this musical astrology?"

I questioned. "Yes," came a soft and sweet reply. I was happy with that "yes!"

Fabien continued, "Human beings resonate with the earth. Therefore, resonating with the tones of the elements (tones of our earth and her kingdoms) heals us.

"Our feet stand on the ground, connecting with the earth, but our body rises to the sky. So, energies from the stars, planets and the sun also affect us.

"Music is energetic sound waves. Light is energy in waveform, also. These energies affect one another when in close proximity, so the energies from earth and sky interact with musical energy."

> "In ancient Egypt music, architecture and astrology were combined... heaven and earth were not isolated realms, and science and religion were part of an integrated, mutually supportive system."
> www.aniwilliams.com

The Energy of Different Seasons

Fabien continued, "The energy of each season has a different feeling. At various times there can be flowers, fruit or neither. There are hot, cold, light, dark, moist and dry influences. The locations of stars change in the sky from season to season. These different conditions affect our energy and music, too.

> "Human life will never reach its fullest potential until our lives become a mirror of nature."
> Egypt's Star – Song Temples
> www.AniWilliams.com

"This is why a song sounds different in various seasons," Fabien concluded.

I thought about singing "Silent Night" on Independence Day in July, or listening to "White Christmas" in April... not a harmonious thought.

"When the acupuncturist measures a pulse he can tell whether the internal energies are in harmony with the season. When we are healthy, our energy pulses in tune with the seasons. When we are not healthy, we have fallen out of tune with the seasons," Fabien added.

"Hmm," I thought to myself, "Musical Feng Shui for the body!"

Fabien found no tones or modes for the seasons in all of the ancient world's traditions, but he used intuition and knowledge of ancient oriental music to formulate keys and modes. For seven years he collaborated with musicians, physicians, mathematicians and the Hindu Brahman to synthesize these disciplines and fine-tune keys that resonate in the seasons.

"Fabien, what are the keys of the seasons?" I asked.

- "Summer resonates with the key of 'C'
- Spring resonates with the key 'A'
- Fall resonates with the key of 'G'
- Winter resonates with the key of 'D'
- Rainy season resonates with the key of 'F'" Fabien answered.

"So music improves our health and gives us more energy if we listen to music in these keys during these times?" I asked.

"Yes!" Fabien whispered.

I love it when he says "yes!" It makes me think I really understand it!

"The impact of songs changes in different seasons not so much because of the base note, but due to the harmonics. The energy from light, stars, moisture and temperature interact with the harmonics depending on the season," Fabien commented.

"Yes!" I blurted out without thinking. "If harmonics resonate differently due to changing light, heat and moisture, then different instruments also impact us differently in different seasons.

"I know that a 'C' on a violin sounds different than a 'C' on a trumpet, because the harmonics have different

203

volumes. Therefore, a brass instrument sounds different than an instrument made out of wood."

Fabien chuckled. "Yes," came his soft and steady reply. (I love that "yes!")

- "In spring, the resonance and harmonics of woodwind instruments (reed musical instruments) resonate your liver.
- In summer, the instruments made out of wood (guitars, violins, cellos…) react best with your energy.
- In fall, the metal instruments (trumpets, gongs, chimes, Tibetan bowls, xylophones and so on) bestow the most benefit.
- In winter, the skin drums raise your energy most effectively.

"On our web site, www.tama-do.com, you can click on samples of music from the seasons," revealed Fabien.

"Wait, Fabien," I cried. "You have a French accent, but did I hear you correctly? Did you say, that the energy of springtime affects your liver?"

"Yes," came the reply.

(It is amazing what I might do just to hear that "yes!")

I remembered that the Swamiji could play special music for your liver!

"We are a hologram with many layers of energy that influence us: a cellular layer, DNA, organs, meridians, chakras, subtle energy and outside energy. All of these energy sources affect us and interact with each other."

"Energy is always moving. It flows through your body every twenty-four hours, governed by seasonal influences. Just as certain pitches (certain energies) can be healing for you, so can seasonal energy," Fabien continued.

"Energy outside your body interacts with your subtle energy fields and enters your body through chakras and meridians," Fabien further related.

"Each season creates energy. Therefore, the energy of each season interacts with your subtle energy body and enters your chakras, affecting your organs," Fabien smiled.

"Why does the same note have a different affect on you in different seasons?" I asked.

"Each organ has a frequency that resonates with a certain pitch. Also, the earth and the sky emphasize different harmonics in various seasons and different harmonics interact with the pitches of organs. Therefore, the impact of the pitches changes with the fluctuating energy of the various seasons," Fabien replied.

"In other words," I mused, "the interaction of seasonal energy affects the quality of tone (not the pitch, but harmonics of the tone.) Further, different harmonics have various effects on the body's organs."

Seasonal Energy

- "Spring corresponds to your liver and gall bladder.
- Summer corresponds to your heart and small intestines.
- Fall corresponds to your large intestines and lungs.
- Winter corresponds to your kidneys and bladder."

One is not harmed when you listen to music at different times of year or in an ineffective key, but with the right pitch and time of year, one can receive physical, emotional and spiritual benefits.

> "I use acoustic instruments because they have strong harmonics. This power is lost with electric instruments."
> Fabien Maman

Fabien took people's pulses before and after his seasonal concerts. He discovered that the pulse harmonized during the concert, which increased energy and vitality in the body.

Music affects your body in other ways, too. Fabien learned that rhythm affects one's blood and circulation. The faster the rhythm, the slower the circulation is. Conversely, the slower the rhythm, the faster the circulation.

"Harmony[151] improves the ganglia (intersections of subtle energy nerves) and endocrine system.

"Harmonics[152] affect the nervous system, chakras and subtle energy fields," Fabien revealed.

"Blockages in our subtle energies result in physical illness if the energy blockages are allowed to crystallize. Sound, color and movement are the most effective tools to dissolve these negative energetic patterns," Fabien continued.

A Picture is worth a Thousand Words

"How did you confirm which pitches affect specific organs?" I asked.

"I researched the benefits of sound on the human body in 1981 with biologist Helene Grimal at the University of Jussieu, Paris," described Fabien.

Fabien photographed cells exposed to various pitches and different musical instruments. "I used Kirlian photography to see the subtle, yet powerful effects of music on the body's cells," he continued. "Using this data, I determined the pitches for the organs."

Fabien noted that one could clearly see the effects of different pitches on human cells. Different pitches changed the size and color of the cells. The same pitch from various instruments (brass, wood, drums, and metal instruments) affected the cells differently.

I also wondered if the pitches would affect the color and size of cells differently depending on what season it was.

Kirlean photographs of sound exploding helia cancer cells are available in Fabien's book, *The Role of Music in the Twenty-First Century*.[153] There are also photographs showing sound impacting cells of the body on www.tama-do.com.

---

[151] In Western music, harmony is the use of different pitches simultaneously. Wikipedia

[152] The untrained human ear typically does not perceive harmonics as separate notes. Instead, they are perceived as the timbre of the tone. Wikipedia

[153] Fabien Maman. The Role of Music in the Twenty-First Century, Tama Do Press: Boulder CO, 1997, Pg. 15, footnote.

More Proof

For further proof Fabien collaborated with the physicist and musician, Joel Sternheimer, who argues that for each atomic particle, there corresponds a frequency, which is inversely proportional to its mass. This "music" of the elementary particles means that we, who are composed of these elementary particles, are also composed of musical frequencies.[154]

As you may recall we introduced Sternheimer's work in Chapter One covering the work of the Swamiji. An article from www.earthpulse.com reported that Sternheimer discovered the mechanism for how plants respond to being stimulated by sound waves.

"The sound sequences used to stimulate plants are not random, but carefully constructed melodies. Each note is chosen to correspond to the stimulation of protein molecules. What this means is that the sound sequenced in just the right order, results in a tune which is unique and harmonizes with the internal structure of a specific plant type. Each plant has a different sequence of notes to stimulate its growth."[155]

"According to *New Science* 'Sternheimer claims that when plants hear the appropriate tune of a protein, they produce more of that protein. Sternheimer also writes tunes that inhibit the synthesis of protein.' In other words, undesirable plants (weeds for instance) could be inhibited."[156]

"Sternheimer also claims to have stopped the mosaic virus by playing notes sequences that inhibited enzymes required by the virus."[157]

"Sternheimer writes that in experiments, tomatoes exposed to his melodies grew two-and-a-half times as large as

---

[154] Maman, Fabien. The Role of Music in the Twenty-First Centaury, Boulder, CO: Tama Do Press, 1997. Pg. 15

[155] http://www.earthpulse.com/src/subcategory.asp?catid=2&subcatid=6 "French Physicist Creates New Melodies – Plant Songs." Sept 3, 2005, Pg. 2.

[156] http://www.earthpulse.com/src/subcategory.asp?catid=2&subcatid=6 "French Physicist Creates New Melodies – Plant Songs." Sept 3, 2005, Pg. 2.

[157] http://www.earthpulse.com/src/subcategory.asp?catid=2&subcatid=6 "French Physicist Creates New Melodies – Plant Songs." Sept 3, 2005, Pg. 3.

those, which were untreated. Some of the treated tomatoes were sweeter in addition to being significantly larger.[158]

"According to Sternheimer's research, each molecule in our body can be reactivated through resonance if it 'hears' its corresponding molecular melody."[159]

Fabien and Sternheimer worked with many people utilizing tones to pinpoint overall, signature frequencies of organs. Often the tone of the molecules corresponded with the tones of the organs.

Fabien learned that tones are different when harmonics vibrate in the air and go into the body via the ear, than when tones enter into the body directly (through physical contact with the vibrations - such as placing your hand on a vibrating drum). The body is denser than air and distorts tones when they travel through the body; also sound travels much faster through the solid body than through the air.

The energy of colors also changes depending on the density of what the energy is traveling through. For example, the frequency *red* is the color of the fire element that corresponds to the heart in the physical body (dense energy). Yet, the energy of the frequency *green* corresponds to the heart chakra (which is outside the body), and resonates with the subtle energy just outside the chest.

I noted that red and green are complementary colors, balancing colors in a way. I wondered if the physical and subtle heart energy were complementary or inversely related!

"I use different healing tones for organs, depending on whether or not someone hears the tones with his ears, or receives tones into his physical body." Fabien

---

[158] http://www.earthpulse.com/src/subcategory.asp?catid=2&subcatid=6 "French Physicist Creates New Melodies – Plant Songs." Sept 3, 2005, Pg. 3.
[159] Maman, Fabien. The Role of Music in the Twenty-First Centaury, Boulder, CO, 1997.

"Fabien," I asked. "I understand how one hears through his ears, but how do you best get sound into one's body?"

"By letting sound vibrate on the acupuncture meridians," Fabien replied. "Tuning forks send vibrations into the body when placed on the skin at these points."

Fabien researched the natural system of channeling energies through the body through chakras and meridians. He created a system of notes linked with the chakras. The vibration of the sound goes into the chakras and the meridians, the body-energy-transport-system.

Fabien also spent seven years researching and creating a sound system linking notes that correspond to the acupuncture meridians and their connected organs.

I imagined a subway system in our physical bodies that transported energy to the various organs. Of course a blockage in the subway transport system would deprive the organ of needed energy.

Tama-Do Courses

I asked Fabien to tell me about the courses in the Tama-Do Academy of Sound, Color and Movement.

"We teach students to use music, colors and chi movement (energy that travels on the meridians, that is, the energy subway system) in their bodies to improve their energy. These methods improve student's mind, body, spirit and energy flow.

"In the first level of training, students are taught to channel energy into meridians and the body with tuning forks. Students learn to be sensitive to frequencies and energies that radiate from nature.

"In the second level of training, students move from the physical to the subtle level of energy. They are taught how sound, harmonics, color and movement affect one's subtle energy fields, which in turn influences one's physical, emotional and mental energies. Students develop sensitivity to feel subtle energy. This increased awareness helps them provide healing services.

"In the third level of training, students develop sensitivity to the energy that radiates from the stars," related Fabien.

Star Tuning

"Stars are light and energy. The time of a person's birth reveals which star energies influence him the most."

"The frequencies of the stars in your astrological sign influence you throughout your life, because information encoded in your DNA is activated by the stars that were in the sky at your time of birth.

"This is like musical astrology?" I exclaimed.

"Yes," came the soft and reassuring reply. (You know it. I was smiling!)

"We receive important energy, which is vibratory information, from our souls and from the stars, which are from a higher realm. As we allow this energy, to guide us, our altruistic nature unfolds.

"The Academy of Sound, Color and Movement is called 'Tama-Do,' which means the *way of the soul.* Our web site is www.Tama-Do.com," said Fabien.

"Our soul resonates with the stars. Light from the stars contains encoded information from our souls. All light is energy, information and a vibratory

"The masses of particles behave and maneuver among themselves as if they were musical notes on the chromatic tempered scale.
We are music in the nucleus of our DNA, in our molecular structure."

Sternheimer, La Musique deis Particules Elementaires" CNRS

influence that affects our DNA and causes us to release inner knowledge. Energy from starlight triggers responses in one's mind, body and feelings, which in turn releases stored information in the DNA and subconscious mind.

210

"Energy from starlight gives us direction in the form of mental and emotional impulses… helping us discover our gifts and how they may benefit others.

"The seed of a spiritual life is found in the physical body, in the heart of the cells. The divine story for each person is written in his spiraling DNA. Star energy can trigger the release of DNA information, facilitating spiritual growth. Music prepares the way for spiritual work and brings us back to our natural crystalline structure, so we can be conduits of harmony on earth."

"I think I got it!" I said.

"Star energy helps us find our divine path in life. A man's quest is to discover his life work (divine path), that is, his soul's work. Once man discovers this path, coincidences and other 'magic' occurs as his career unfolds and blesses others," I couldn't stop talking!

"We experience a hierarchy of learning throughout our lives. First we learn about our body, then our environment. Later we ask questions like, 'Why am I here?' Energy from the stars give people encoded information, that later enfolds, about their life purpose," I concluded.

"That is correct," Fabien replied.

"Rebirth occurs with realization of our soul's purpose. By following our soul's path, we shine like the sun. Strength and beauty return, while celestial overtones add increased radiance," Fabien summarized.

I scratched my chin. "How does a star give us information?" I asked.

"We get star energy just like a radio receives radio waves from outer space. Radio waves can be heard and we understand their messages. The same is

"We are musical beings, because the substance of our universe is music – ready to serve and inspire through its vibration. All vibration in our aura and energy fields is full of musical notes in suspension."

Sternheimer, Joel. "Compte de l'Academie des Sciences" de Janvier 1983. "La Musique des Particules Elementaires

211

true for starlight waves.

"Energy is information. The messages from stars are held in our subtle energy fields until our consciousness can accept and integrate this information," Fabien continued.

"Energy travels in the universe from stars, planets and nature into our subtle energy fields and then enters into our physical forms through the chakras.

"We may not understand the specific energy at the time, but later we learn something or develop a value," Fabien said.

"Like patience," I concluded.

Fabien asked me, "Which star catches your eye in the night sky?"

I pointed to a star.

"You are resonating with that star's energy and on some level with its message," he explained.

All of the sudden, the night sky became more magical to me. It was like an advent calendar with hidden messages waiting to unfold when the time was right.

Stars and Our Quest in Life

"How do you teach someone to receive star information?" I queried.

"The students experiment by facing in each direction (north, south, east, and west) and they note their different feelings. With the students' increased awareness of energy from the stars, they identify which direction affects them the most," Fabien said

"We also expose students to frequencies based on their birth time, giving them amplified star energy," Fabien answered.

"I invented a huge, outside instrument, a bagwa, a 13 foot cathedral of sound with 25 tubes. The bagwa produces extremely low and high harmonics, which activate one's consciousness and awareness. A student stands inside the bagwa so the bagwa's music surrounds his body, opening his consciousness and awareness. In the bagwa a person's energy better balances and harmonizes."

The Bagwa

Copyright Tama-do 1997, used with permission

"Different stars have different energy - the qualities of their energies help us develop qualities within ourselves, through sonic resonance," Fabien explained.

Fabien's words were like a spotlight shining deep into my memory. I remember being told that the stars could awaken qualities such as:

- Determination
- Intuition
- Consciousness
- Aligning with Higher Will
- Liberating spirit from matter

- Awakening the soul vision
- Adding light to our chakras
- Bringing spirit into matter
- Increasing the light in our aura[160]

The clear midnight sky seemed remarkable to me now!

www.JillsWingsOfLight.com – Art Gallery

Singing in Harmony with the Stars

I asked Fabien to give us advice on how we can most benefit from his work and products.

Fabien recommended listening to his CDs while paying attention to where the music resonates in one's body. "If you don't feel anything from the music," Fabien cautioned, "then use tuning forks on your body."

"Pure acoustic sound clarifies your aura and opens up space for new consciousness, new ideas and energy," Fabien reminded me.

"Come to a workshop. We will let you experience everything I have talked about," Fabien invited.

---

[160] Sanaya Roman and Duane Packer. Courses from Orin and DaBen.

People respond to Fabien's work differently, because their feelings are affected differently by movements, color and sound. Fabien uses all of these modalities in his healing practices.

Fabien smiled, "We are starlight, all part of the universe."

I smiled back and began to hum, "When You Wish Upon a Star." This song held new meaning for me now.

And Fabien whispered, "Yes!"

The Tamo-Do website has much to explore, with numerous sound clips, enlightening photos, books, CDs, Fabien's instruments, tuning forks and articles.

www.JillsWingsOfLight.com – Art Gallery

Chapter Sixteen

Songs of the Earth

One man singing. What is the fuss over Tom Kenyon all about? I fortunately got the opportunity to interview Tom and discover a few of his secrets! I was excited to figure out what makes his singing so unique. What is that draws so many people drawn to such unusual sounds?

Tom channels interplanetary and evolved beings. (What is channeling? It occurs when a "spirit" uses a person's mind to communicate; the person relays the spirit's message.) In addition to writing books to reveal the teachings of these extraordinarily evolved spirit-beings, Kenyon receives the spirits' energy and expresses it in songs. But since when is a song that powerful? Our society is clueless about vibrational power and consequently, we do not take advantage of the wide, wondrous potential of sound. Ancient wisdom held that sound had the power to influence all things; today our science agrees that *all is vibration* and certain waves (in close proximity) can alter each other - in important ways. Sound energy transfers through resonance to other levels of our being. That is what is going on, when music evokes strong feelings in us, such as the effect an orchestra performing Mozart can produce, or maybe the stress we feel from the movie sound track building up the tension in a suspense scene. Vibratory sound can heal people, boost a plant's growth, control thoughts, uplift spirituality and even change physical bodies. A "song" can be a powerful thing, indeed.

With the creation of sounds never heard before, new vibratory patterns access untapped pathways of subtle energy (that may sound strange at first), within and around us. Listening to new vibrations - sound and music compositions, which enable listeners to experience new energies - can express as *NEW* thoughts and feelings! Pretty important stuff. "My songs opened me up to levels of energy that I did not have access to before. I could receive richer and increased information after these new channels of energy were available to me," Kenyon related.

The new movie about the work of Tom Kenyon, *Song of The New Earth*, begins with Tom as a little boy swinging from a tree and singing to the stars, while being nurtured by Mother Earth. The movie is about the man, who today, sings duets with Mother Earth. His tender and moving songs enable listeners to grow, morph and join in on the love song to our earth! Wow! What a big undertaking – changing the planet with a song!

All this time, my dear friend Raticus, was hiding in the shadows. He followed behind me and listened in to my interview with Tom Kenyon. I spoke softly, but strongly to my dear furry friend, Raticus. "Your assistance is critical. You are needed to follow the modern-day Pied Piper (Tom Kenyon) to restore the earth to a kinder and more-cared-for-place." Raticus straightened his spine – feeling important.

Raticus was thoughtful and listened carefully, as I continued to recount all of the information that Tom relayed to me. He was "quiet as a mouse" and did not say another word the entire interview with Tom Kenyon.

Tom told me of a time when he was tired and beat down, and then stumbled into a humble Mexican restaurant. Kenyon watched a woman cook, which she did with great love. Tom cites her food as the biggest healing he ever received. For a man who regularly participates in a loving-song-fest with the earth – this is quite a complement. The woman loved to cook. Her food, infused with her love, provided a powerful healing and transformative experience.

Each one of us, whether unemployed, a cashier, an executive, or a rat - is capable of feeling love, joy and gratitude. We can sing, adding love and gratitude to the music. Such feelings can be amplified within our voices. Our songs can be powerful "loving transmissions." So, each one of us can walk in the big footsteps of Tom Kenyon, just by playfully singing a happy tune. This is what the world needs now.

Tom, known for his channeling of the Hathors (highly evolved planetary beings), discussed his role as a conduit, revealing amazing information; he hears sounds (but not with his ears) and sings what he "hears" and feels. Kenyon commented on channeling: "Channelors are like hollow reeds. They receive and send energy through the container of their bodies. The goal is to surrender to the energy that comes through you. You must be in a high energy state to channel successfully. Also, you can not interfere with the transmissions by inserting your own ideas or wishes into the message. I enter into a high state of consciousness where time and space disappear. This is conducive to enjoying deep communication with spiritual beings."

I like to think - that by raising his energy and entering a deep meditative state - Tom creates a porthole to receive beneficial energy transmissions, which express as sound. Tom has dedicated a significant portion of his life to meditation and esoteric techniques to raise his energy. This allows him to receive "sacred sounds" and transmit them to listeners, with as little human energy interference as possible.

Kenyon offered more information regarding: raising the energies of your body, mind and emotions, "One method of raising your energy is cathartic release of negative energy. Think of Michelangelo, who started his masterpieces with one block of stone. He cut away the pieces that didn't belong, to get the prized work of art."

So it is with your personal energy. You must release the negativity stored within. Tom added, "The last song of the movie, the *Song of the New Earth,* was cathartic for me and the earth as well. I had countless people tell me of changes in their energy and life – after listening to this song."

I reflected how I felt about this same song. When I heard it, I felt like crying - although there was nothing for me to cry about. I was letting go of past pain, invisibly stored within my being. When we heal, the earth heals too; everything in the vibratory universe is connected.

Tom told me about an experience he had of being in a cave, where he recognized and communicated with an invisible "earth spirit"; this was a deep and usually silent spirit. The spirit was expressing sadness, because of humanity's lack of love and respect for the earth. The earth will survive, but many species (such as humans) come and go. With great concern, Tom reflected, "Our careless actions and plunder of the Earth are toying with our destruction. Earth energies cry to be balanced. The *feminine energies* of feelings and nurturing need to be honored and strengthened. This emotional strength must be respected – becoming equal with the actions and *masculinity* of mankind."

The movie, *Song of the New Earth*, described the story of Kenyon being employed by "spirit entities" to sing the "songs of earth." Tom and his wife Judi, have traveled the globe six times over,; he traveled to sing his songs – songs like none other. Tom feels energies flowing through him. This awareness allows his body to replicate the feelings through sound. While singing, Tom is not aware of what the next note will be. That takes some guts! He observes his song as it springs from him via internal vibrations and feelings. In this way, Tom sings from the inside out. When other people sing, they learn a song (the words and the tune) and sing from the outside in.

Tom's "special sounds" are not ones that we normally hear in a vocal solo. He produces whistles, groans, cello and percussion sounds, along with the wails of the wind. Sounds shoot from his mouth like a water pistol, or echo forth from deep within his chest. Muffled vibrations ricochet down his throat and off the inside walls of his mouth. His sound shoots into his nose or splits into two simultaneous voices. This is definitely not your ordinary concert. The singing reverberates from different locations inside of his mouth and then various parts of his body vibrate in turn – each adding their own unique flavor to the final sound. For example, sounds vibrating up into the pineal gland appear dreamy, while sound echoing off the back of the teeth are percussive-like.

Throughout the ages, wise sages knew that new sound frequencies create new states of consciousness. As Tom channels the *Songs of the New Earth*, he presents healing tones, grounding feelings and other mysterious gifts to listeners and the surrounding environment.

We receive gifts from listening to the songs of earth, yet the music is sung to *heal* the earth. I asked Tom, "Who is healing whom? Are you healing Mother Earth or is she healing us when we listen?"

The answer was comforting: these healing concerts work both ways, blessing the earth, and all who listen or sing. This form of song revives ancient practices that mankind has long forgotten. For example, today we think of a musical rhythm as a sound pattern that is heard over several seconds. Mother Earth has a much broader time perspective; her rhythms are the seasons, the sunset and sunrise, the equinoxes and earth's movement throughout the midnight sky. She has a much larger time scale than we humans. Although unplanned, Tom performed these concerts in time with the earth's rhythms - on equinoxes, full moons and important celestial star configurations. Such a schedule for concerts was important to ancient sages. Tom believed that his concert tours were divinely guided because of this and other reasons.

Ancient man strongly felt the presence of energy at certain locations (some are spiritual sites today). At these special locations, one feels heavenly and peaceful. Churches and sacred sites grace these spots. Ancient masters traced rivers of divine subtle energies that traveled from one sacred site to another; thus the *ley lines* were mapped. Ancient people believed that these special subtle-energy-currents were the earth's "Energy River," nourishing and defining the health of the planet. Do you want to guess - what are the stages for the Kenyon concerts? The Earth's ley lines and chakra points (locations where subtle energy enters the earth, such as the bed of the Grand Canyon). Again unplanned, Kenyon's concert tours have traveled along ancient ley lines and sacred spots. Tom believes that these concerts "tune" the surrounding energy matrix, including: crystals in the soil, negative residual energy of the site, pollution, the vibratory legacy of local inhabitants and of course the energy of the audience. The song lifts and raises all vibrations nearby. This beautiful energy, absorbed by the earth, then could travel along ley lines - like nutrients to depleted soil.

One listener recognized that Tom used ancient Asian scales – comprised of notes that replicate sacred geometry and patterns found in nature. Once again, this ancient practice linked the listener to the vibrations of the earth.

If this story wasn't tantalizing enough, I had a deeply personal experience (a lucid dream-like occurrence) while watching the movie, *Song of The New Earth*. As I watched, I recognized Tom's eyes with a deep sense of knowing, although his face was new to me. Shortly thereafter I was transported, in this lucid dream, to a strange yet familiar world on earth – *the underwater world;* here Tom was the master. This is where I knew those eyes from. Tom was a kindly, yet dedicated Master-King of the earth - deeply committed to managing, nurturing and saving the planet. He appeared regal and stately, even though he was of a squid-like species. In this dreamy experience I was a spirit, full of the naivety and purity of a young girl - with only thoughts of playing, singing and cuddling. I did not enter the King's radar screen - for I was longing only for song and play. His dedication and deep responsibility to manage things for the good of mankind, was lost on me. Feeling ignored, I announced that I was leaving; his focus was on "important" tasks elsewhere. The King-Master was surprised and saddened.

The scene morphed and Tom now represented the spirits of long-lost Masters from Atlantis and Lemuria. Distinguished, strong and scholarly (he had thick black hair, combed back with a gray stripe), he maintained a vigil in order to shepherd the souls of earth - directing every little detail. He was devising practices and meditation techniques to lift people up and provide for their safely. I came to watch them, but found the impossible to be true. There was even less room here for love, laughter and play than in *the underwater world*. Again, I flew away like a butterfly, shimmering in the light. This time, the Atlantean Masters (symbolized by Tom), knew what my departure meant and were enraged. I symbolized their "Higher Selves," (high energy that we are subtly connected to - this soul or energy form does not reside within our bodies) and I would not merge with their human souls at this time.

This dream was so vivid, surely it changed my very essence. The symbolism of the experience was revealed to me. Tom represented souls on this earth. I represented the energy of human souls' Higher Selves. In real life, Tom sings the song of the earth, while I channel the music of the stars and celestial realms. Many Golden Ages ago (each Golden Age is approximately 26,000 years), the first souls on the earth did not inhabit human bodies and their forms included their Higher Selves). As souls incarnated, they became deeply engrossed with their earthly affairs. They became so entangled with matter that the energy of their Higher Selves separated and left their human bodies - with only an energy chord to connect them. The Higher Selves reside in higher dimensions, where they can love, laugh and play – without touching the negative energy and duality of this physical world.

People of the long forgotten epochs of Atlantis and Lemuria tried to regain their heavenly claim to divinity (they could do this by reuniting with their Higher Selves); ultimately they went for a deeper ride into duality, immersing to a greater degree with the matters of the earth. As their thoughts and energies focused on controlling, managing and directing their worlds, they slipped further away from their Higher Selves. Yet, the *Song of the Earth*, sung by Tom Kenyon with love and reverence, captured the attention of their Higher Souls. The pure, untouched, childish essence of joy and love has been rekindled by Kenyon's tender *Songs of Earth*. A shift in perspective and love has now reached human awareness. It is time for us to bathe in loving, energy – in fact to be the essence of love – as pure as that of a little child.

Going back to the beginning, remember a young Tom Kenyon singing happily in a tree swing ... singing to the stars. As an adult he has become a loving and joyful "voice" – to elevate energies and cathartically release the sorrow of the earth. The heavenly stars want to play along in joyful song and return Divine Energy to the earth, but all (including Rats) must join in! One man's singing may lure the celestial spirit of our Higher Selves, but she will not unpack her bags to stay until more of us sing a heartfelt song unto the earth! Amen!

At Tom Kenyon's website enjoy: a wealth of free sound healing mp3s (including tracks for human body organs and endocrine glands, stressed parts of the earth, expanding your heart energy, developing consciousness & awareness and much more), videos and Tom's lectures, and a wealth of articles. Articles contain channeled information/wisdom of the Hathors, Mary Madeline and others. Also included is acoustic brain research. Visit **www.TomKenyon.com**

Conclusion

The curve of the incense smoothly morphs as it rises around the swami. The smoke dances with the music of "the inner silence" that is projecting from the swami. The incense cloud sways in time with the slow swish of the swami's tail.

Hey! Wait a moment! Swamis don't have tails! Hmmm…. We'd better take a closer look.

This can't be Osborn Raticus wearing a turban and deep in meditation, can it?

I decided to clear my throat to make the swami come out of his peaceful meditation. "Ahem! Ahem!"

There were the deep brown eyes, almost black and barely visible when he raised his eyelids. And there was a slight smile.

"Raticus," I blurted out. "Since when did you become a spiritual guru?" I suppose that was rude and forward of me, but the words slipped out before I realized what I said.

Raticus just closed his eyes, retreating into the deep abyss of silence.

Before that tail started to swish again, I changed my tune, "This is quite a change, dear old Raticus." I remembered that you get farther with people (and rats) when you are kind."

"Yes," came the slow reply. "I have discovered things far more precious than gold, jewels and dames… except not more precious than dear Mrs. Raticus, who now abides with me again."

"What a relief that is," I murmured.

"Sound has made a believer out of me. First, I learned that sound affects matter, which is a powerful insight, indeed. Next, I learned how to use sound to enhance my health.

"Sound enabled me to master meditation and control my thoughts. I improved my memory, I.Q., meditation and intuition. Meditation gave me internal prescriptions leading to greater health.

"At first, I used this powerful knowledge to help me improve my intelligence, energy, health and beauty. Then I realized that life could be richer.

"Music then gave me the ability to harness the power of my emotions. Rarely do people realize the strength that lies in the control of their own emotions. Strengthening positive feelings and thoughts enabled me to manifest my dreams and uplift those I loved in my life.

"The music of nature and the songs of the stars tuned my consciousness into harmony, a harmony that unfolded what truly makes me happy in life. I later became aware of the things that I love to do and I pursued them.

"I embarked on a spiritual path and used sound, as a fast track method, to travel that spiritual path. Now, I experience bliss and peace. I am sharing this blessing with the world. I sing and use sound to uplift myself, my world and everyone else too!"

"I have something to say to those readers of yours." Raticus's eyes were wide open now, displaying the warmth of a beautiful Christmas in them.

"Everything is made of energy and sound is energy. Sound is powerful, indeed.

"The power of sound and vibrating energy is just beginning to unfold in the minds of mankind. Our journey into understanding this power, the power used in creation, is in its infancy. There is a long road to travel before we master the secrets of sound.

"All the universe is a song, and everything in it makes music. Sound and music affect everything in our world, even if we can't see the effects with the limited frequencies our eyes can see.

"Every level of you is singing a song, however softly. You are a musician and a composer, creating your music with the words that you speak, the thoughts that you think, and all that you feel. Sound and music help you elevate what you think, feel, say and do.

"You learn to sing your song, by trial and error. At times you sing in tune and other times you do not. However, when you create harmony in your world, the world sings with you.

"The universe is not complete without your unique song. You are a child of the universe (uni-verse, meaning one song). Your destiny is to be a 'star' singer in the universe's song of life. This will bless and uplift others."

Raticus slowly closed his eyes and slipped into a blissful state of being, as he gently hummed his song.

www.JillsWingsOfLight.com – Art Gallery

Ancient Sounds ~ Modern Healing

www.JillsWingsOfLight.com
www.Ancient–Music.com
http://www.MusicForBeauty.com
http://www.RedBubble.com/Jill Mattson

All of the artwork in this book - inside and out - is based on original oil paintings by Jill Mattson. Many of the paintings are available along with prints. Visit JillsWingsOfLight.com for more information.

If you enjoyed this book, please consider leaving a review at amazon.com/Jill Mattson – to help spread these ideas! Thank you! Jill Mattson

Jill Mattson: Author, Composer, Musician and Artist

Jill Mattson is an author, artist, musician and widely recognized expert and composer in the emerging field of Sound Healing. She has written four books and produced seven CD's that combine intricate Sound Healing techniques with her original Award winning musical compositions *(Best CD of 2015 – People's Choice Award for **Contacting Angel & Masters**; 2012 Best New Age CD – Silver Award **Deep Wave Beauty CD**).* The CD's consist of intriguing, magical tracks using ancient & modern techniques - with sound energy & special healing frequencies to achieve profound benefits.

Her cutting edge music includes: Sound Based Beauty Treatments, Frequencies of Flower Essences (emotional catharsis & virtue building), Celestial music with Tones from ancient Egypt and Celestial Bodies, Solfeggio/Reverse Solfeggio & Fibonacci tones, Binaural Beats & Meditative Music, Countering Negative Astrological Energies, Ascended Master & and Angelic

Channeled Energies, Ancient Languages of Light, Tuning Notes for your body and more! These multilayered, multidimensional, deep layered, soulful works will uplift your heart - while offering a myriad of benefits.

Jill lectures throughout the United States on *"Ancient Sounds ~ Modern Healing"* taking followers on an exciting journey revealing the healing power of sound. She unveils secrets from ancient cultures as well as the latest findings of the modern scientific community showing the incredible potential and healing capabilities of sound, including how sound travels through your body. Jill draws on her extensive research of modern Sound Healing, and over 30 year study of ancient civilizations and secret societies in her music, lectures, workshops and writings.

Free Sound Healing MP3s
for Amazing Results
From Jill Mattson

All found at www.JillsWingsOfLight.com – home page!

Song #1. Enchanting music with **Fibonacci Tones** and 18 **Solfeggio Tones**.

Song #2. **Star Tones** are converted into sound and shine through heavenly music! Also are tones of the elements: hydrogen, oxygen, carbon and nitrogen.

Song #3. **Flower Music** – The actual composite frequencies of flowers is mixed with fluid & emotive music to clear negative emotions & build positive feelings/virtues!   The aural version of Flower Essences!

Gift #4. A Fascinating **Sound Healing Newsletter** – comes out every three weeks!

Read on for a free excerpt from Jill Mattson's newest book...

The Lost Waves of Time

We have reached the nexus point in man's destiny.
We are further from God and the divine than we have ever
been. Look around you – can you doubt that this is so? So
what happens next?

Today, many believe that we are staring into the abyss:
environmental disaster, war, revolt and global upheavals,
economic collapse... despite the seemingly insurmountable
problems, some think that we are on the brink of re–capturing
what the ancient masters tightly guarded and employed with
incredible success: *Music.* Pliable music was the foremost
ancient tool to perform unbelievable feats. Special sound
vibrational energy manifested as music, has always molded
our world - much more than we can imagine. The mirror of
music reflects a culture's deepest social and moral values.
Using their understanding of music's power - ancient man
shaped his world and maintained his creation for millennia.

Jill Mattson's *The Lost Waves of Time* is the story of music through the ages – how it built and maintained and then destroyed and tore down – each great civilization. The point that I believe is unique in *Lost Waves* is that Music played a far greater role throughout time than any historian has ever recognized. And it impacted on every level. Music was crucial at pivotal points in time in history.

Praise for Lost Waves of Time from Readers and recognized Experts:

"*Lost Waves of Time* will take you back to the beginning and ahead to the potential that we have forgotten. Prepare for a ride through history in a way that will move you to your core. You will recognize information from a deeper inner place that you likely didn't know even existed within in you" - Sharry Edwards, Founder Bio Acoustics

"From the mythic days of Atlantis through all the histories of the major civilizations: An idea echoes around the ancient world; the vibrational power of music slowly shapes human emotions, behaviors and actions. These influences accumulate and solidify, resulting in entire cultural reform. ... Like the slow erosion of a tall mountain into a gentle rolling hill, music's subtle energy relentlessly molds everything in its path." - Hank Selata, Founder Holistic Healing

The Lost Waves of Time is the mind-blowing story of how *music* - (the sound vibrational matrix of infinite variety) - literally shaped human history. -Testimonial

"Three time author Jill Mattson breaks through in *The Lost Waves of Time*, revealing ancient vibrational energy techniques for sublime results. Enormous in scope. Reach new levels of consciousness. It will alter your ideas of sound and the ancient world – forever!" - Bessheen Baker, Director and Founder of NITE.

This book reveals - more than anything else - what the conventional history books never will! Almost no one knows this story - and I doubt academia would dare to tell it! -Testimonial

Music has always molded our world - much more than we can imagine. The mirror of music reflects a culture's deepest social and moral values. Using their understanding of music's power - ancient man shaped his world and maintained his creation for millennia. Pliable music was the foremost ancient tool to perform unbelievable feats. -Testimonial

Excerpts from Jill Mattson's new
Lost Waves of Time

Energy.
Energy is life.
Energy is information.
Energy is matter made quick.
Energy enables all.
Without Energy... we have nothingness.

The energy of gravitational attraction drives the formation of stars in deep space. The energy of our sun powers all life on Earth. The power of our winds and storms have their roots in the nuclear fusion reactions constantly going on the sun (nuclear energy) – transmitting energy to the Earth in the form of photons (sunlight – electromagnetic energy). The relentless ocean tides are due to the gravitational attraction of our moon (gravitational energy). Bio–chemical energy allows new life to begin – as an egg is fertilized and cells begin to divide, multiply and specialize. Electro–chemical energy powers our brains, thoughts and memories. On a finer level, *subtle* energy flows through our bodies, minds and souls – representing and nourishing our consciousness, our "self," our qualities and inspirations.

This book is about Sound energy – an often overlooked and vastly underrated form of energy. Sound energy has a multitude of capabilities, as it consists of a large spectrum of vibrational frequencies that can be adapted for an incredible variety of applications. The energy is selective and powerful for focused uses. We are all familiar with many common types of sound energy: ultrasounds and sonograms in the medical field, sonar for naval and aquatic purposes, sonic booms, car horns and high pitched dog whistles... there are many, many more examples encountered in everyday life.

Subtle, influential energy – disguised as music – has affected mankind for many thousands of years. In ancient times, music was considered critical for survival. It was used for diverse applications: strengthening warriors, striking enemies, inducing rain, building psychic skills, enhancing crop growth, creating trances, curing physical, emotional and mental health issues and even more. Music was a powerful "vibratory wand" wielding magical–like energies. Thousands of years later, music's mystique has faded; it is considered only as a form of entertainment, a tragic loss to mankind.

Some sounds (frequencies of specific energy) interact with our minds fostering a certain type of brain wave state and hence a specific state of awareness or consciousness. Other sounds, *help our bodies heal themselves* – in the face of almost any illness or malady (including cancer, emphysema, flu, muscular and skeleton injuries and much more). Sound energy can enhance our consciousness by interacting with our subtle energies and associated systems, such as the chakras and meridians. Sounds can heal emotional and physiological problems. Often, sound can replace or simulate physical items – such as vitamins or other nutrients; even pathogens or beneficial microbes can be neutralized or simulated by sound. Other special sounds can enhance intelligence.

Modern man applies sound in a variety of useful ways; we can greatly expand on this – to the good of all – by returning to our ancient forefathers.

Sound: A Window on the World

Ancient peoples understood many things by connecting them to music. Sound was a "window on the world". Music was a way of viewing reality – just like science or religion. Music was a paradigm to understand the universe. The mechanics of music explained everything for the ancients, just as science does for many people today. Pythagoras explained the universe with mathematical equations derived from simple vibrations of a lyre string.

Music was often a prerequisite for all higher learning – as it explained the Heavens and Earth (again music bridges science and the spiritual). Ancient leaders believed that minuscule sound vibrations impacted all facets of life. In fact, sound was intimately related to math, science, religion, philosophy and many other studies.

Music was viewed as a lens for viewing the universe and sound was used in ways that we would not even dream of today. These cultures deliberately used special music for practical and spiritual purposes. It was used to control areas ranging from the environment and health, to the population's values and attitudes.

An entirely new way of thinking is required to accept these ancient ideas. We can easily miss their reasoning. Fatal errors of understanding occur when we interpret ancient music based on today's norms, namely music's prime value is to entertain us; *not so for the Ancients.*

Worldwide religions[161] describe sound as the source of creation.[162] Indeed, the *Bible* says, "In the beginning was the Word, and the Word was with God, and the Word was God."[163] Creation was related to the vibrational energy of words. It is no wonder that sound and music were sacred in the ancient world. Sound was God's tool.

Music can display intricate, coherent information when you translate it mathematically. Think how much information the combined output of a large symphony orchestra playing a classical masterpiece contains. Music's hidden mathematical patterns, not listening preferences, were of supreme importance to ancient leaders. Ancient music mimicked naturally occurring numerical patterns or laws, such as those found in a star's movements across

---

[161] Hindus, Egyptians, Mayans, Hopi, Buddhism, Christianity and others
[162] Hindu tradition states in the Vedas, "In the beginning was Brahman with whom was the Word. And the Word is Brahman." Thot, an Egyptian God, was believed to have created the world with His voice. According to Mayan tradition, in the *Popul Vuh* (the book on creation), humans are given life by the power of the Word. In the Hopi Indian tradition, "Spider Woman" sings songs of creation to produce animated life. The *Satapatha Brahmana* reads, "In the beginning was God with power through speech. God said, 'May I be many...may I be propagated through subtle speech, he united himself with that speech and became pregnant.'" In Chinese Buddhism, the Divine Voice calls forth the illusive form of the universe.
[163] Bible, John 1:1

the heavens. Music emulated nature, reflecting its perfection. When man vibrated in sync with Heaven and Earth, he was in harmony with God and all cosmic forces.

Ancient man used numbers to understand God's creation. Numbers were not considered to be only symbolic, but infused with sacred essence. God surrounded us with mathematical revelations, hidden in nature. Recall that Pythagoras said, "All is number." As numbers and music were interchangeable, ancient people believed that music was another means of expressing God's sacred language.

Music and Subtle Energy

Subtle energy is sometimes viewed as a universal life force – present within all things, even inanimate objects. Subtle energy connects things. Subtle energy has infinitesimally small vibrations that are currently undetectable; not identified within the electromagnetic spectrum. It has been called qi, chi, orgone, prana and kundelini energy. Yet others link this fine energy to the energy of thought, intention and intuition. Some disciplines refer to this fine energy as an aura, a field or universal life force.

Some modern scientists scoff at the concept of subtle energy, however, consider that after 400 years of modern scientific study we still do not understand how the force of gravity works. Further, in the past 15 years, modern physics has discovered that the universe consists mainly of *dark energy* and *dark matter* – neither of which we can directly detect! Ancient mystics knew of subtle energy since the dawn of our existence.

Ancient people believed that the properties of subtle energy explained psychic occurrences. They described subtle energy acting more like waves than fixed particles (similar to modern physics theory for how things like electrons work). For example, during the psychic phenomenon of remote viewing or past life regression, a person animates one body, while viewing events at another time or location. The ancient Buddhists exposed people to specific colors to activate healing energy within their bodies. The ancient Greeks listened to sorrowful music to vibrate and release negative emotions. In a classic example of sound resonance, a plucked "A" string on one violin makes a nearby violin's A string vibrate. The energy of the A note transfers to the other violin. Analogously, subtle energy readily transfers between things.

In the physical world we perceive fixed, permanent things. We perceive a table to be separate from its surroundings. Yet if we observe the infinitesimally small atomic energies within it, we see that the table is largely empty space occupied with small forces of constantly moving energy. Ancient people described subtle energy as infinitesimally tiny, moving streams of energy. This clearly displays their vibrational understanding of reality.

We are holistic vibratory beings constantly interacting with many types of energy. The energies of our mind, body, and spirit and the environment surrounding us are deeply connected and interrelated; each aspect impacts the others. Every cell in our body emits and absorbs frequencies.[164]

Our internal vibrations resemble music; all music that we listen to intermingles with our internal vibrations. The effects of a single song may be too small to notice, but the cumulative effects – after extensive listening – can be significant.

Our ancestors were well aware that subtle energy, influenced by music, could be used to shape our world. By focusing on small subtle energies they discovered amazing capabilities of sound and music.

www.JillsWingsOfLight.com – Art Gallery

[164] Thaut, Michael. Rhythm, Music and the Brain, Scientific Foundations and Clinical Applications, Routledge: NY, 2005, Pg. 205.

Lemuria and Atlantis: The Story & Music

The title of this book: *The Lost Waves of Time,* has its roots in numerous myths and legends – none more controversial or mysterious or wonderful than the legends of Atlantis and Lemuria... These two long lost lands were Eden to early master races that lived tens of thousands of years before the full emergence of our direct ancestors – homo sapiens. Of course, both island continents met with separate cataclysmic demises – perhaps due to massive floods, Earthquakes or polar shifts. Or, perhaps, the inhabitants sunk their own island homes after their work was accomplished.

Folklore originating from all over the globe makes reference to the Motherland of Mu (Lemuria). Mu or Lemuria clearly is older in origin than Atlantis; it is possible that there was a period of time that the two mysterious lands were simultaneously occupied. It is widely accepted that Lemuria was situated in the Indian or Pacific Ocean basin. The beings that were the Lemurians may never have been fully involved into matter. Many sources cite ethereal Lemurians who may have been more spirit than matter. To be fair, there is not enough evidence that allows us to definitively categorize the Lemurians. They did live on this planet for many years, starting at least 100,000 years ago – perhaps even far earlier. Their music and their relationship to the Atlanteans – as well as their heritage to us – will be addressed later in this chapter.

The evidence for the existence of Atlantis is voluminous – truly remarkable in its scope and depth. Some background on Atlantis will be provided for the uninitiated reader, however, our focus will be on addressing this legendary race's music and wondrous application of sound.

Atlantis – The Story and People

Atlantis is probably the most enduring grand mystery of all time... an enigma that was famously recorded by Plato around 360 BC (and it was an ancient tale at that time). Atlantis has captured the interest and imagination of countless generations; over 2,000 books have been written on this most famous "Lost Continent." Some suggest that the longevity of the "myth" and mankind's fascination with Atlantis is due to the memory of Atlantis written into our collective subconscious.

Plato's account of Atlantis is based on a trip that Solon, a respected Greek lawyer, took to Egypt around 580 BC. While traveling in Egypt, Solon learned of Atlantis from priests who received knowledge passed down from very old reliable sources. They told of a land beyond the Pillars of Hercules (Strait of Gibraltar) that was lost to the Atlantic Ocean 6,000 years before (this account gives a final demise date for Atlantis of approximately ~ 6600 BC – 8,700 years ago; sources usually date the disappearance of Atlantis beginning 30,000 to 40,000 years ago and finishing up 8,000 to 11,000 years ago; the destruction occurred in phases).

Edgar Cayce, famous for revealing alternative health information while in a trance state, has provided us with prolific and carefully documented, channeled sessions, about Atlantis and its people. During trances, Cayce learned of people who had lived previous lives in Atlantis. He provided startling detail on this ancient land and its destruction. Amazingly, many of Cayce's channeled revelations were later confirmed with scientific discoveries – after his death! Ancient sources referring to Atlantis are incredibly numerous and pervasive. Information on Atlantis is also found in Central American cave writings. The ancient Tibetans refer to Lemuria as *Ra Mu*.[165] In the Yucatan, monuments are dedicated as a memorial to those lost in Mu's flood.[166] Stories of a devastating flood are part of old oral legends of the Lancandon Indians in

---

[165] Andrews, Shirley. Lemuria and Atlantis: Studying the Past to Survive the Future, Llewellyn Publications: Minnesota, 2006, Pg. 1.
[166] Andrews, Shirley. *Ibid,* Pg. 30.

Mexico. The Cherokee history begins with beings from the Pleiades star system, who migrated to America prior to the sinking of Atlantis.[167] The book, *Popul Vuh*, from Central America described a visit by three princes "in the East on the shores of the sea whence their fathers had come."[168] The Toltecs of Mexico trace their heritage to Atlan (Atlantis). Montezuma (Aztec) told the Spaniards that his people came from the East, where their homeland of Azlan sank into the seas. The Dakota Indians insist their ancestors lived in a city now underwater. Similar stories are found in stories from: the Iroquois, Sioux, Delaware and Mandlan tribes.[169]

Geological finds support the existence of "lost" continents in the Atlantic and Pacific oceans. For example, nearly identical flora and fauna exist on lands widely separated by oceans. Fossil remains of the camel are found in India, Africa, Kansas and South America. Many similar fossil remains, of closely related species, are found around the globe. How did they cross the ocean barriers? The banana tree, native to Africa and Asia, with no small seeds, got to the Americas. The mid–Atlantic ridge has some of the highest peaks (submerged) of any mountains on Earth – are these remnants of the original Atlantis island continent?

Traces of mysterious language links abound; the old language of Basque from early Western Europe resembles the aboriginal languages of America. One third of the Mayan language is *pure Greek*. The first 13 hieroglyphs of the Mayan "alphabet" resemble the Egyptian Hieroglyphs. Many Hebrew words resemble the Chiapenecs' language of Central America.

In 1920, the British–born James Churchward published *The Lost Continent of Mu*, after 50 years of research and explorations throughout Asia and the South Asian Sea. Churchward described the Naacal, the people of the lost continent of Mu (Lemuria). Churchward claimed that he gained this knowledge after befriending an Indian priest, who taught him to read the ancient (dead) Naacal language. The priest revealed several ancient tablets, written by the Naacals. Churchward found that the writings of the

---

[167] Andrews, Shirley. *Ibid*, Pg. 57.
[168] Scott–Elliot. <u>The Story of Atlantis and the Lost Lemuria</u>, The Theosophical Publishing House: London, 1925 with editions up to 1968. Pg. 13.
[169] Andrews, Shirley. *Op. cit.*, Pg. 58.

early Naacal tablets were in the same language as geologist William Niven discovered on artifacts in Mexico.[170] How did these language influences cross the oceans? Did land once connect the east with the west?

The Guatemalan sacred text, *Popul Vuh,* claims that all people originally spoke the same language; this link was lost as groups moved away from their homelands. When the Spaniards first came to America they were surprised that natives had religious customs similar to their own, such as the worship of crosses, baptismal practices, fasting, confession, marriage, virgin mothers and communion. Ancient stories all over the planet tell of an archaic flood.

Numerous underwater archeological ruins of ancient cities have been discovered. One of the most notable is near Cuba on the Bahaman Plateau. Massive stone tiers that look like streets and walls have been found underwater, with carbon dating to 12,000 BC. The shapes are tetragonal and polygonal and precisely interlock. One formation appears to be the base of pyramid, 55 by 43 meters.[171]

Book after book presents extremely specific evidence of Atlantis. Numerous stories – from widely diverse cultures around the globe – refer to Atlantis. We find skeletal remains of homo sapiens (anatomically modern man) dating 150,000 to 200,000 years back.[172] We also know that cataclysmic events changed the surface of the Earth many times over. It is not hard to believe that the civilization of Atlantis existed at one time... only to disappear with hardly a trace.

Legends tell of a fantastically advanced Atlantis – with sophisticated technology AND spiritual and psychic capabilities unlike we have ever known. At the same time, numerous species of hominids as well as homo sapiens were walking the planet – using stone tools and wearing animal hides. How can we reconcile these mysteries?

---

[170] Andrews, Shirley. *Op. Cit.,* Atlantis: Insights from a Lost Civilization, Pgs. 17–18.

[171] Muck, Otto. The Secrets of Atlantis, Times Books: NY, 1976. Pg. 34.

[172] Tattersall, Ian. The World from Beginnings to 4000 BC, Oxford University Press: NY, 2008, Pg. 67.

An Atlantis Theory

Science tells us that there have been numerous – surprisingly many – possible ancestors of modern homo sapiens (modern man). Often, several of these races of "early men" were present at the same time, co–inhabiting the same geographical regions. Why where there so many of these early hominid species and why did only one emerge – and emerge so quickly – to become modern man? Enter Atlantis theory... with the idea that some form of *"Divine Designer"* was watching developments on Earth and waiting for the right moment to arrive – when one species of early man was ready – or when the overall environment – or the planet or cosmos was right. Perhaps then the Divine Designers intervened and elevated the "chosen" race of early primitive man to the status of *modern man* – where the preceding species was animal only.

According to some schools of thought, Atlantis was where the early "chosen" human ancestors were taken by the Divine Designers. Perhaps in this isolated, pristine land – the spark of divinity – the soul, or the everlasting spirit – was added to the animal form and what we know as true human man was born! These Divine Designers could have been truly divine – say the Angels of a traditional God; myths tell of Atlantis being home to Poseidon and his descendants. Even *Bible* stories echo this idea, as some versions of *Genesis* describe Giants who found Earth women pleasing and mated with them. If you are rooted in a more physical or scientific explanation, these super beings could have been advanced extraterrestrial aliens who had visited the early Earth for many millennia – watching and waiting until the time was ripe... This "creation" event dates at approximately 100,000 years ago, as closely as it can be traced.

Perhaps guardians watched over the small population of early "true men" for thousands of years in the isolated, paradise–like Atlantis. There, the Divine Designers educated them, nurtured them to grow and explore. The ability to use agriculture to enable permanent settlements started in Atlantis, as did advanced language and artistic skills. Early true men multiplied across Atlantis; then, starting about 50,000 years ago small vanguard parties of the true men began to move out into the wider Earth where they initiated small outpost settlements. These ancient vanguards – our earliest true fathers –

went out in many different directions. Europe, Africa, Asia, and the Middle East were the first destinations for establishing proto–civilizations. (This theory, if true, could explain many enduring mysteries that have long baffled scientists and archeologists.)

As the years went by, more parties departed Atlantis – to supplement and extend the populating of our planet. The new settling parties went in varied directions – venturing into North and South America including Mexico and Central America. Others entered remote islands in the Pacific including Australia; some groups went to the same areas as previous settlers, to insure that a healthy population was developing.

Early true humans from Atlantis began to interbreed with suitable animal–like primitive men. The results of their offspring were mixed – some of the offspring thrived and the divine spark burned bright in them. Others retained a baser nature and lead to inferior species or died out altogether. The Designers saw that their efforts were succeeding.

Earlier we posed this question: why did modern humans emerge so quickly, after numerous hominid species existed for millions of years with little progress? Homo sapiens man, was chosen for his biological features; these allowed souls to develop emotional, mental and physical control. After emergence of this physical body, Middle Earth's purpose was concluded and the other human–like species faded away. This time period, called Middle Earth in stories, featured many human species existing at the same time. Perhaps these stories awaken our subconscious recognition and emerge repeatedly in works such as Tolkien and others.

It has been convincingly argued that some Atlanteans departed their doomed continent and spread around the globe, joining established populations of early men. These Atlantean refuges began the Shaman or Wiseman traditions in the primitive peoples that they "seeded." Often these transplanted Atlanteans and their direct heirs, passed on remarkable powers and skills to the primitives. This can explain many of the early wonders of primitive and early cultures – such as the monument building accomplishments and reported psychic abilities.

When the preeminence of modern man was certain, forces were put in motion that would eventually destroy all traces of Atlantis. The first destruction is traced to approximately 45,000 years ago when Atlantis was divided into five major islands. At 28,000 years ago the Earth's magnetic poles shifted and an Ice Age began. Complete destruction of Atlantis occurred approximately 9 to 10 thousand years ago.

From a spiritual point of view, a physical body can be likened to a container, skin or vehicle for a soul to use. Just as a variety of people can drive the same car, a Lemurian, Atlanean, dwarf, ogre or higher celestial soul can incarnate in the vehicle of man. The gamut of souls could incarnate into the human body. Not only is Earth a melting pot for different ethnic races, but for a wide variety of souls. The hermetic saying, "So as above, so below" reflects the mixing of spirits and races. If one believes in reincarnation then it follows that the souls of these earlier races can be reborn into today's human bodies.

Everything that was proposed earlier in this chapter, as an explanation for the rise and fall of Atlantis, can easily be considered as also true for Lemuria. It is probably unknowable today, but it seems logical that Lemuria and Atlantis fit together in the overall master plan for Earth and mankind. The main differences being that Lemuria came earlier than Atlantis (and was situated in the Pacific); we have far less evidence surviving for the Mother continent of Mu.

... Moving on in Chapter 3: Lemuria and Atlantis:

www.JillsWingsOfLight.com – Art Gallery

Hominid Species approximate Time Spans of presence on Earth

Species	Approximate Time Span
Homo erectus	2 million years ago to 200,000 years ago
Homo Heidelbergensis	600,000 years ago to 250,000 years ago
Homo Neanderthalensis	200,000 to 25,000 years ago
Homo Floresiensis	800,000 to 40,000 years ago
Homo Sapiens	200,000 to present

The Lemurian and Atlantean time periods overlapped somewhat according to channeled sources. The Lemurian civilization was an older culture than Atlantis, and experienced its demise much earlier. Channeled stories describe "beings" visiting between the continents and "inter–racial" children. At this time the fossil records show numerous species of hominids with different facial characteristics, varying heights and different arrangements of the brain cavity. Stories from this time describe a variety of races, with skin color ranging from red, black, blue, yellow and white. Many types of men walked the Earth in these days, namely: anatomically primitive men (of several unique strains), modern man (homo sapiens) and the near–divine Atlanteans and their cousins. Popular stories parallel this scenario. Perhaps the Lemurians can be likened to the Elves.

Helena Blavatsky (1831–1891), a Theosophist, described the early spiritual development of humanity. In the First Age, humans were pure spirit. They were sexless beings in the second state.[173] In the Third Age the giant Lemurians used spiritual impulses to develop awareness of the physical world and sexual reproduction.

---

[173] Other sources indicating that these early beings were sexless at first: Steiner, Bailey, list, Willugut, Randall–Stevens, Cayce, and Tom.

In a similar vein, *Genesis* (6:1–6:4) refers to the "sons of God," or in other Biblical translations references are made to "the giants." [174] Perhaps these "giants" or the "sons of God" are from an older civilization, such as the Lemurians.[175] These giants found favor with the Earth women who bore their children. Atlantean mythology has similar stories with advanced beings mating with Earth women. Other sources also report that some Atlanteans were giants.[176] The story that the Greek's Poseidon (a god) mated with Earth women is in a related tradition. Similar stories exist in Sumerian texts;[177] the gods from Sumer are referred to as "visitors from heaven" in Mesopotamian tablets. The extraterrestrials seemed powerful and came from above, which classified the extraterrestrials as gods.[178]

Blavatski mentioned a race, cited in the *Popol Vuh,*[179] whose sight was unlimited and they knew all things at once.[180] These early beings were not fully materialized and exhibited an intuitive, clairvoyant state of consciousness. Perhaps these were the advanced beings mentioned frequently in ancient texts.

Life in Atlantis

The last phase of the Atlantean culture endured over 50,000 years; there were significant and lengthy earlier phases, according to channeled sources. Life was different in the beginning and changed significantly as the continent endured. The Atlanteans started out more involved into physicality than the earlier Lemurian race; they were spiritual and harmonious beings that gradually mixed their energies with matter. The early Atlanteans were not like today's human species.

---

[174] Giants were also referred to in Numbers 28–31, Deuteronomy 1:28, with David and Goliath.
[175] The composite frequency of an object changes with its dimensions, according to Barbara Hero. See her chart: *Unified Theory of Color and Sound as Related to the Physical Body, The Chakras and Human Dimensions*: Hero, Barbara. The Glass Bead and Knot Theory of Relationships, Strawberry Hill Farms: Maine, 1992 –1996. Pg. 45.
[176] Bellamy, Saurat, Steiner, Heindel, Oahspe, Scott–Elliot and Heindel
[177] Andrews, Shirley. Atlantis, Insights from a Lost Civilization, *Op. Cit.,* Pg. 32.
[178] Andrews, Shirley. *Ibid*, Pg. 32.
[179] *Popol Vuh* is a mytho–historical narrative from Guatemala. The title translates "Book of the People."
[180] Godwin, Joscelyn. Atlantis and the Cycles of Time: Prophecies, Traditions and Occult Revelations, Inner traditions: Vermont, 2011, Pg. 67.

They were highly capable of manipulating malleable and subtle energies. For example, the power to produce rain at will was common, as water is pliable.

The early Atlanteans did not see objects with clear and sharp edges, but as hazy objects surrounded by auras or soft lights. The early Atlanteans possessed clairvoyance and clairaudience. To them, the astral world was enormous and rich, while the physical world appeared diminished and small. Music that we hear only with our external ears is described as a shadowy reflection of the "inner music" that they enjoyed.

The people of Atlantis communicated telepathically.[181] (Comprehensive speech as we know it emerged relatively late in human evolution, roughly corresponding with the emergence of homo sapiens.[182]) This may seem fanciful, but today even humble ants receive long distance, nonverbal communication from the queen of their colony.

Telepathy was widely used to communicate with beings other than humans, such as plants and animals. The Atlanteans believed in *nature spirits* – the intelligent consciousness of energy in all living things. The ancient Hindu religion calls this consciousness, divas.[183] Sound is used by some Hindus as a bridge to other dimensions, such as the divas.

In the later days of Atlantis, people were involved into matter to a far greater extent. Their physical bodies were perfected to better interpret vibrations in the physical world, such as sight and hearing. In the later years, when telepathic skills lessened, thought transference was taught in the temples in attempt to retain these skills. The students practiced specific techniques – they relaxed while breathing deeply to low pitched, rhythmic sounds. This enhanced the mental state required to produce telepathy.[184] In any society in which everyone can read minds, secrets were uncommon. With transparency, people's behavior was impeccable.

---

[181] Andrews, Shirley. Atlantis: Insights from a Lost Civilization, *Op. Cit.,* Pgs. 68, 80.
[182] Perrault, C. and S. Mathew. "Dating the origin of language using Phonemic Diversity." *PLoS ONE* 7(4): e35289. Doi:10.1371/journal.pone.0035289. 2012.
[183] Andrews, Shirley. *Op. Cit.* Pg. 138.
[184] Andrews, Shirley. *Op. Cit.,* Pg. 74.

Edgar Cayce reported many details about the Atlanteans. Prominent was their great mind power; they could use their minds to strictly control their bodies. Many of the priests could levitate; others were "magicians." Religion, science and magic were considered almost the same thing. Their schools of magic served the role of both church and school. This land did not have stark contrasts between rich and poor. No one lived in want. Items most valued were not material, but psychic skills and abilities. Their country relied on seven famed oracles – who foretold the future by accessing subtle energies from future times.

Atlantis had rich soil and enjoyed a temperate climate (as you would expect for a large island in the Atlantic). Their diet included fish and fowl, but no red meat, although there are stories that they drank fresh blood.[185] Lions were kept as pets; felines enhanced psychic work and protected against the "lower astral" energies.

Atlantean houses were built with the help of sonic gongs; huge stone blocks were raised without machinery or human effort. Power from the sun was harnessed for energy. Stories of these abilities are found all over the world. We will go into more detail about using sound for moving large objects in the chapter on Egypt.

The Atlanteans developed amazing skills unimaginable today. In one account, they used hypnotism and magnetic therapy to raise the consciousness of criminals, to rehabilitate their thinking, so that they would never commit a crime again.[186]

The sound of one's name was believed to resonate with the gifts that the soul wished to create while in the physical body. Care was taken to say someone's name with love. If a child heard his name in a judgmental, demeaning way, the child was expected to experience difficulties in expressing his potential.[187]

Even when they were young, these highly evolved beings often chose to pass over once they accomplished what they had incarnated

---

[185] Scott–Elliot. *Op. Cit.,* Pg. 51.
[186] Andrews, Shirley. Atlantis: Insights from a Lost Civilization, *Op. Cit.,* Pgs. 80, 90, 92.
[187] Cooper, Diana. Discover Atlantis: A Guide to Reclaiming the Wisdom of the Ancients, Findhorn Press: Scotland, UK, 2005. Pg. 172. (channeled information)

for.[188] The process of dying was perceived as simply separating from the physical body. When a person died, the body was "disintegrated by the occultist priests with the use of certain cosmic forces."[189]

The Mayans have a legend about a practice of willful death. When a medicine man or shaman got too old to perform his duties, a young person, who was trained to replace him, would sit with the aged shaman and a crystal skull. During a ceremony, they would both put their hands on the skull; in this way the knowledge and wisdom of the older person would pass to the younger. When the ceremony was completed the older person passed. The Mayans credit the Atlanteans as their ancestors. Mayans believed the people from Atlantis created the crystal skulls, which according to some reports, several have now been found.[190]

In Atlantis seeds were given an energetic boost with music. Loud drum beats and passionate dancing were believed to inject energy into the Earth. The soil's energy was activated with vibration for best results. Additional instruction was received telepathically from the growing plants to produce optimal results. Examples include: plant root vegetables during a full moon for best growth; tomatoes prefer to live alone and a quartz stone in the middle of gardens amplifies plant growth.[191]

"Boji" stones were composed of dense sand, in which the outside felt like iron particles. These perfectly round balls were smooth, while others had protrusions. The smooth ones were considered feminine and the others masculine. Both varieties were arranged in gardens to benefit crops.[192]

In *The Secret Life of Plants,* a study showed that ultrasonic frequencies stimulated plants' enzyme activities and respiration rates. Plants that were exposed to frequencies for insect control grew faster than those not exposed. However, the frequencies that

---

[188] Andrews, Shirley. *Ibid*, Pg. 86.
[189] Helio–Arcanophus, Atlantis Past and To Come, (London: The Atlanteans, 1959), Pgs. 8–9. Godwin, Joscelyn. *Op. Cit.,* Pg. 194.
[190] Morton, Chris and Thoman, Ceri Louise. The Mystery of the Crystal Skulls, Bear & Co.: Santa Fe, N.M., 1963, Pg. 26.
[191] Andrews, Shirley. Atlantis: Insights from a Lost Civilization, *Op. Cit.,* Pg. 139.
[192] Cooper, Diane. *Op. Cit.*, Pg. 47. (channeled information)

stimulated one plant often inhibited the next. In conclusion, exposure to frequencies greatly impacted the growth of plants and seeds.[193]

The Kairos Institute of Sound Healing in New Mexico tested if sound vibrations enhanced crop growth. They played tuning forks and hand chimes over seedlings. The forks were tuned to the frequency made by Mars and Venus moving in their orbits and other special frequencies found in space.[194] Their findings showed that sound vibrations improved seed germination, quantity and quality of produce, longevity of production, pollination, and plant size.[195]

The Atlanteans used a healing technique that specified treatments depending on brain hemisphere dominance. Dr. Richard Gerber reported that ancient civilizations, such as the Atlanteans, altered their medicine depending on a patient's primary brain usage. Today, Sharry Edwards, who developed the science of BioAcoustics, does the same thing. One of her discoveries is that each brain hemisphere uses opposing methods to determine frequencies.

Rosenzweig, a scientist with studies published in *Scientific American*, conducted experiments to validate that each brain hemisphere is hardwired with its own sound processing center.[196] This has significant implications. For example, medicine and food have their own unique frequencies. A medicinal or chemical compound is in essence a frequency, a vibrational energy. Since the right and left hemispheres of our brains process frequencies differently, which brain hemisphere is being used makes a critical difference in which frequency (or medicine) is most effective. Perhaps this explains why some antibiotics work on one person, but not another. The Atlantean civilization altered the type of medicine used on people depending upon their brain dominance.[197]

---

[193] Tompkins, Peter and Bird, Christopher. Secret Life of Plants, Allen Lane, 1974 Article by Sherwood, Ed. http://www.cropcircleanswers.com.
[194] They also used planetary gongs tuned to the "three cycles of the Earth: the four seasons, the Earth spinning on her axis, and the Earth going through its processional cycle."
[195] Leeds, Joshua. The Power of Sound: How to be Healthy and Productive using Music and Sound, Healing Arts Press: Vermont, 2001, 2010, Pgs. 207–209.
[196] Rosenzweig, 1961. The Science of Audio Based Beat Brainwave Entrainment, http://web–us.com/thescience.htm
[197] Gerber, Richard, MD. Vibrational Medicine, third edition, Bear and Co.: Vermont, 2001, Pg. 330.

Author and teacher Diana Cooper presented a channeled explanation for the many stone circles that we see around our planet. She reported that the heavy stones were transported by telekinesis (dematerializing something and rematerializing it elsewhere), together with sound and crystal power. The stones were often concave, so that the circle created great acoustics for chanting. The circle location usually included an underground stream crossing. The people's chanting and prayers blessed and purified the water that the people drank. The stone circles were built on ley lines (subtle, magnetic energy currents of the Earth). The circles were also aligned to special star systems. For example, when the stones matched the star positions of Orion, they connected with the wisdom of the Orion Masters. Perhaps they aligned the stones to the Pleiades star grouping, to receive healing energy from the Pleiades. In another example, the stones may align to Sirius to receive energy to create spiritual technology, originating from that star.[198]

In the ceremonies, people entered the circle by walking on the ley lines, to receive uplifting energy. They chanted as they walked in clockwise circles that got smaller and smaller. This was done to amplify the energy of the participants, as well as the power of the circle stones, the earth and water. Eventually, the location and stone accumulated healing powers; people brought their sick to these stone circles. In their ceremonies, the priests gave thanks and led people in further chanting. At the conclusion of the session, chanters walked in circles that gradually got larger in a counter clockwise direction to close the ceremony. The creation of labyrinths evolved from this practice. Walking a labyrinth strengthens one's right brain, meditative abilities.[199]

Sound temples were often located in circular buildings; the height of the building was half of the length. The windows were made of quartz crystals. This created a reflection pattern that was excellent for sound waves. Sound was used for healing, regeneration of limbs and detoxification. To regenerate a limb, a person was placed within a crystal chamber. Chanters sounded the resonant frequency of each tissue to be regrown. Within their minds they held the image of the

[198] Cooper, Diana. *Op. Cit.,* Pg. 66. (channeled information)
[199] Cooper, Diana. *Ibid,* Pg. 67. (channeled information)

regrown limb. In this same way, they provided a rejuvenating treatment to counteract the impact of aging.[200]

I have had numerous "visions," in which I woke up in what I believe to be Atlantis. On one occasion, I perceived I was in a building, formed with several wings; there were no straight lines in the design of the building. The building segments were circular and connected. The windows were made of quartz crystal. There was a crystal skull in the center of the building. It glowed with red dots of light, and I believed the crystal skull was the generator or power source for the building.

A person missing an arm stood in the center of one of the circular rooms. Six of us (and at other times five) surrounded this person in a circle, equidistant apart. We were wearing hooded, midnight blue robes, similar to that of medieval monks. We used our voices, aiming our voice streams to the section of the arm that we were trying to regrow. Our voice energy-streams created the shape of a five or six pointed star (depending on the number of people in the circle). We had crystals and colored lights behind us that also amplified this energy.

In another vision, I believed that I had twelve strands of DNA. I understood DNA to be like radio antennae. The longer an antennae, the better the reception. Likewise the more strands of DNA one had, the greater his connectivity to other energy sources. People with "developed DNA" were more psychic and possessed other useful skills. I believed that DNA was resonant with love. Love could be compared to white light, which can be broken down into the component colors of the rainbow. Love was made up of many qualities. For example, two aspects of love were compassion and wisdom. As people lost their telepathic and clairvoyant abilities, they hid their mental and emotional energies – if they expected condemnation. When they denied their emotions, this energy hung around them like little balls of dark energy. As it accumulated, their DNA recoiled, losing strands of connectivity.

Theosophy sums up changes that the people of Atlantis experienced towards the end of this civilization: Their spiritual world gradually

---

[200] Cooper, Diana. *Ibid,* Pg. 85. (channeled information)

diminished as the Atlantean society came into its ultimate prominence. The soul became more attached to its physical environment. People relied on information from their senses; the use of intuition and subtle energy information faded. As spirits increased their identification with matter, the Lemurians and Atlanteans utilized sound as spoken words to communicate in place of mental means.

Theosophist, Helena Blavatsky, wrote that modern humans developed on the continent of Atlantis, and that this developmental age is not over. The final accomplishments will be the reawakening of psychic gifts. Blavatsky hinted that the psychic gifts that mankind will develop may be intuition and telepathy.[201]

Sounds and Music of Atlantis

Atlanteans enjoyed musical instruments made from reeds and animal bones. Before an animal died, they would ask permission to use its bones for the instrument; they respected the animal in this way. Bones of different lengths could be wrapped together and used like pan pipes. They would hit the pipes with something covered in a soft material to create beautiful notes. They also made music with the sounds of hanging crystals. Stringed instruments, such as the harp, were widely enjoyed.[202]

People liked to chant together. They isolated a specific emotion that they wished to experience, such as peace or playfulness. Their music would create this wonderful feeling, allowing everyone to experience this vibration of peace internally. Likewise, they created art. It was displayed so that people experienced a playful feeling when viewing the artworks; in another room the art would radiate a feeling such as peace. They would desire a beautiful feeling and then create art and music to experience it.[203]

Being clairvoyant, the people saw that certain sound patterns lit up their auras, making them feel uplifted. They listened to these sounds often. Today, Kirlian photography allows us to see one's aura. Certain sound patterns – such as solfeggio frequencies, tones

---

[201] http://www.katinkahesselink.net/blavatsky/articles/v12/y1890_053.htm
[202] Cooper, Diana. *Op. Cit.,* Pg. 42. (channeled information)
[203] Cooper, Diane. *Ibid*, Pg. 42. (channeled information)

associated with the Fibonacci pattern of numbers and sounds calculated from the planet's orbits – all create light in one's aura.

Intuitive channeler, Margaret Brown,[204] described the Atlantean command of sound: "They had a mastery of sound that we cannot imagine. They had instruments not played by the hand, but by electric mechanism. The Atlanteans had different vocal chords from ours, which enabled them to produce more efficacious vibrations."[205]

Cyril Scott reflected on Atlantean musical practices, "It was the priests who by degrees improved the primitive types of song and transformed it into a species of chanted spell. These spells were committed to memory and handed down generation to generation…. They increased religious fervor, with the result that men swayed with their bodies, to dance and clap their hands…. The priests discovered the potency of 'mantrams' or spells. They realized that if certain notes were reiterated, definite results could be obtained and powers brought into action. They used this particular form of magic – for magic it was – for noble and constructive ends during the earlier periods of the Atlantean history."[206]

Edgar Cayce related channeled stories describing healing chants in Atlantis. People intoned sounds such as *Arrr, Urrr*, and *Ouuu*, while using crystals and symbols to obtain purity, raise their vibrations to a higher level and absorb more light for healing.[207]

Music was a central component of the Atlantean society. Part of training for the priesthood included learning to play musical instruments, such as flutes and harps. The Muses taught students chants for healing and ceremonial purposes.

---

[204] 1867–1925?

[205] Gareth Knight. Pythones: the Life and Work of Margaret Lumley Brown, Thoth Publications: Loughborough, U.K., 2006, Pgs. 220–221.

[206] Scott, Cyril. Music: Its Secret Influences throughout the Ages, Samuel Weiser: London, 1958, Pg. 152. Reprinted in 2013 by Inner Traditions.com

[207] Andrews, Shirley. Lemuria and Atlantis, Op. Cit., Pg. 114.

Women could go to a "Temple Beautiful" to learn to be good mothers. Music was used when they were ready to prepare their bodies and minds for procreation.[208]

These ancient people applied sounds to tune patients to their natural harmonic states. This was particularly helpful with depression and other mental issues. Rhythms restored normal, calm and internal balance.[209]

Like the Lemurians, the Atlanteans enjoyed a descending musical scale. This descending pattern of sounds lowered frequencies linked to their minds, bodies and spirits. This resulted in a greater association with physical energies.

The Atlanteans believed that everyone had a composite frequency. Author Ted Andrews described how the ability to know and work with their fundamental frequency benefitted them, "The Atlanteans developed the ability to transmute physical conditions – to alter the physical vibrations – through fundamental tones. Many believe that the misuse of this knowledge contributed to the collapse of the civilization."[210]

Stones and crystals were thought to have consciousness and absorb energy. Healing ceremonies were conducted near circles of large rocks, while people chanted. The musical energy hovered around the rocks, infusing them with harmony. The priests added tantalizing, hypnotic music for tranquilizing effects. Gauss meters, which measure static magnetic field strength, have recorded elevated energy around ancient stone circles. Further tests suggested that the stones acted as amplifiers.[211] In a manner reminiscent of plants responding to music, the rocks' subtle energy was altered with music. This musical harmony combined with the energy from the Earth at sacred spots to induce healing. These healing energies were then easily accessible to the entire community.

---

[208] Andrews,Shirley. *Ibid,* Pg. 45.
[209] Andrews,Shirley. Lemuria and Atlantis, *Op. Cit.,* Pg. 80.
[210] Andrew, Ted. Sacred Sounds: Magic & Healing through Words & Music, Llewellyn Publications, Minn., 2008, Pg. 26.
[211] Michell, The New View over Atlantis, Pg. 208, as quoted in Andrews, Shirley. Atlantis: Insights from a Lost Civilization, Llewellyn Worldwide: MN, 1997, Pgs. 97and 85.

Atlanteans associated metals with the celestial bodies – associating certain metals to energy from the planets and sun. Gold and an unknown metal, orichalcum, were associated with the sun. Copper was associated with Venus and tin with Jupiter.[212] Likewise, Tibetan masters insist that the sounds made from different metals produce specific effects. They prescribe singing bowls of different metals for specialized purposes.

Exactly why Atlantis was destroyed we may never know... many who have closely studied the available information believe that the Atlantis masters destroyed all trace of their homeland – when their work was done. Some others blame black magicians and their "black" music for the destruction of Atlantis. After the fall of Atlantis, information regarding subtle and spiritual energy, including information about powerful sound frequencies and their application, was hidden by priests and leaders who possessed this knowledge. The vibratory and musical secrets were buried deeply; it was feared unscrupulous people could use this information to control and destroy others. Only those who proved themselves to be virtuous were allowed to carry the torch, keeping the information alive though oral transmissions.

www.JillsWingsOfLight.com – Art Gallery

---

[212] Andrews, Shirley. <u>Atlantis: Insights from a Lost Civilization</u>, *Op. Cit.,* Pg. 120.

Tomorrow's Total Wellness Today

CDs

Jill Mattson's CDs are multidimensional, deep-layered soulful works that offer a myriad of benefits.

Paint Your Soul

Vibrational Path to Spiritual Enlightenment using Fibonacci and Solfeggio Tones, and the Golden Ratio

Healing Flower Symphonies
vols 1 & 2

Frequency-based Flower remedies providing Catharsis and deep emotional healing

Star Dust

Enhance Astrological Energies; grow with Star Tones and Elemental Tuning

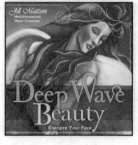

Deep Wave Beauty

» Revitalize and enhance your beauty with Vibrational Energy
» Includes Frequency equivalents of nourishing compounds and vitamins
» Tone skin, and muscles of face and neck

CUTTING EDGE VIBRATORY CDS AND BOOKS

Contacting Angels and Masters

INATS PEOPLE'S CHOICE AWARD FOR 2015 BEST CD OF THE YEAR

FINALIST FOR *INATS* BEST FREQUENCY HEALING CD OF 2015

An educational CD with guided meditations to bathe in the divine subtle energies, and meet your guides, angels and masters.

Absorb subtle energies for healing and enlightenment: Channeled Energies of Angels & Ascended Masters, Schumann Frequency (associated with Healing & Grounding), Frequencies of Master Numbers, Chakra Tones, Crystal Tunings, Healing Elemental Sounds, Sacred Geometry Sounds and Music relating to the Ray of the Angel or Master.

Deep Wave Body Healing

Ancient wise Masters established conscious control of their physical bodies, specifically the organs. When they detected disharmony within an organ, they tuned it into harmony, which was associated with the health of the organ. In this meditation, establish healing connection and tuning of organs, with the help of frequencies associated with healthy body organs.

CUTTING EDGE VIBRATORY CDS AND BOOKS

Cosmic Streams

Multi-level guided meditations and techniques of Ascended Masters for Chakra Balancing

Books_____

Mystical Accounts of Healing through Sound Energy

Secret Sounds ~ Ultimate Healing

Mysteries of the voice revealed; tuning the body with sounds; Sharry Edward's life story and BioAcoustics

The Lost Waves Of Time

This is the ultimate collection of sound energy secrets taken from every important ancient culture. Sound mysteries from Lemuria and Atlantis through Egypt, China and Sumeria are presented in this comprehensive work.

Websites & Social Media

Wings of Light
www.JillsWingsofLight.com

Ancient Music
www.Ancient-Music.com

Music For Beauty
www.MusicForBeauty.com

Twitter
https://twitter.com/wingsoflight

Facebook
https://www.facebook.com/pages/Jill-Mattson/286604571357944

YouTube
https://www.youtube.com/channel/UCAEuQdsjfce4m-ORTbxI6sA